To: Be

My trusted broker and best friend! Your generous support of my book also benefits the Wounded Warrior Project!

Brad Willis

2011

MARBLE MOUNTAIN

Bud Willis

authorHOUSE®

AuthorHouse™
1663 Liberty Drive
Bloomington, IN 47403
www.authorhouse.com
Phone: 1-800-839-8640

First published by AuthorHouse 3/21/2011

ISBN: 978-1-4567-4348-2 (sc)
ISBN: 978-1-4567-4349-9 (hc)

Library of Congress Control Number: 2011903029

Printed in the United States of America

Any people depicted in stock imagery provided by Thinkstock are models, and such images are being used for illustrative purposes only. Certain stock imagery © Thinkstock.

This book is printed on acid-free paper.

Dedication

For the sons and daughters of the
men who fought in Vietnam

With a special family memorial to

Medal of Honor recipient John Harlan Willis, a first
cousin, killed on February 28, 1945 on the Japanese island
of Iwo Jima while serving with the United States Marine
Corps as a Navy corpsman and to his son, born two weeks
after his father's death.

and

Colonel Daniel McKisick, my great, great, great, great
grandfather, who joined the Patriot militia in 1775 and rode
with the North Carolina Dragoons. On Jun 20, 1780, he lost
the use of his left arm to a musket ball while leading the
predawn surprise attack against British forces at the Battle
of Ramsours Mill at Lincolnton, NC. On July 4th, 1810, he
founded and charted the city of Shelbyville, Tennessee, the
home place of my grandparents and my mother.

The Cover ... Earth and Sky

The cartoon-like image of Vietnam inside the belly of a Dragon symbolizes the dominance of China on its culture. The Vietnamese believe they descended from an ancient dragon. Their customs are steeped in imagery and superstition passed down through generations for thousands of years. In Western society, we often refer to the *heart* of a man, but in the Vietnamese culture, they view the *belly* as the core of a human being. According to them, the umbilicus (abdominal scar) represents the exact center of man ..."nơi đất đáp ứng các bầu trời"... *where earth meets the sky."*

By coincidence, the geographic center of their country is a place called Marble Mountain, about four kilometers from Danang. The Marine Corps constructed a helicopter facility there for the pilots of Marine Air Group 16. From the navel of this ancient country, the Marines would attempt to dominate the sky while tens of thousands of North Vietnamese soldiers invaded by land. This classic confrontation between the forces of Earth and Sky would to be the longest war in American history.

When Ho Chi Minh was asked how he could possibly defeat a power as great as the United States, he replied, *"They will kill many of us, and we will kill a few of them. They will grow tired of it."* He fought us for 15 years, losing over two million of his people. Whatever motivation may have kept his soldiers moving forward is still a mystery to this day. However, we do know where their energy came from. As with all Asians, eighty percent of their energy came from a single source – *rice.*

Napoleon claimed that an army marches on its *stomach*. It has been said that Asians have two stomachs, one for rice and one for everything else, and the first one must be fed every day. Rice is their fuel, and therefore their energy. Whoever controls energy controls his future.

(The cover was created by Joe Wlodarczyk from artwork by Justin Champagne, both of Naples, Florida.)

In 1965, the United States Marine Corps installed several acres of Marston Matting just north of Marble Mountain to serve as a parking lot and runway for the helicopters of Marine Air Group 16. This base camp was called Marble Mountain Air Facility (MMAF), or simply, *"Marble Mountain."* Marines were sent there by our president, Lyndon Johnson, to protect the rice farmers of South Vietnam and prevent the spread of Communism throughout Indo-China.

This prominent landmark consisted of a cluster of five limestone outcroppings jutting out of the rice-rich belly of South Vietnam along the coast of the South China Sea, four kilometers southeast of Danang. The hills are named for five elements: metal, water, wood, fire and earth. The tallest stands 350 feet, with steps carved to the top, leading to a Buddhist Temple.

The base was home to a squadron of Huey pilots and the setting for my story, which took place more than 45 years ago. My memoir was constructed from a stack of letters and a journal that I kept in 1966 while serving a tour of duty with a group of extraordinary men. I've had virtually no contact with any of them until recently while doing research for this book. Like most returning Vets, we rarely spoke of our experiences after we returned home. Reconnecting with some of my old friends has been a tremendous reward for me.

I apologize to them for writing this book in first person and centering the stories on myself. Mine is the only version I know. However, anyone who served in Vietnam, or had a father, grandfather, brother, or an uncle who served may substitute his name in the stories for mine -- we all did essentially the same things. Some of these events were painful to recall. There are certain feelings that soldiers are reluctant to share with people who might not understand. I stuck with the project because I felt our story needed to be told and because our country's current military situation in Afghanistan makes *Marble Mountain* as relevant today as it was then. Our government should be required to explain exactly *why* it sends its young people into strange lands to fight and die. Their families and loved ones deserve this explanation.

My greatest writing challenge, apart from conflicting emotions, was the obvious disconnect between the 24-year-old pilot *in* the stories and the 68-year-old writer trying to craft them into perspective. Some of the things in my journal seemed immature years later, such as my tongue-in-cheek criticism of high ranking officers. Still, others were remarkably insightful. In the choice between honesty and manipulation, I chose to trust the words as I wrote them in 1966 and to be true to the experience. My editor advised me to write exactly what happened and simply allow the reader to decide how to process the information. *"Tell it, not sell it,"* she said.

One major issue that I had to confront is how to cope with my personal life in the book. I was a married man with a two week old son when I left home to go to war and later divorced. Receiving letters from my wife with pictures of my son was the brightest part of any day. Most of the men in these stories were married or had significant relationships. I chose not to write so much about how we missed our loved ones because it would have taken up most of the book. A warrior manages his emotions privately, keeping his vulnerabilities to himself. In my letters home, I tried to avoid the gore of combat, choosing instead to write lighthearted details about the weather, what we had for dinner, or something funny that happened; anything to keep them from knowing what we were really doing. In my journal, I wrote what was on my mind.

Hat's off to the men who were able to keep their relationships together when they returned home. We weren't the same when we came home, and this can take a toll over time. *Emotionally unavailable* is a popular term for it. Divorce is just one more unfortunate statistic for deployed soldiers. But the truth is, the types of people who willingly perform these rough assignments are a different breed and not always easily explained. According to Cicero, "... *they have a sense of duty that is born into them.*" Rarely inspired by small plans, they need ... no ... *require, lofty* assignments. To quote George Orwell, "*We sleep soundly in our beds because rough men stand ready to do violence on our behalf.*" Perhaps *Marble Mountain* will provide some clues for my own two sons about the complicated father who drove them to school in the mornings.

Sometime in the late 70's, a group of my friends who knew I didn't like to talk about that war, suggested I go with them to see the movie *Apocalypse Now.* I decided to go, but to go alone. I lasted about an hour before I had to leave. The movie captured the fear factor of combat so intensely, that I found myself living each scene with the actors. The memories were too much to process in one evening. After some reflection, I decided it might be good "therapy" for me to continue to go until I could sit through the entire movie. It took five trips to make that happen. Like most movies, this fictionalized story was far from reality, mainly because a movie can concentrate a lifetime of drama into a short time frame. That, in itself, is unrealistic because it ignores the important dimension of time. If time were not important, it would not have taken me 13 years to screw up the courage to watch a movie about Vietnam.

After five visits to the movie, I was able to see one of the final scenes when Marlon Brando's character tells the graphic story of his own epiphany. Brando portrayed a Green Beret colonel who went rogue, and in this important scene, he explained why. He told the story of the day his unit went into a small Vietnamese village to inoculate its children for smallpox. This was part of the program to win the hearts and minds of the Vietnamese people. Shortly after his men left the village, a man came screaming after them. They returned to find that the Viet Cong had come in behind them and chopped off every vaccinated arm of each of those children. *There was this pile of little arms.*

"What a perfect act of terror," he said. There was nothing that our government could ever do for that village to win their hearts and minds that could possibly compete with that single act of horror. For many Americans, that movie was their first real glimpse into the twisted world of terrorism. But for the two million of us who served in that war, we already knew.

Marble Mountain is not intended to be a military book. This is a coming of age story of a small group of Marine Huey pilots who were caught between our compassion for the troops on the ground and the complicated drama of global politics. I wanted to write the human side of combat: what goes on in a young man's mind when he knows he is being asked to give up all he has for his country.

I tried to avoid the jargon that usually accompanies stories about the military, explaining the slang along the way or converting it to ordinary language. Some of it could not be avoided, so I included a short glossary in the back of the book. Entries from my journal are distinguished by a special font and are dated. The dates are important to me because they add historical value. Besides the drama, there is significant history. Flight logs and squadron chronology records were used to verify some of the dates.

Thank you for reading *Marble Mountain.*

Bud Willis

"Helicopters are different from planes. An airplane by its nature wants to fly and if not interfered with too strongly by unusual events or by a deliberately incompetent pilot, it will fly.

A helicopter does not want to fly. It is maintained in the air by a variety of forces and controls, working in opposition to each other; and if there is any disturbance in the delicate balance, the helicopter stops flying immediately and disastrously. There is no such thing as a gliding helicopter.

This is why being a helicopter pilot is so different from being an airplane pilot; and why, in generality, airplane pilots are open, clear-eyed, buoyant extroverts and helicopter pilots are brooders, introspective anticipators of trouble.

They know if something bad has not happened, it is about to."

Harry Reasoner
ABC Evening News

CONTENTS

January 12, 1966

During his State of the Union address before Congress, President Johnson comments that the war in Vietnam is unlike America's previous wars, "Yet, finally, war is always the same. It is young men dying in the fullness of their promise. It is trying to kill a man that you do not even know well enough to hate...therefore, to know war is to know that there is still madness in the world."

CHAPTER ONE

SHOT DOWN

26 January, 1967

On the southern edge of the DMZ, just north of the Rockpile, sits a relatively flat piece of real estate which we named the *Punch Bowl*. The perimeter of the bowl features several well known landmarks. At the 12 o'clock position is Mutter's Ridge. At nine o'clock is the infamous Razorback Ridge, one of the more non-negotiable vertical formations of jagged limestone rock imaginable.

Nearly a year into my 13 month tour, this was my fifth time to shoot up the caves of Razorback Ridge, and each time we were greeted by enemy fire. The rocks in front of their caves were being chewed up by our machine guns, and I wondered what would possess the North Vietnamese Army to take a position in such an untenable location. And then, I looked down at the Rockpile, where a dozen Marines were camped on top of a cone shaped observation post with barely enough room to spread their sleeping bags. None of this had to make any sense to me. This was Vietnam, and straight answers to any question were hard to come by.

As my wingman and I were returning to Dong Ha to refuel and rearm, my rudder pedals suddenly went mushy. These are the two foot-pedals that control the pitch on the small tail rotor, providing horizontal stability to the chopper. Without the tail rotor, the centrifugal energy of the main rotor would cause the fuselage to spin in the opposite direction. Control of all this is delivered to the pilot's feet and fingertips by the hydraulic system. The short version is that the tail rotor keeps the Huey pointed in the right direction, and the hydraulic system makes it easy to operate the rudders that tell the tail rotor what to do. In my situation, the hydraulics seemed okay, but the rudders didn't work because the rudder cable had been severed by small arms fire.

At high speeds, the shape of the "tadpole" Huey acts like a dart, and the wind streamlines the dart. Slowing down for the landing would be the tricky part. I would need to land with at least 60 knots of airspeed and skid to a stop, using the friction of the ground for directional control. If this sounds complicated, look at it from my perspective; I'm flying over hostile territory in a busted chopper with three other people in the plane with me, all counting on me to make the right decision.

The first thing we're trained to do in an emergency is to look for a safe place to land. I needed flat and friendly for a long, run-on landing. We'd been into places where bullets had been flying, and who knows what else may have been hit. Trouble usually travels in pairs and we're trained to think that way. If the hydraulic system decided to give up the ghost, it would take the Incredible Hulk to muscle that monster to the ground. Instinct told me to put that Huey on the ground while we still had some control over it.

I asked my wingman to follow me down into a rice

paddy that looked accommodating enough to make a running landing. The paddy was adjacent to a small village and soaked with rain from the recent monsoons. We had flown over this place many times en route to the badlands and we didn't consider it hostile, but if it happened to be, we had a wingman with us and plenty of friends within shouting distance at Dong Ha. As I descended to 300 feet, I saw the other half of trouble. The rice paddies were sectioned off by dykes that are three to five feet high. These dykes hold water in the fields, and there were more of them than I thought. This shortened my "runway" considerably. I had intended to land farther from that village rather than ski down through the middle of it. I had to make it over one dyke and stop short of another while maintaining 60 knots of airspeed -- the standard procedure for a landing with no tail rotor. When my airspeed went below 60 knots, I would lose the advantage of the slipstream effect, and I would start to lose directional control. This would have to be a landing that I would need to nail the first time. There would be no second chances. Adding power to the main rotor for a wave-off would be disastrous.

The short landing area forced a rapid descent with the village looming larger in my windshield. Coming in hot required a big flare to stop the airplane. As I pulled the nose up in the air, my freewheeling tail rotor clipped the rice paddy. When the back of my skids caught the soggy turf, we were already in a 15 degree crab. My eyes were glued to the fast approaching dyke, which now had three people standing on top of it, watching me sled toward them. One of the men was down in that familiar, Oriental squat. They didn't understand the situation because they had the worst seats in the theater.

If I hit their dyke, the main rotor would strike them about head high. Taking the head off the village chief would not be the kind of civic action that Lieutenant General Lewis Walt was looking for. But if I forced the plane straight down into the mud pie too abruptly, the side torque might flip the plane on its side, and they would be attacked by a giant Mix Master. The crew might survive that, but not without a visit to the Repose (hospital ship).

Fifty yards from the dyke, I had no other choice but to plug it into the mud. Plunging into the soggy paddy, the plane bogged down to its belly and tried to pitch forward as if it were tipping its hat to the oncoming spectators. They were only a few feet away now and still clueless. Their expressions never changed. As we pitched forward, out of control, the rotors took a big swipe at the mud in front of them, taking rice stalks with it. The plane fell back on its haunches and hunkered down like that old man on the dyke. My eyes were locked on his. The skids were completely underground, and if the plane had a butt, it would have been sitting on it. The landing was successful, and nobody was scratched, but we didn't do their rice crop any favors. None of the spectators changed their expressions. They neither smiled nor applauded. It was like making a hole-in-one in front of an audience that didn't play golf.

Nobody inside the plane was clapping either because now we had another set of issues to manage. Who are these people in front of us? The audience quickly doubled in size to maybe six or seven, and there were a couple of kids there now. This was encouraging, as we didn't think the villagers would involve children in a gunfight. I asked the crew to stay inside the chopper while our wingman made a low circle around the area to take a look at that village. There was normal activity, which was good. We all waved and smiled at the villagers and tried to look like friendly spacemen.

While the crew chief worked his way back to open the hatch to confirm the rotor cable had been severed, we released our seat belts and shoulder harnesses and retrieved our flak jackets, which we usually sat on. We put the flak jackets on, zipped them up, and opened the doors, but stayed put. I asked the door gunner to lock and load and stay at the ready, but he didn't need to be told. The copilot activated the armament. We had enough machine gun ammo to hold up our end if it came to that. There was no strain on the idling Huey, so I kept the engine running while I talked our rescue over with the wingman. We surveyed the survival kit and pulled out an M-79 grenade launcher which we sometimes carried. There was a box with five rounds in it.

While we waited, more village gawkers appeared on the dyke. A CH-46 and a Huey would be dispatched from Dong Ha to pick us up. While we sat and stared at them, I had plenty of time to think about what had just happened as I fondled my loaded Smith and Wesson .38 revolver and wondered why I had never bothered to exchange it for a .45. A few lucky breaks helped us through that landing. First, the muddy landing area accepted the skids immediately as we gradually sank into the mud to slow down the plane. The depth of the goop also prevented the plane from spinning, just as it would be difficult to turn anything stuck in mud. The wet ground may also have prevented us from tipping forward, by "sucking" the skids back to earth when they tried to free themselves. If I had tried to make that same landing at Phu Bai or Dong Ha, skidding across a metal runway at 60 knots, I might have spun out of control and flipped over, making a triple bogey in front of an audience of professional "golfers."

We talked and laughed and waited. No one seemed anxious. Nothing bad had happened to any of us, not yet anyway, and help would soon be on the way. We assumed that the severed cable was caused by a lucky sniper. I never even bothered to follow up on that. What difference did it make? After a few more minutes, our wingman radioed to tell us that help was coming from Dong Ha. We shut the plane down while the wingman came to a low hover beside us. The crew chiefs and door gunners on each Huey stayed behind to prepare the plane for evacuation while the pilots waded through the muck to hitch a ride back to Dong Ha.

Part of the fun of being a pilot is that after an incident like that, your buddies want to hear all about it, so they can weigh in on it, see what they can learn, and give advice on how they would have handled it differently. It hones the learning process. But when nobody says a word, you have to figure it was a good day. You had a problem, and you handled it. I consider my biggest responsibility as a pilot, other than the mission, is to take care of the crew. They seemed happy enough about the way things turned out.

UNLIKELY MARINE

I learned at an early age that people are capable of almost anything; bravery, cowardice, good, evil, you name it. You see all kinds of behavior out there. It's only natural to wonder what the future holds for us in this regard. In my case, I tried to look to my own family for some clues. My father was not what I consider a brave man, quite the opposite really. He drank too much and behaved badly. From observing his conduct, I knew by the time I was five years old that I didn't want to be like him. Whatever life-or-death choices were waiting for me, I would do my best to avoid dishonor.

When you grow up in Tennessee, you are likely to be taught the Pledge of Allegiance before you learn the Lord's Prayer. That's just how we roll. In my hometown of Tullahoma, tens of thousands of soldiers were trained during WWII at Camp Forrest, and pictures of men in uniform decorated the living rooms of practically every home. When boys graduated high school in the Fifties, they had to register for the draft, and we all knew that military service would have to be addressed sooner or later. It was all quite natural, really. We were raised on a steady diet of patriotism, and Douglas MacArthur had already lectured us that *"no man should consider himself entitled to the blessings of freedom if he was not diligent in its creation."*

There may have been some crafty ways to avoid the draft, but most of us weren't handicapped by that kind of privilege, nor did we care for the label *"draft dodger."* Throughout the South and in Tennessee in particular, we belonged to a culture that made us want to do our part. After all, if Elvis Presley could be drafted, anybody could! What other place in the world can claim the title of *The Volunteer State?* I'll wager that none of the 70,000 men who fled to Canada to avoid Vietnam were from my hometown. McArthur would have been proud.

In the of spring of 1954, a group of older kids in my neighborhood convinced me that it was okay to lie about my age to join their Boy Scout troop. Since petty lying and bragging had been the basis of every one of those childhood relationships, I saw no harm in it. I took this suggestion as a sign of acceptance and jumped at it. My first scouting task was to memorize the Scout Oath in order to earn a Tenderfoot badge. At my very first meeting, after hearing two other plebes stumble through the process, I decided to go for it. I held up three fingers on my right hand and looked the scoutmaster square in the eye.

"On my honor, I will do my best to do my duty, to God and my country. To help other people at all times; to obey the Scout law; to keep myself physically strong, mentally awake; and morally straight."

A piece of cake!

Even though I didn't have 10 cents to pay for the badge or a uniform to put it on, all this made perfect sense. I was born to be a scout: loyal, brave, and trustworthy. Never mind that I had lied about my age to be in the club. At last, I stood for something. I *belonged!* And in less than 15 minutes, I'd earned an award. It was in the shape of a fleur-de-lis and had an eagle on it. Two beautifully embroidered images representing the French symbol of valor and the American symbol of freedom! This was an important and serious moment for me. The fact that fleur-de-lis means "lily flower" was not something that I would have found amusing at the time.

In the fall of 1961, shortly after my 20th birthday, I was struggling through my junior year of college in hopes of becoming a writer. Dr. Ingram's Shakespeare class was assigned a project on *King Henry V.* Instead of the standard college paper, I planned to re-enact Henry's inspirational speech on the eve of his battle with the French at Agincourt on Saint Crispen's Day. In the middle of my rehearsal, three men walked into my dorm room. One of them was the quarterback of the football team and a good friend. The commander of the ROTC drill team and the student body president were with him. They were all business and told me flat-out that they were looking for *a few good men* to join the Marine Corps and become officers. *"How many*

are you looking for?" I asked, thinking that they might be putting together a prospect list.

"Just one more ... you!" one of them said.

I looked out across the Tennessee Tech campus and saw at least 100 good men that they might have called on, some with twice my credentials. It didn't occur to me that they probably had already done that. They talked for a while, and I listened with King Henry's words ringing in the back of my brain ...*"we few, we happy few, we band of brothers; for he today who sheds his blood with me will be my brother."* This was reminiscent of my Boy Scout recruitment except that I didn't have to lie about my age.

The following Monday at 11 a.m., the four of us sat quietly listening to the spiel of the Marine Corps recruiting officer. He explained the *"no commitment screening process"* that would determine if any of us would even be eligible to be among the few and the proud. I decided to go ahead and take the screening exam that same afternoon, so it would be behind me. I was suspicious when he told me privately that I had scored higher than anyone he had ever tested and was tempted to ask if I was his first. The simple test didn't break any Phi Beta Kappa ground. Most of the answers were common sense. A few formalities later, and after several pages of triplicate government paperwork, I was an officer candidate. As soon as the summer break began, I was on an all-expense paid trip to Quantico, Virginia, for ten grueling weeks of training.

Quantico is a 385 acre wooded, Marine Corps officer training base located 36 miles from Washington, DC. The FBI Academy is also located there. The PLC (platoon leaders class) summer program allows college boys to complete their officer training without interrupting their college class work, and college juniors could complete the course in one summer over a ten week period without entirely wrecking two summer vacations.

Even though I was an aspiring writer, I must have missed the fine print because this was the most grueling ten weeks of my life. It was a combination of boot camp, outward bound, survival training, and college football practice, with a few West Point type military classes thrown in for good measure. We did all the classic tasks that we'd seen in the movies, like taking weapons apart and putting them back together while blindfolded. That wasn't difficult for me since I was in the dark most of the time. There were hand-to-hand combat drills with pugil sticks representing bayonets.

The mental and physical torture began every morning at 0400. We started in total darkness with a couple of laps around the *"grinder,"* which was a few acres of steaming asphalt used for drill instruction and running in formation. More a three mile shuffle than a run, we did this in combat boots, tee shirts, and heavy green utility trousers, guaranteed to make the body fluids flow. Then, we showered like a herd of naked cattle while a skilled harassment expert screamed insults at our every move. "K" Company, 2nd Platoon went to breakfast and everywhere else in formation. We competed against the other platoons 24 hours a day at everything, and each activity was carefully measured, critiqued, and scrutinized.

The odor of huge mounds of scrambled eggs and biscuits hung in the air so thick that you could smell the greasy breakfast clear across the Potomac. They cooked the bacon in a deep fryer, like French fries, ten pounds at a time. The metal trays in the chow line were stacked five feet high, and in front of the trays was a large red sign:

"TAKE ALL YOU WANT, BUT EAT ALL YOU TAKE!"

I connected with that portentous message on many levels. It was a metaphor for my life to that point and reminded me to be careful what I signed up for and to take responsibility for whatever choices I made. *"Finish what you start"* and "Don't *bite off more that you can chew"* were two of my mother's favorite sayings.

There was nothing mandatory about any of this officer training. We could drop on request at any time and forget about the Marine Corps forever. But once you start the habit of quitting, it's a tough habit to break. Some people realized their mistake in the first few days and were sent to a special area called the "goon platoon." There, they were free to do whatever they wanted with minimum supervision until they were processed to go home. Instead of hiding them away in some remote corner of the complex, they purposely located the goon platoon right next door to the mess hall where we marched past them three times a day. Some of them taunted us with cold beer and made fun of us in good humor as we marched by. They were like Ulysses' sirens representing forbidden desires and beckoning us to crash on the rocks. Had there been any actual female nymphs among them, there would have been no Marine officers that year.

The instructors knew exactly what they were doing. The whole process was carefully crafted to separate the wheat from the chaff, and the Marines have been making quality bread for nearly 200 years. There were times when we envied those lucky bastards, knowing they would all be home with their girlfriends in a few days. But the message was loud and clear; they were going to find our breaking points. If we came out the other end, we might be fit to be Marine officers.

There are miles and miles of hill trails on the banks of the Potomac River. One sure way of extending the attrition rate was to take an entire company of trainees on a single-file forced march up and down those steep hills with a heavy rifle and a fully loaded backpack. The unfortunate souls who were stuck near the end of the long green line for two hours became victims of the accordion effect from all the stopping and puking. Once anybody stopped, everyone in the back had to wait and then sprint to catch up. If you were carrying a few extra pounds of blubber or were slightly out of condition, your legs would fire up like a coal furnace. The sweltering summer heat and the humidity trapped in those woods made it feel as though you were gagging on boiling water. The heat alone wilted many a good man who thought he wanted to be among the few and the proud. During the first six weeks, we ran these hill trails twice a week.

We took a stretcher on these monster marathons in case someone collapsed with heat exhaustion. The leader always asked for two volunteers to carry this eight foot long canvas cot held together by two wooden poles. It weighed 30 or 40 pounds, but it traveled at the front of the line where there was always a steady pace, and, therefore, very little stopping and starting. Always looking for an angle, I saw the stretcher bearer's job as an opportunity to be with the big dogs at the front of the pack, so I wouldn't be subjected to that energy sapping accordion. Stupidly, I volunteered to help carry the stretcher and talked my buddy into joining me.

It was probably 95 degrees that day in early July. About half way through the run, we received the call from down the line to bring the stretcher. A good half mile behind us, the only obese candidate in the platoon had gone down. We were instructed to run back there and carry him out on the stretcher. We could barely lift Candidate Lard Ass on the stretcher much less carry him up those hills. We made the poor guy walk the uphill parts, and the only time we let him back on the stretcher was when we came out of the clearing at the end of the run for the last 50 yards. We walked out of the woods carrying the guy as if we had carried him for two miles. They had been waiting for us for more than half an hour.

The irate company commander, a major, made him get off the stretcher and walk in front of the entire company while a single drummer slowly tapped on an empty canteen to each one of his footsteps. About 15 feet into his journey, the major ordered the company to do an about face, turning our backs on him. I, and the other hapless volunteer, and now former friend, placed the ten thousand pound stretcher back on the truck while we watched as our patient was "drummed out" of the Marine Corps. By the time we came back in the barracks after our showers, his foot locker was gone, and we never saw him again.

A few weeks of this kind of torture was enough to convince me that I was not cut out to be an infantry soldier. Leading a platoon of 44 good men up a steep hill to knock out a machine gun nest was not my vision of the future. I knew I couldn't quit, but I needed a job with a little more control over my destiny. At the first available opportunity, I raised my hand for aviation.

The biggest problem with that decision was that practically every other officer candidate at Quantico had the same idea. I think they took about 350 of us to the infirmary for the first screening. As soon as they checked our eyesight, about 40 were eliminated. Several people had problems with deviated septums, which we learned from the doctor can be a problem with oxygen masks at high altitudes. More were excused. Some of the California boys, who spent a good bit of time in the water either surfing or swimming, had some sort of inner ear issue. This might cause problems with pressure equalization, and it eliminated about 50 more. Four people directly in line in front of me flunked the ear canal test. When the Doc looked in my ears, he said I was lucky that my ear canals were shaped the other way. I made some wisecrack about swimming on my *back,* which he appreciated by laughing and repeating it to the other doctor handling another long line. I could tell that some of those guys weren't too disappointed at being rejected and were only there to avoid whatever was going on back in the barracks.

The next day, those of us who had survived the physical screenings gathered at the air-conditioned FBI training center for a 750 question aptitude test that would eliminate another 50%. The questions seemed to focus mainly on the areas of endurance, adapting to stress, judgment under pressure, and decision-making skills. I could see the difficulty of trying to identify our strengths because of our youth and lack of experience. The test lasted for hours and seemed to focus more on weaknesses, asking similar questions over and over but in different ways in case you were trying to make yourself look too good. There was the usual psychological nonsense about whether you looked back at your poop or if you had ever thought about suicide.

Who knows what they were looking for on those tests? Everybody has a joker in their deck that might cause a problem down the road, especially under pressure. One of the test questions haunted me, and it will sound silly when I tell you. I must have gone back to it 20 times to change my answer and wore a hole in the paper. It simply asked if you would rather be a snob or a slob. I marked slob immediately because I can't tolerate a snob. A couple of minutes later, I realized that they probably didn't want a slob in a Marine officer's uniform and certainly not in the cockpit of an airplane. As much as I hate snobs suddenly I was one, and I didn't like my own self. For the next few hours, I went from being a slob to a snob every few minutes until I decided to hell with it. Any organization whose slogan is *"The Few and the Proud"* isn't looking to recruit a bunch of slobs. Sometimes, you have to do things that you don't feel good about because you know it's the right answer. It was just a screening test. I didn't have to be either one of those things.

Eventually, they whittled us down to a group of about 50 guys who were earmarked to go to flight school in Pensacola assuming we graduated from college. I'm sure we were ranked in our class at Quantico, but I wasn't even smart enough to know what my ranking might have been. All I know is that I survived and came home in a Marine uniform with the temporary status of Lance Corporal until I could receive my BA degree and accept an officer's commission. When college classes resumed, I was not even aware that nine units of military science electives had been applied toward my college requirements. This unexpected, but well-earned bonus turned the complicated process of graduation into a walk in the park.

I was the only military officer in my 1963 Tennessee Tech graduating class bedecked in tailored, summer parade dress-whites complete with ceremonial sword. There were about a dozen Army ROTC boys in olive drab receiving their commissions, and they chose me to lead us in our commissioning ritual. I barked out the military commands for our grand entrance as everyone in the building leaped to their feet.

Fellow English major, favorite study partner, and some-times girlfriend, Janie Fulmer, who had tolerated me as a friend for a year or so, was totally perplexed by my decision to become a Marine, especially that I would be willing to fly airplanes into what was sure to be a life or death propo-sition, at least from the images and stories being shown on television every night. She was not an adamant pacifist, but my decision to become a warrior had deepened the di-vide between us in those last few weeks before graduation. Nevertheless, since I was the only graduate out of several hundred on that beautiful spring day in May of 1963 who was dressed like an ice cream salesman with a sword, she accepted my invitation to help pin on my lieutenant's bars. With my sweet mother on one side and the beautiful Miss Fulmer on the other, they each pinned a gold bar on my uni-form while my journalism professor snapped the picture. I had a fever blister on my lower lip the size of a dime from all the stress and was afraid to kiss either one of them.

My journalism professor was also a news correspondent. The next morning, his picture of the three of us showed up on the front page of every morning newspaper across the state of Tennessee, fever blister and all. That was the last time I ever saw Betty Jane Fulmer. Three weeks later, I was on a train to Pensacola for flight school. A fellow at the train station in Pensacola went out of his way to drive me to the main gate at the Naval Air Station, and the sentinel called for a military driver to pick me up. The driver said he would take me anywhere I wanted to go and wait for me as long as it took. The very first official muster after registration was at the gymnasium for a fitness test. They wanted to make sure that we were physically able to withstand the rigors of flight school, which included timed three mile runs, swimming a mile, being turned upside down in deep water while strapped into a cockpit simulator, obstacle courses, and survival training in the tropical Florida heat. The initial PT test required a minimum number of pushups, pull-ups, sit-ups, a long run, and a variety of standard drills that any decent athlete would consider a normal 90 minute workout … nothing heart-stopping for a Marine. Afterwards, we cooled off on the risers in the gym while an officer gave us an orientation talk. The first thing he did was ask us to look at the man on the left of us and the one to the right.

"Only two of you will graduate from flight school," he told us. *"Of the two who become pilots, one of you will be killed before your tour of duty is up. That will leave only one of you standing. Are you sure you still want to become pilots?"* We all knew the drill and responded with what little breath we had left, ***"Yes, Sir!"***

CHAPTER TWO

FLIGHT SCHOOL

"If you hold a piece of typing paper by the corners and blow across the top of it, the paper will rise. This is called the Venturi principle. Molecules of air, moving farther and faster along the curved top of the paper, spread out and become less dense. Since nature likes balance and hates a vacuum, the more dense molecules on the bottom push up on the paper in an effort to equalize the molecular volume. Voila ... Venturi's principle of flight. When an airfoil is pulled or pushed through the air, as with propellers or turbines, the lift created underneath the curved wing pushes the wing up.

Gentleman, the engine mock-up in front of you is a 225 horsepower, Continental O-470-13 which propels the T-34 airplane to maximum airspeed of 188 mph. You will solo that airplane in the next three months.

Tomorrow you will be expected to name all the parts of this engine.

Welcome to Preflight, Gentleman. Open your manual to page one."

After a couple of months of rapid-fire class work, we were assigned a flight instructor to begin our flying program. I drew a Navy lieutenant (equivalent to a Marine captain) by the name of Anderson who told me right up front he had not had any good experiences with Marine flight students.

"I haven't met one yet that was very bright," he told me.

I told him he was still batting 1,000, but if he would show me what to do, I assured him that I would make it through the program. I said that I could at least read and write and could be very funny when given half a chance. We became friends in an odd, big-brother sort of way, and I really liked the man, especially after I met his wife and she told me what a pussycat he was, right in front of him. He just grinned and winked at her as if they had been together forever, and she had his number.

Pensacola was intoxicating. The cobalt summer skies and puffy white clouds reflecting in the turquoise harbors of the Gulf of Mexico and the blinding sun beaming off those sugary, crystal-quartz beaches would make any Marines' biceps stand at attention. The beaches were teeming with girls who were there expressly to meet some of these fly boys up close and personal. The curriculum was tough enough without all these distractions. Once again, the sirens in Homer's Odyssey were casting their magic spells. Temptation was everywhere as though it had been carefully staged to suck us in.

After 12 flights with the instructor, it was time to solo. On the 13th hop, after a few touch-and-go landings with the instructor in the backseat, he exits the plane and watches you make a couple of landings on your own. On a normal good-weather day, this should be no problem, assuming you don't panic and start hyperventilating at the thought of being alone at the controls of your own aircraft. But who really knows what demons are lurking in the mind of a student pilot, or what all they had lied about on those screening tests? The moment of truth can be a defining one for student and instructor alike. On my first solo landing, I set the wheels down right beside Lieutenant Anderson who was standing on the runway with the fire truck just in case I went "tango uniform" (a clever military phonetics pun for "tits up," meaning exactly that). If my pulse rate changed, I didn't know it. Perhaps, it was good that Marines weren't that smart because it never occurred to me to be scared of something that I had been doing with a good teacher for several weeks. Anderson was probably as relieved as he was proud, but I had soloed, and we could both check off that box.

When I returned to my quarters, my roommate, Lenny Young, was not there. He didn't show up for dinner either. Later that night he stopped by the room to tell me that his solo hadn't gone well. It took him four passes to land the plane after three harrowing attempts in which he bounced hanger high. He said it didn't help that after the first attempt they manned the fire truck, and he could see the red emergency light flashing. I could tell he was still shaken because he was chain-lighting cigarettes and had two or three going. Lenny never bought cigarettes. He had already quit the flight program and had spent the rest of the day processing out. We had one last night as roommates and that was the last I ever saw of Lenny Young.

Lenny and I had spent a great amount of time together. He had introduced me to his girlfriend's roommate and finagled tickets for the four of us to attend a fantastic Hawaiian luau at the Mustin Beach Officer's Club. The girls were charming Southern belles from Columbus, Mississippi, fresh out of college. Kay Fleming was an Ole Miss sorority beauty who told stories of the Mississippi National Guard digging foxholes outside her dorm room during the famous James Meredith crisis. After the girls cooked us a spaghetti dinner in their apartment with a jug of cheap Chianti, we could hardly let them out of our sights on weekends. Now, Lenny had been erased from the picture, and I would be flying solo back and forth to Miss Fleming's apartment.

The relentless game of attrition continued in the classroom with subjects like Physics, Engines, Aerodynamics, Meteorology, Recognition, Astronomy, Morse Code, Flight Theory, Navigation, and Hydraulics. We used a hand-held flight calculator for wind speed and direction problems, fuel consumption, and time of arrival for complex cross country calculations. They locked us into claustrophobic flight simulators to practice instrument flight rules, complicated instrument procedures and landings in bad weather. We went to a simulated altitude of 30,000 feet for hypoxia training to demonstrate the effects of oxygen deprivation at altitudes. We packed our own parachutes and studied alongside Apollo astronauts who were there to master helicopter controls that mimicked the controls in the lunar landing module. One day you made a friend during the mile swim, and the next day he was no longer in the program. The only thing for which I had a natural knack was the obstacle course, and I sometimes finished with the best time. The key was to be the first one out of the blocks and be the first to reach each obstacle, so you wouldn't be hung up in the bottlenecks along the way. Waiting in line behind someone who can't climb a 15 foot wall with a knotted rope can waste valuable time. If you could hit the wall running, you only needed the rope for a little leverage to reach the top. Once your hand caught the top of the wall, it was just a pull-up from there.

The biggest secret to surviving all these tests was simply the ability to adapt. I tried not to use all my energy fighting the system or being negative. By doing whatever task was in front of me at the moment, I managed to satisfactorily complete all the requirements. Keeping an open mind and looking for opportunities is as good a survival strategy as I know. The ability to excel at any one thing was not as important as avoiding hang-ups or falling victim to a critical weakness. A good balance of physical, mental, and emotional can pull a person through almost anything, and a sense of humor can knock the rough edges off a tough assignment. The most important thing I tried to remember was that if thousands of aviators had gone through that program, then so could I.

Five months after I arrived in Pensacola, the president of South Vietnam was assassinated, another bungled attempt at espionage by John F. Kennedy. In early November of 1963, in one final, desperate effort to achieve a rational foothold in South Vietnam, Kennedy sent Ambassador Henry Cabot Lodge to Saigon to orchestrate Ngo Dinh Diem's overthrow. This was a curious political reversal considering that Kennedy's vice president, Lyndon Johnson, had been referring to Diem as *"the Winston Churchill of Vietnam."* In reality, both Diem and his despised brother, Ngu, had a notorious reputation among their own people for murder, mayhem, and drug use. They simply killed anyone who was in their way. Other internal coups had been attempted but had failed. Diem's removal was intended to be bloodless and had been carefully staged and coordinated by the CIA. On the day the brothers were to be deposed, they were instructed by the CIA to escape through a secret tunnel, a plan to save their lives. At the last minute, the arrogant pair decided not to co-operate. This infuriated their captors, who already hated them, and the well-planned coup took an unexpected dark turn when they were both shot in the head execution style. When this news reached JFK, he was shaken to the core, and the incident served to further undermine JFK's faith in our Vietnam involvement. Sources close to him believed he would withdraw after his re-election.

JFK might have altered the collision course of the Baby Boomers and Vietnam by pulling out of Vietnam as predicted. But, as fate continued to deal the cards, just 20 days after Diem's botched coup, JFK himself fell victim to an assassin's bullet. On 22 November, 1963, the future and the idealism of our little flight school class were going "tango uniform." To make matters even more sickening, JFK's assassin was a former Marine. Over the long Thanksgiving holiday weekend, one of the major television networks ran a special report on ex-Marines who had gone rogue. Families across America sat in their homes and watched these morbid stories for days. It was impossible to feel proud in a Marine uniform for several weeks. None of this felt good to anybody, especially young, idealistic Marines. "Someone left our cake out in the rain," and our sweet green icing was melting fast.

For the next few months, as the nation grieved the loss of our president, his vice president, Lyndon Johnson, took the reins. There was an unprecedented amount of unrest on college campuses, much of it centering on race relations. A perfect storm was brewing in our own country. Had someone recognized this, perhaps our new president might have shifted his focus away from the specter of Communism to some of our domestic problems, but for some reason, America has always held a strong fascination, if not an outright obsession, for coming to the aid of people who can't do a damn thing for us. The way this was shaping up, the only space that my new aviator friends and I would be exploring would be the gray skies over the rice paddies of Southeast Asia. Our new president, the third one to support the Vietnam War, pulled on his cowboy boots and saddled up like a true Texan.

One month after the assassination of Kennedy, I was married to Katherine Dennis Fleming, in her hometown of Columbus, Mississippi. That same evening, December 20, 1963, we left for a short honeymoon at the Fontainebleau Hotel in New Orleans, driving through a rare snow blizzard that produced nearly a foot of snow.

BOY SCOUTS AND PRESIDENTS

In America anyone can become President. That's one of the risks you take.

Senator Adlai Stevenson

Within days of my becoming an illegal Tenderfoot Scout in 1954, Dwight D. Eisenhower, our highly decorated five-star president, was busy making a decision in Vietnam that would eventually impact every Boy Scout and Baby Boomer in America. Vietnam was a French colony then, and the French had their hands full with a Communist organization in North Vietnam called the Viet Mein. On March 13, French troops were surrounded by Viet Mein fighters at a place called Dien Bien Phu, and they were calling their allies for help. Eisenhower had already supplied two or three billion dollars and 300,000 weapons to aid the French effort, but for some reason, he decided against sending help in their most critical moment. Instead, he offered two atomic bombs which they would have to drop themselves. The French refused that extreme solution and were subsequently massacred, causing North Vietnam to fall into the hands of the Communists under a brilliant strategist named Ho Chi Minh. I remembered from reading my American history about the American Revolution that the French had come to the aid of George Washington. They supplied gunpowder, not atomic bombs. Apparently, our then president felt he had given enough support to the French in Vietnam.

Ike was a skilled military strategist and knew full well that wars are fought over *material assets*. He immediately shifted his total support to the infamously corrupt government of South Vietnam and its French installed president, Ngo Dinh Diem. Ike's strategy of allowing the French to be removed from the Vietnam picture would supposedly provide the US access to valuable assets. As he put it, war is an investment, and in the end, it's the cheapest way to obtain essential materials from certain parts of the world. At a governor's conference in Seattle in 1953, he explained his reasoning for his recent 400 million dollar military commitment to the French effort:

"...the cheapest way that we can prevent the occurrence that would be of most terrible significance to the United States. Now, let us assume that we lose Indochina. If Indochina goes, several things happen right away. The Malay Peninsula, which is the last little bit of land hanging on down there, would be scarcely defensible. The tin and tungsten that we so greatly value from that area would cease coming. One by one, other Asian nations would be toppled. So you see, somewhere along that line, this must be blocked, and it must be blocked now. That is what the French are doing."

"So," he continued, *"when the United States votes $400 million to help that war, we are not voting for a giveaway program. We are voting for the cheapest way that we can prevent the occurrence of something that would be of the most terrible significance for the United States of America..."*

our security, **our power and ability to get certain things from the riches of Southeast Asia."**

Straight answers like that are not common in politics, but Ike's candor sheds light on our Vietnam "investment." He could have reinforced his comments by adding, *"We don't want China and Russia to have those assets."*

Ike's analogy of the one-by-one toppling of nations to Communism was the first known reference to the *domino theory*, suggesting a blow to our national security if these resources should fall into the wrong hands. Vietnam had been divided into two countries after WWII: the Communists, under self-appointed President Ho Chi Minh in the North, and the "Democratic" Republic in the South, separated by a line in the middle at the 17th parallel. The division of the country was to be temporary and would be followed by an election that would eventually unite the North and the South. The U.S., however, would not allow that election, knowing the more popular Ho Chi Minh would easily win. This created a slow simmering civil war of hatred instigated by Ho Chi Minh. He began a methodical siege to infiltrate the South and overthrow the weak and arrogant U.S. supported South Vietnamese government headed by Ngo Dinh Diem.

By 1962, Ike's youthful and inexperienced successor, John F. Kennedy, took over where the French and Eisenhower left off. Advisors and military supplies were being sent to Saigon to support a fledgling, unpopular, and notoriously corrupt political regime. Diem and his despotic brother dictated with an iron hand until November of 1963. JFK had reluctantly inherited Ike's Vietnam position, and he sent more than 16,000 American advisors, Special

Forces personnel, fighter jets, and equipment to support Diem's unstable regime.

JFK soon grew weary of this money pit and the murderous Diem. Many of JFK's staff, including his secretary of defense, Robert McNamara, expected a withdrawal from Vietnam as soon as he became re-elected in 1964. While we were sending advisors and military equipment to Diem, Russia and China were doing the same thing for Ho Chi Minh, with shiploads of Russian surface-to-air missiles, munitions, and supplies coming into Haiphong Harbor. More than 60 tons of food and munitions per day were being smuggled across the demilitarized zone through Laos on the infamous Ho Chi Minh Trail.

During this era, our country was obsessed with the notion that Communism might take over the world, and many political decisions were guided by that irrational fear. JFK, a man who read his share of Ian Fleming's (James Bond) spy novels, orchestrated an outrageous plot to assassinate Cuban leader Fidel Castro in April of 1961. This spurred the wrath of Russia, who sent long-range missiles to be concealed in Cuba. We then had nuclear missiles 90 miles from American soil. In October 1962, JFK barely averted WW III in a standoff with Russian Premier Nikita Krushchev. The Boy Scouts were in college by now, and we were watching all this high drama unfold on television from our dorm rooms. Classes were closed for two days while the Cuban Missile Crisis and our entire future played out before our eyes. This was a very scary time for this Boy Scout, as none of us knew for certain if college classes or life as we knew it would ever resume again.

A generous supply of Baby Boomers was available by the time I came along. They supplied most of the teenagers who served with me in Vietnam. Their average age was 19, but regardless of where they grew up, most of them volunteered. That's right--*volunteered!* Some weren't old enough to vote and couldn't have found Vietnam on a map, but the Boomers supplied nearly two million young men for that war. When it was finally over, these former Gerber babies led this nation into an era of unprecedented growth and financial prosperity, and they still dominate our economy.

Our North Vietnamese enemy was an even younger group of scrappy fighters, and their training was significantly different than ours. American soldiers were trained to *fight against* Communism, and those fellows were being trained to *die* for it. In that pursuit, they were being told to kill as many Baby Boomers as possible, and as it turned out, they were pretty darn good at it. However, they weren't nearly as effective as we were at killing them.

Destroying another human being has absolutely no appeal to an American teenager, but it pales in significance to the idea of *being killed.* Any child can figure out, entirely on his own, that he doesn't want to die. When you grow up in the Bible belt and your bedtime prayer includes, *"If I should die before I wake,"* God knows, it's something that is always in the back of one's mind. It's a terrific burden for young boys to grow up knowing that they may someday have to die for their country. Nevertheless, it's a cross they continue to bear.

For several years the US government referred to our involvement in Vietnam as a *conflict* because Congress never officially declared war. In fact, Congress hasn't declared war since 1941. Since the prolonged Vietnam conflict spanned five US presidents, a relentless media eventually promoted the Vietnam Conflict to the status of *War.*

The Eagle, Globe, and Anchor represent the three elements in which the Marines perform their combat duty; it is the only branch of service to operate in the air, on land, and sea.

[Inclusion of this image does not imply that either the Department of the Navy nor any other component of the Department of Defense has approved, endorsed, or authorized this book.]

Some went off to fight the war

halfway 'round the world.

Some lost touch with reality.

Some lost their steady girls.

They were dying in living color

every night on the six-o'clock news.

We were safe and sound,

with our windows rolled down,

on Summer Avenue.

Singer/songwriter Everett Brown, Murfreesboro, TN

From lyrics to *Summer Avenue,* by permission.

A naval aviator must know the wind and weather. He must understand the stresses of heat and cold and be able to function on land and sea. He must know the elements and command them all. Most of all, he must command himself.

[Inclusion of this image does not imply that either the Department of the Navy nor any other component of the Department of Defense has approved, endorsed, or authorized this book.]

26 Feb, 1966

It's noon Saturday in Okinawa. We spent four hours yesterday being processed after our plane landed, and we were checked into the officer's quarters. Apparently, the nine shots they gave me 36 hours ago to bring my shot records up to date and to prepare me for the "strains" of Southeast Asia, were not enough. In two hours I will receive 10cc's of gamaglobin for hepatitis. It's a horse needle in the butt, but at least it doesn't make you sick. I've had a fever and chills for three days from the reaction to those other vaccinations.

After being on a plane for nearly two days and a bus for three hours, the freedom to stretch out on a bed after a hot shower has put me in a better mood. When we landed in Anchorage, Alaska, to refuel, I nearly froze to death when they opened the plane door. I grabbed every blanket I could find as the others went out to see what Alaska is like in February. Those shots are wearing off now, but I can tell I'm not in Kansas anymore. There are a dozen Asian maids running around here doing laundry, ironing, shining shoes, and handing out fresh soap. This is a different culture, especially when it comes to modesty. These women walk right into the shower or into your room without knocking. They mop, dust, or pick up your laundry all day long. All these services come at the bargain price of 70 cents a day. This is *their place,* and we are only transients passing through. Mercifully, none of these gals are showstoppers.

I rode on the plane from California with Major Bob Plamondon, Captain Harold "Gus" Plum, and Lieutenant Tony Pecoraro. We were all in VMO-1 together in Jacksonville, NC, but were not seated together on the crowded plane. I just wanted to sleep and wait out the effects of those shots. This hasn't been a great start for my deployment. After the long, grueling flight, we spent nearly two hours sitting on a shuttle bus waiting to be delivered to our quarters. There was the usual amount of horseplay, but I wasn't part of it.

Anyone who has ever had anything to do with the military knows that every group activity revolves around *waiting*. Tony entertained me with stories about losing every bet at the Meadowlands Race Track and joking that he and Helen had blown through every penny of their savings. Like me, he has just come off a long leave in anticipation of being separated from his wife and son. He saw no reason for delayed gratification. Right now, we're all just frozen in time, five days into our deployment and not a single one of us knowing what we will be facing next. Such is the life of a soldier, I guess.

I was advised by some jungle veterans that most of the clothes I brought with me are not suitable. This included just about anything that resembled civilian clothing and some of my uniform clothing as well. Comfortable, green cotton utility trousers and blouses, as we call them, plus a dozen or so olive green tee shirts and skivvies (underwear), will be our basic wardrobe. In the combat zone, we will be living in our flight suits around the clock. I had a little time to visit the PX (Post Exchange store) to make some minor uniform adjustments and was able to leave a full duffel bag of useless gear in storage. They said it would be waiting for me on the way back through. *Yeah, right!*

At 0530 tomorrow morning, we will board a plan for Danang.

MEMORANDUM

From: Commanding Officer, Marine Aircraft Group-26
To: 1/LT WILLIS, B
Via: Commanding Officer, VMO

1. For planning purposes you can expect orders to WESTPAC, in place date not later than 28 FEB 66 to fill a UH-1E billet.

2. At this time the method of issuing orders, proceed and leave enroute is not known.

By direction

A soldier doesn't have the luxury of rhetorical debate when he's handed his orders and asked to execute them. Whatever questions might be tumbling through his mind have to be sorted out between himself and his own code of values. Every single day of training for the previous three years had led to this point, and it came as no surprise. No one asked if I had a young wife and a two-week-old child when they issued my orders, nor did I try to offer that as an excuse. Those decisions were mine to make, not theirs. None of us were *drafted* into our circumstances; we were all volunteers.

27 Feb, 1966

Greetings from Pan Am Flight 1148 from Kadena AFB Okinawa to Danang Air Base in the Republic of Vietnam. We have a full airplane. My seat back and tray table are in the full upright and locked position, and I hope I can say that when this tour is over. It's only 1120, and we have already logged four more hours of military waiting. We receive no medals for waiting. Someone should look into that.

To calculate the time difference, subtract 10 hours from central time and add a day. We have a three hour flight ahead of us. I'm not sure if the time will change again in Danang. We won't know until we check in if our orders will take us to a place called Chu Lai or to Marble Mountain near Danang. Scuttlebutt has it that the living conditions might be slightly better at Marble. We'll see.

Last night the four horsemen from VMO-1 decided to have dinner together at the officer's club in Kadena. My *new best friends*! Nothing breeds camaraderie quite like a common crisis. I hope it wasn't our last supper together. We made a corny pact, led by the major, to look after each other and come out of this thing alive. How we plan to look after each other is not entirely clear. Maybe, we will simply stay in touch and pull for one another to survive. How would I know?

We also spent some time at the extremely large PX,

which resembled a football-field-sized department store chocked full of bargain-basement merchandise made in Japan and deeply discounted to the military. This stuff is wildly popular among servicemen, and I've seen plenty of it at New River while visiting senior officers' homes for social hours. Tony was excited, but none of it appealed to me. I had other things on my mind, and all that seemed like junk to me. The major held up a piece of Noritaki china and showed us how the light shines right through it. *Whatever you say, major!* It isn't important to me to see through my dinner plate.

Tony bought a watch for Helen who already has a watch but not one from Okinawa. He never found a place to mail it, so Helen will have to mark time with her old watch for a little while longer.

As we were leaving the PX we ran into Gary Hebert, a first lieutenant also from VMO-1, who came over about a month ago. He was selected to play on the All-Marine basketball team. I played in a few pickup games during lunch hours with him at New River. Gary could score 20 points before I could tie my shoelaces. He was in Okinawa for a game against the Air Force team. This is one of those dream jobs that would be nice to have, like playing first chair trumpet in the Marine Corps Band. Anything to keep out of sniper range!

Gary filled us in on what we might expect in the days ahead. It started with plenty of flying, and he warned us that we should be prepared to *"hit the ground running."* He didn't see the irony in that as I pictured him in his little basketball shorts *running* a fast break. He was stationed at Chu Lai in VMO-6, a Huey sister-squadron. Other mutual friends had been sent to Marble Mountain with VMO-2. They were doing the same kinds of jobs at both places. By this time tomorrow, I will know which of these two squadrons will be blessed with my service.

A man with his head in a cloud must keep his feet on the ground.

MILITARY INTELLIGENCE

New River Air Facility Jacksonville, NC 1965

After flight school we were assigned to fly either rotary wing (helicopters) or fixed wing (jets). Since the war in Southeast Asia was shaping up to be a helicopter war, the strategists at the Pentagon were ramping up for chopper pilots. The top five percent of each class could have their choice of jets or choppers, and most of them wanted jets, or said they did anyway. Everyone else, especially Marines, were assigned choppers. There was no way that I could have been anywhere near the top five percent of any of those classes. We filled out a form requesting our preferences, and I imagined a couple of officers sorting through that huge pile of *"dream sheets"* with a big red pencil. I decided to save them some trouble by making helicopters my first choice. There was a Huey squadron on the East Coast in Jacksonville, NC, and I asked to be sent there.

New River Air Station was the home of Marine Observation Squadron One (VMO-1) commanded by Colonel Burneal Smith. It was an old tobacco farm purchased by the government back in 1941, the year I was born. There were about 40 pilots, and nearly half were fresh out of flight school. The veterans among us were there to whip us rookies into shape for combat in Vietnam. We were flying the world's first turbine powered helicopter, built by Bell Helicopter, a division of Textron.

Early in 1962, the Department of Defense held a competition to supply the Marines with a new helicopter. The UH-34, still being used as a workhorse by the Marines, was early 1950's technology. Its performance suffered under the rigors of heat and humidity, and it lacked firepower. It was originally designed as an anti-submarine helicopter. It also lacked agility, and its size made it a vulnerable target. The results of the "contest" were announced on 3 March 1962. The Bell UH-1 was the clear winner. The first "Huey" was delivered to the Marine Corps in February 1964. We were its pioneer pilots. This is the airplane that would become the symbol of the Vietnam War. This new turbine powered, rotary-wing aircraft was the envy of all the chopper pilots. We called it by many names: airplane, aircraft, chopper, bird, helo, Huey, helicopter, plane, gunship, gunbird, ambulance, and slick, to list a few. A sister squadron on the West coast was doing exactly the same thing that we were doing in its training for combat.

The makeup of a squadron includes pilots with a mixture of ranks and experience. There is an unspoken, but obvious pecking order among them based on flying experience, not rank. We all wore our names on everything. It didn't take long to know everybody's name and which officers were more receptive to the rookies. Those who were rank conscious were carefully avoided since us young lieutenants were on the tail end of the pecking order, only one notch higher than plankton on the food chain. Each pilot had two or three additional collateral job assignments that were randomly selected for us by Colonel Smith and his second-in-command, the executive officer.

The new squadron also had a few fixed wing airplanes. These were O1-C's used as spotter planes for calling in artillery and fixed wing airstrikes. Since we had all been trained to fly fixed-wing, we would be expected to fly both in Vietnam. The 01, aka Birddog, was a Cessna C-170 except that it had additional radios and a two-man crew, consisting of a pilot in the front seat and an artillery observer in the rear seat. I was given a check-out flight prior to taking a Birddog out for a solo run.

It was a beautiful day for flying when I signed the operations log for my very first solo in the O1-Charlie. I climbed out of the traffic pattern and headed for the airspace northwest of New River to practice acrobatic maneuvers, stalls, and spins. Loops and barrel rolls are things you can't do in a helicopter, which is not made to be turned upside-down. I was looking forward to having some solo fun. I leveled off at a safe altitude of 8,000 feet and flew around for a while at full throttle checking to see if I had any company before I started my stunts. When I tried to back the power off, the throttle wouldn't budge. I tried pulling it back with both hands and jiggling it sideways, but there was no moving it. Short of breaking it off with brute force, which would accomplish nothing, I was stuck. After tinkering with it and racking my brain for a few minutes, I began going over in my head the emergency procedures for a dead-stick landing. This meant flying back to the runway, cutting the power, and turning the Birddog into a glider.

I wasn't concerned about the landing because it made an excellent glider. My concern was the same one that haunts every military pilot. Had I done something stupid to cause the problem that might bring the humiliating wrath of the squadron down on me? I finally pressed the radio transmitter to broadcast the dreaded words that no pilot ever wants to hear, especially out of his own mouth. These crisp, clean, unmistakable words I knew would cease all other radio traffic and bring the entire New River Air Facility to a complete halt and possibly reduce me to less than plankton.

"Mayday! Mayday!"

"This is Birddog one two. I am 15 miles northwest of New River at 8,000 feet in straight and level flight. My throttle is stuck in the full open position. Over."

The men in the tower then began pushing buttons that I could only imagine from my lofty predicament. After a few conversations in which I had to assure more than one person that this was indeed an emergency and that there was no way to land that plane with the engine running at full throttle at sea level, I told them my plan. I would fly back to the runway at my current altitude and descend until the manifold pressure and the airspeed were redlined. Then, I would cut the engine by turning the fuel off and make two lazy circles down to the runway and land. By now, one of our veteran squadron pilots, very familiar with the O1, had been summoned to the tower. He agreed that my plan was the best way to kill the engine. By cutting the fuel, I might be able to restart the engine safely if I happened to butcher the power-off landing. It's amazing how uncluttered your mind can be when it's your butt that's on the line.

The runway was a mile long. I only needed a couple of hundred yards, so I wasn't worried about the landing. At 2,500 feet with the engine wide open, I came across the runway numbers and killed the engine. Then, it was just a matter of judging the two wide 360 degree turns. I would need to manage the altitude in order to hit the ideal spot -- hopefully, near that precautionary red fire truck they had conveniently summoned for the occasion. I had four half turns to lose 2500 feet or about 300 feet per quarter turn. I would start with those checkpoints and adjust after the first full turn.

With the powerless prop wind-milling to a halt, the wheels didn't even squeak when I floated in and rolled to a stop right next to the fire truck. Three men were standing there in white fire retardant suits with hoses in their hands. The man who was perched on top of the truck gave me a big thumbs-up and a smile, followed by a pantomimed clapping motion; the kind that's symbolic but makes no sound. A "Follow-Me" truck came out to pick me up and give me a ride back to the flight line. Then, I began the long walk up the stairs to the squadron ready room to talk to the skipper and file the dreaded incident report. By the time I climbed to the top of the steps to the ready room, my legs were wobbly. Colonel Smith told me this was because my adrenaline had spiked.

The first thing everybody thinks about with a rookie pilot, of course, is pilot error. By now, they all knew that was my first solo in that airplane. The next morning, at the all-pilot meeting, the skipper called on me to describe every detail of the incident and answer questions. I told every detail just as I wrote it here, and nobody asked questions. Afterwards, he said that he had never heard of anything like that happening in an O-1, but it looked like *Mister Willis* had devised a textbook emergency procedure for it if it ever happened again. The term *Mister* in the military can mean one of two things: a verbal flash of respect or a subtle reproof. I tried not to overanalyze that, knowing that any pat on the back is only a few short vertebras away from a kick in the butt anyway.

Official explanations are never as satisfying as alternative theories, so after the meeting everybody had to "weigh in" with me on the incident. A senior captain named K.D Waters, who came in late to the meeting, "got in my face" demanding to know what I was doing up there at 8000 feet in the first place. One of the other senior captains chimed in, *"He was doing acrobatics, Numbnuts, leave him alone."* Waters was the only person to challenge me, but that was the one that stuck. I did an excellent job of keeping my mouth shut with him. This was the typical initiation into the pilot fraternity, supported by peers and suspected by superiors. That kind of intense scrutiny, right down to the stubble on your chin, helps to hone the pilot-preparation process. All the 0-1's had to be grounded until they could determine the cause of the problem.

Every Marine pilot had secondary duties. At New River I served as the squadron *Intelligence Officer*. This was a fitting assignment for a second lieutenant without a clue. This job gave me the keys to the room where all the classified (secret) information was stored. I was to familiarize myself with the constant flow of classified material and bring any new or unusual items to the attention of our commanding officer. The term "military intelligence" has since been ranked as one of the top ten oxymorons of our time. However, in 1965 it was slightly more highly regarded, at least among the faithful. In a year of doing this, I never once read anything that I thought would interest our fearless leader or affect our squadron parties. Most of it could be found in *TIME* and *Newsweek*.

This room was one of the few rooms in the building

that was air conditioned and had peace and quiet, so I went there to read and feel important. I was too green to interpret some of the documents. On the first day of April 1965, for example, President Johnson changed the mission of the Marine Corps from a defensive role (protect our bases) to an active combat role (seek out the enemy). This was part of a plan to involve the Marines more directly in Vietnam. This was hardly shocking information but somewhat historic in the sense that the Marine Corps was founded for one particular reason, and after nearly 200 years , it seemed as if we were being folded into the Army. It was ironic that Johnson signed this order on April Fool's Day.

Military strategists divided South Vietnam into four tactical areas: the I Corps and the II, III and IV Corps. The Marines were assigned to protect the northernmost section called the I Corps and would headquarter in Danang. Everybody pronounced it, the *"Eye Corps."* On April 29, 1965, an advance party of Marines erected three general purpose tents near the southwest corner of the old airstrip at Danang, Republic of Vietnam. Nine aircraft and their crews were waiting aboard the USS Princeton after a hurried departure from Okinawa to join the struggle to defeat the Vietnamese Communists (VC). On 3 May, six UH-1E's led by Lieutenant Colonel George Bauman flew into the country to begin a new era in Marine Corps aviation history. By mid May, the tiny squadron, operating from both the Princeton offshore and from Danang, participated heavily in a regimental amphibious landing, dubbed Chu Lai. The Chu Lai enclave would be home to a second squadron of Hueys (VMO-6), 56 miles southeast of Danang.

The Marines had landed! The Chu Lai landing created

the III Marine Amphibious Force (III MAF) which would be commanded out of Danang.

Hunkered down in my intelligence library at New River, I was determined to find out what all this Vietnam fuss was about. Are North Vietnamese Communists really a threat to our national security? Something was missing. I found several long articles that had to do with the supply and demand for rice in Asia and the strategic role that South Vietnam played in those economics. South Vietnam was the third largest producer of the world's most sought after grain and a neighbor to nearly a billion people in China who would eat the stuff three times a day if they had it. South Vietnam had enough *surplus* rice to feed millions of starving Chinese and was considered the bread basket of Southeast Asia.

So my mother was right when she told us, "People *in China are starving.*" I took this rice theme and ran with it. At least I had found a reason for the war. Roughly, 90% of the world's rice supply is consumed by Asians. The explosive growth of world population was threatening our ability to feed it. China didn't want anybody else controlling the rice fields of the Mekong Delta. Russia was going along, not for the rice, but because they simply hated everything America stood for. North Vietnam was merely China's sock-puppet in the rice scheme and was led by one of the most skilled terrorists of all time. Ho Chi Minh had established his credibility in the Communist world by kicking the French out of North Vietnam. This ruthless genius, lightly regarded by the US, would play the role of our antagonist in the Communist's play to capture the rich South Vietnam bread basket. China and Russia would gladly supply most of the military hardware to Ho Chi Minh.

South Vietnam was an undeveloped country with a weak, corrupt government, hardly worth a loud argument. There were only three major cities, Saigon, Danang and Hue, and except for the rice, there was little else worth fighting over. Danang was so primitive that it didn't even have a sewer system. There was speculation about oil reserves in the South China Sea that had not yet been confirmed. I had a journalism teacher in college who taught me that just because something is in print doesn't mean it's the gospel. Above all else, he encouraged his students to be objective.

Killing people has never been a high-minded exercise. When I dug a little deeper, I learned that wars are not fought over ideology, religion, or philosophy. People fight and die for purely economic reasons and for material things such as land, natural resources, or regional necessities like food and water. Communism, Socialism, Buddhism, Capitalism or any other *ism* is not a concept that would inspire an ordinary person to kill his neighbor. Wars are fought over useful things that can be loaded in a truck and shipped around the world with a price tag on them. You can't load the domino theory onto a forklift.

But there was more to read in my secret library in 1965 than articles about cereal. The late President Kennedy's pet project to land a man on the moon within the decade had produced the Apollo Space Program. There were some interesting military implications to our space initiatives, including computers, cameras, and satellites already in orbit. The race for space went into high gear after the Russians put Sputnik into space. The proposed lunar landing module was being engineered to mimic the controls of a helicopter, exactly the same as a Huey. The LEM would use thrusters instead of rotors, but the controls would be virtually identical to a rotary wing aircraft. This way, the astronauts would be able to practice landing the module by manipulating a helicopter. We had those clever German engineers on our side, and they had thought of everything.

The Apollo astronauts who sat in on some of our flight school sessions in Pensacola were a big part of why most of my new pilot friends had volunteered for all this in first place. We were the new generation of risk takers -- Eagle Scouts, high on Coca Cola! We may not have been as gung-ho as John Glenn, but we were all trying to give to Marine aviation what he would have called "*a hunnerd percent.*" We sure as hell hadn't planned on landing our capsules in the leech-infested rice paddies of Vietnam.

In spite of Kennedy's embarrassments, LBJ spurred ahead. We were America, not the French, and we'll put a Texas-sized boot in your butt in a New York minute. Our new president had several powerful options. He could decide on an all-out attack to subdue North Vietnam, or he could employ a patient strategy of winning over the enemy with pacification and civil action programs. We could teach the South Vietnamese farmers to grow a bug resistant rice hybrid that would increase their yields from 1½ tons per hectare, once a year, to four or five tons per hectare *twice* a year. We could do anything because we were the most powerful nation in the world. We could turn those farmers into capitalists in no time and put a chicken in every pot and a Rice Honda in every hut.

Our military leaders eventually split on the best way to approach the war. LBJ's Supreme Commander, Army General William Westmoreland, was promoting a game of attrition, meaning we can kill more of them than they can kill of us because we have more and bigger toys. This would have made an interesting recruiting poster, *"We're having a war of attrition. Sign up here!"*

Five Star General Westmoreland was in command of the entire Vietnam Theater, but the Army controlled only the Southern portions of South Vietnam. The Marines were in control of the northernmost section, but they had to answer to Westmoreland. Top Marine generals Victor Krulak and Lewis W. Walt were not enthralled with Westy's "war of attrition" and tried to steer the strategy in a different direction. Krulak wanted to cut off supplies coming from China by mining Haiphong Harbor, which he considered the mouth that was feeding the war. Walt was promoting far-reaching civic action programs designed to *"win the hearts and minds of the people."* The Marine Corps had been founded on a simple principle: go in, kill the enemy and get out! Taking over a piece of land is a concept that every Marine can wrap his head around. We are trained for that. Sitting around playing defense to protect it is somebody else's job. Now, we've been inserted in the middle of a great civil war, playing political ping-pong with no clearcut objectives.

From the beginning, there seemed to be no real game plan for Vietnam, certainly nothing that would serve as a rallying cry for the young men who would have to execute it. If our own generals couldn't come up with a singular strategy, how could they explain it to the troops? We weren't sure if we were still the Marine Corps or a new version of the Peace Corps. Our politicians were also having difficulty grasping our imprecise motives, and Congress was unable to present a unified front to the American public. The nation was divided on how to proceed. Everybody who was lucky enough to live in a free country voiced their opinion, and a record number of "armchair quarterbacks" were coming out of the woodwork. I knew this war was going to present some interesting survival challenges for me and my new pilot friends.

"There is nothing more gratifying to a Marine on the ground than the sound of an inbound Huey." SSgt Gary L. Weatherford, USMC

ALWAYS FAITHFUL

On the first day of March, 1966, I flew my first combat mission out of Marble Mountain Air Facility, VMO-2's new location just across the Han River, two miles east of Danang. This storied squadron was popularized by Tom Selleck when he wore the VMO-2 ball cap during his long running *Magnum PI* television series. As a Marine, I belonged to an elite, 190 year old organization that carried the vanguard of American freedom squarely on its shoulders. There is a code among Marines that they all hold sacred: S*emper Fidelis,* which simply means "always faithful."

This group of young aviators would be controlling millions of dollars worth of airplanes, munitions, equipment, and taxpayer's money! We were engaged in a *helicopter war,* and we would be in the thick of things, flying an elite new jet-powered aircraft. These helicopters would shuttle Marines directly into live action on an hourly basis unlike any other war in history. While soldiers in WWII might see an average of 20 hours of combat exposure during the entire war, in this unique war, choppers would make it possible for men to see 10 or 20 times that exposure in a *single year.* The turbine powered, overachieving, heavily-armed Huey emerged as the alpha-dog of the chopper arsenal. Without question, it ran the war during the time I spent there, and our small band of rookie Huey drivers, operating closest to North Vietnam, found ourselves on the bleeding edge.

There was no way that the Marine Corps or anyone

could have prepared us for what we would find over there. The first few combat missions were terrifying, and they were nothing like what we had trained for at New River. The events chronicled in these stories during 1966 and early '67 would prove to be a tipping point for defining that war and American policy toward it.

CHAPTER THREE

SNAPPING IN

28 Feb, 1966 Danang

We de-planed around noon and waited for an hour just to form a line. A couple hundred of us were herded into a metal building to be processed like stockyard cattle. The majority of Marine chopper pilots have to fly that lumbering hulk of an outdated contraption called a UH-34. These fellows were the first to be called, and most of them were sent down south to the Chu Lai enclave. Our little group of Huey pilots was hoping to be sent together to Marble Mountain, which is rumored to be the preferred location. The two low ranking first lieutenants, Tony and I, had sort of "grown up" together for the last year or so and had formed a friendship.

Huey's are the most coveted seat in the Marine chopper fleet, so if you had to be in Vietnam flying choppers, why not be in the best place to fly the best? Tony was called before any of us. He was assigned to Chu Lai. So much for staying together! This was not entirely surprising. If anything unusual is going to happen, it's going to happen to the little Italian. When you're with him, you're either going to win the lottery or be struck by lightning; there's no middle ground. He grabbed his duffel bag and headed for the designated chopper that would take him south to Chu Lai. Plamondon also received orders to Chu Lai. It soon became apparent that everyone going to Marble Mountain would be processed last, so this was one long wait that Plum and I didn't mind. However, in typical Marine Corps fashion, there was not a chair or a bench in sight for the endless process. We stood with dozens of others on the blistering concrete, waiting for the branding iron.

Gus and I were surprised to find Major Plamondon on our chopper to Marble Mountain. He said someone had *"pulled some strings"* for him. We had no idea what that meant. No sign of Tony, though. It was almost dark by the time the three of us touched down at our new home, only a three-minute chopper ride from Danang. Bill Kirby, another friend from our old squadron, was our "taxi" pilot, and he looked no worse for wear in the month or so that he's been over here. We could see the vertical limestone rocks of Marble Mountain a few kilometers south of the base.

We visited with some of the guys in the ready room who had come over in the months before us. They were already tanned and lean from the heat and daily grind. None of us had been assigned places to sleep that night, almost as if they were not expecting us. It would be up to each of us to figure all that out in the morning. Meanwhile, we would just sleep in a bunk that was vacated by one of the pilots who had been temporarily sent somewhere else for various overnight assignments. The operations duty officer, whom I had known from New River, took it upon himself to find beds for us for the night, and asked me if it would be okay if I slept in Ron Jennings' bed. I didn't know Ron Jennings, but they told me he was getting medical attention for some sort of foot injury caused by shrapnel wounds. The duty officer called for a motor vehicle to drop us off at our respective hooches.

The next morning I discovered why this location received its three-star rating. It's right on the South China Sea, which may as well be the Atlantic Ocean to this country boy. It's not comparable to the pristine beauty of Pensacola Beach, but much better than living in the middle of the jungle with snakes, blood-sucking leeches, and people trying to kill us. Instead, we can see the foaming surf from our *"hooches."* The view of the shoreline was marred slightly by a seven foot tall roll of razor sharp concertina (barbed wire) extending as far as I could see, maybe three miles down the beach.

Six officers share a wooden framed tent, resembling a crude Quonset hut with plywood floors and brown tarps covering the tops and sides. These are called hooches or huts. The officers sleep on canvas cots with crude mattresses on them. Some are blow-up, military issue, rubber air- mattresses, with layers of standard-issue green wool blankets between the sheets and the hot, sticky rubber. I've slept on these *"rubber ladies"* before, and there is no room for tossing and turning on these cots. You lie down, you go to sleep, and you wake up. That's about it. This is a far cry from the private rooms in Okinawa with female servants handing us soap in the shower.

Each officer has an area of the open hut that is about 10 by 12 feet customized with a makeshift barrier between the spaces. A homemade bookcase or a sheet of Luan paneling provides the only privacy. All these makeshift walls have a similar theme, punctuated with pictures of Playboy pinups. One guy has taken a pair of scissors and cut out dozens of circles of women's breasts which cover his plywood partition over the head of his bed. With all the leftover Christmas decorations strewn about, he's created a vision of overly plump sugarplums that appear to be dancing in his head.

The corner of the hooch contains a confiscated, mini-refrigerator with two small ice trays. There is a parachute for ceiling decoration, and a shipping crate for a common closet. The heat from a 100 watt light bulb attempts to keep the contents of the closet dry. The men wear flight suits and black flight boots with steel toes and very little else. Marines are known for their green tee-shirts which are worn under the flight suits during the cold season. During hot weather the flight suit can be stripped off the shoulders, and the sleeves tied around the waist while lollygagging around, thus another need for the tee-shirt. The majority of the pilots wear a tan cotton flight suit or a green fire retardant Nomex suit. Earplugs are required, but nobody ever uses them. The high pitch sounds of the turbine engine might cause hearing loss over time, but that is the least of our concerns. The common headgear (hat) is the USMC utility cover on the flight line, with a flight helmet stored in the squadron ready room or on the seat of the designated helicopter while on a scramble alert such as medevac. Fire retardant gloves are mandatory on all flights. They are stuffed into the flight helmet along with the pilot's kneeboard while on standby.

Dog tags are also compulsory. These are two small metal tags, worn around the neck with your name, serial number, blood type, and religious preference embossed in raised letters: our identification in case of an emergency or last rites. The notch in the dog tag carries its own legend. Rookie soldiers are told that the notch will be placed between their two front teeth if they are killed in combat and secured there by a swift kick under the chin. The legend is that a WWII private actually did that and woke the victim up. It's really there for holding the tag firmly into the hand-held embossing machine.

The notch in the dog tag carries its own legend.

The breeze off the South China Sea keeps the flies and mosquitoes to a minimum. The little buggers don't fly well in a stiff headwind, but just in case they do show up, a truck comes by in the evening and sprays insecticide. We have no running water and no hot water. For shaving and simple hygiene, we have to walk to the nearest water truck to fill a five gallon can. A personal metal bowl serves as a sink basin for brushing teeth and shaving. The shower is a couple of hundred yards away and has a painted black 55 gallon drum suspended overhead. The water heats up nicely in the hot afternoon sun, which is good for those who shower while the water is still warm. I wasn't one of those. The barrel holds 55 gallons which is less than a gallon per person. Nobody goes there first thing in the morning.

The tent next door has a 12' by 12' makeshift wooden deck crafted from leftover wooden pallets. The deck is littered with dilapidated folding chairs, presumably for beer drinking and story-telling. The chair legs need to be carefully positioned on the boards between the wide cracks in the pallets. This "patio" is covered with an old tarp to provide shade, and inside their hooch I can see a fake Christmas tree that is still poorly decorated and "frocked" with red dirt and sand. There's a barbeque grill made from a steel drum that's been cut in half and balanced on scrap metal legs. Spools that once held communications wire appear to serve as outdoor tables for group picnics. Bring your own chair or stand up. Down the beach, about 200 yards just inside the barbed wire is a crude Tiki hut with a straw roof that serves as an officer's club. It opens early in the afternoon and stays open until lights out, serving drinks with ice.

Between or under every hooch is a bunker about five feet deep lined with burlap sandbags stacked like cement blocks. These are our hiding places during mortar attacks. During our spare time, we are expected to maintain and fortify these bunkers. Two six-hole officer's latrines are strategically placed, as well as several open-air urinals. These pissers, as they are called, amount to no more than a three foot length of "stove pipe" that sticks out of the ground at a convenient angle. They are just randomly located near the main traffic areas. The zippers on the flight suits are one long fly with a double zipper that goes up to the chin and down below the crotch. Underwear is optional in hot weather, and caution is advised with the zipper.

During my short, self-guided orientation, my skin turned pink from the burning sun. We are going to be beach people, I guess, and except that there is a war going on and we are the main characters, this could otherwise be fun. We're camping on the South China Sea.

I saw some unopened mail postmarked back on the 23rd and surmised that mail must take about five days to reach us. Everybody here knows to the day when they will be going home, so seeing new people reminds them of that. We are their replacements, and it makes them feel better somehow to see the new palefaces coming in. Some like to be helpful, while others like to see the rookies squirm for some reason. Dozens of people I know from flight school are here. It doesn't seem that long ago that we were sitting in a cockpit trainer trying to identify the instruments. Now, look at us. We're fighting a real war. Writing about all this relaxes me and makes me feel more like an observer than a participant. Jotting down my thoughts freestyle without trying to organize them seems productive somehow. There isn't time for editing and rewriting … just 30 minutes here and there. Keeping a pen and paper handy is a good release for everything that's racing in my head.

A 30 KW gasoline powered generator cranks out electricity to our huts. It broke down two or three times last night until 2215 when they shut it down for the night. Condition Dim Out! After that, everybody uses flashlights. Everybody except me! I don't own a flashlight. I will need to make a long list of all the things I need, including plenty of batteries. A number of people will be finishing their tours and heading back to the states over the next few weeks. I will be able to negotiate some of the things I need from them.

Just before I fell asleep in Ron Jennings' bed last night, Charlie Plunkett and Steve Waltrip, two of the fellows in the hut came over and filled me in on Ron's injuries and gave me a general idea of what I might expect over the next few days. According to them, there isn't much that my new squadron doesn't do. Much of it seems to take place in a 20-25 mile radius around Danang which they call our *'tactical area of responsibility'* or TAOR. They asked me if I had figured out why the duty officer had assigned me to Ron's bed. I told them that from the looks of the pictures of his wife or girlfriend that it was because he was black. Everybody knew I was a Southern boy from Tennessee and that I had married a girl from Mississippi. Race and civil rights were major news topics, and I guess they figured this was some kind of test for the new Southern boy. They didn't have any clue that I had grown up with black kids and played with them all my life. Ron's hoochmates just wanted me to know that they weren't part of that little joke. They didn't appreciate it any more than I did.

1 Mar 1966

Well, this afternoon I was snapped in. It was a gunship escort of a truck convoy from here to Tam Ky about 30 miles south of here along Route One. So much for the aforementioned TAOR radius! There were two hops: one with Bill Kirby and one with Major Plamondon. I was co-pilot on both, and they were quiet and uneventful. We just flew in circles at a comfortable altitude, flying cover for the convoy for four hours. Kirby and I talked on the intercom, and he gave me a few pointers. Plamondon was as new as I was, and we both figured it out as we went.

When we finished at 1800, I learned that several pilots had been diverted to Chu Lai to check out some kind of enemy activity down there. They will be gone all night, and I am currently standing in for one of them, which means I will sleep in the ready room in case we're called. That's just as well since I don't have my own bed. I'm still sleeping on Ron's dirty sheets. Other beds came open, but I decided to stay in Ron's bed until he comes back because I like his roommates. The downside is that Ron's bed is filthy. He's been gone several days, and the sand covers everything in the hooches. If you don't make your bed and cover it with your poncho, it gathers a thick layer of dirt while you're away. He may have some clean sheets somewhere, but I don't want to go rummaging through his stuff.

The chaplain just brought a big Claxton Christmas

fruitcake into the ready room. That shipment took awhile to come from Texas, but you know fruitcake; it's still okay if you don't mind trimming off a little mold here and there. Obviously, that Christmas package was not a five day delivery.

The food in the mess hall is good … no complaints here. No real milk, some sort of dehydrated eggs, no soft drinks, but plenty of meat and fresh vegetables. Tonight, we had ham and pineapple sauce with several other things. Plenty of it, for sure. In this part of the world, I expected to be eating rice at every meal, but I haven't seen any, which is a puzzle since we flew over several thousand acres of it today.

Because of my all-night standby, I'm being told that I have a day off tomorrow. Maybe, I can use that time to stake out a place with my own bed and pillow. I might even find the time to wash Ron's sheets.

2 March, 1966

During the night the duty officer left a note on my pillow informing me that I was scheduled for an afternoon flight. So much for my day off! I guess I haven't been around long enough to earn one. I was hoping to go into Danang and try to feel out the neighborhood. There's a post exchange there where I could purchase some items for my new quarters.

We're not allowed to use real money here, but you can have US dollars to send home if we ask for it. Otherwise, we receive Military Payment Currency or MPC. It looks like Monopoly money, and it's worthless anyplace but here. There's a thriving black market here that devours American currency, so we use this *'funny money'* for haircuts, PX supplies, poker, or whatever to keep the US dollars out of circulation. If we go into town, we need to exchange the funny money again -- this time for Vietnamese currency which is called piastres, a French word. The locals call it *dong*. One U.S. dollar buys 118 piasters. However, on the black market, a dollar might bring *160-170* piasters, 30% more. This illegal market for US cash keeps the traffic flowing in the streets of the city.

There is a rich irony in all of this. These people are very poor, and this war has dumped carloads of dollars into their economy. War is a big industry that brings employment. It also brings inflation, which dilutes the value of any dong that honest Vietnamese may have saved. There are thousands of Americans throwing money around, and the black market is one of the few ways that savvy locals can protect their purchasing power. The law of supply and demand works in any language, and greed has always been the father of inventive schemes.

Our base commander has worked out some sort of civil action arrangement for local Vietnamese from Danang to come onto the base to do odd jobs like cleaning hooches and cutting hair. Each Vietnamese maid is paid about 1800 piasters each month for cleaning one of our hooches. This amounts to 15-16 dollars which comes to less than five bucks per officer with tip. They are lined up for those jobs. Since tipping is built into the American culture, these ladies have come to expect a little extra cash when they actually *do something.* For what they actually do without being asked, they are overpaid. Mostly, they socialize with each other and raid the refrigerators for our Koolaid and soft drinks. Ron's dirty sheets would be an excellent example of something they won't do without being told.

My afternoon flight was exciting for a guy who has been "in country" for only a couple of days. It was a routine perimeter check with two gunships, one high and one low. The idea is to make sure that they aren't planning a sneak attack on our vulnerable airplanes that sit out on the tarmac all night protected only by our perimeter ground defense. One plane flies low to try to draw some attention, and his armed escort insurance policy circles overhead like a hawk. We were the high ship, and the one that would make the gun run if needed. Normally, it's a routine flight, just not tonight!

About 15 armed VC were spotted in a nearby village not far from our perimeter. The low chopper dropped a red smoke grenade to mark their position, and we had to radio group headquarters for authorization to fire on them, just in case there were any South Vietnamese (friendly) soldiers in that area. It took a little while to receive clearance, maybe five minutes. Finally, our gunship made several passes on the tree line where they were last spotted. I will have to be honest and tell you I didn't see a single person down there, nor did I ever know if we hit anything, but my first live rounds fired at human beings was a night to remember.

It was all over in a few minutes and amounted to nothing, but the feeling of shooting at real people made me dizzy and sick to my stomach. As soon as we stopped, the feeling went away. I tried to imagine that we were just shooting at the trees, which was probably the reality of it. We're told they have spider holes dug in those tree lines. They could have been plotting some overnight mischief, so maybe we sent them a strong message to leave us alone for the evening.

Meanwhile, back at the hooch, my pillow for the night is a canvas duffel bag with a blanket crammed in it, and I still don't have my own bed. Lying there staring into the blackness of my strange new world, I knew I had to figure out a way to survive 13 months of this. For starters I would need to learn everything I could about the Huey and its armament.

The VMO-2 Huey gunships are armed with a TK-2 Weapons Kit, consisting of six electrically operated M60 machine guns firing 30 caliber, 7.62 NATO approved (full metal jacket) rounds of ammo. There is a rocket pod on each side of the helicopter carrying a total of fourteen 2.75 inch white phosphorus or high explosive rockets. These weapons are fixed and have to be pointing directly at the target which requires the pilot to make a kamikaze type gun run into the target area sometimes into a hail of returned fire. Each door has an M-60 machine gun on a door mount for traversing gunfire when the Huey is pulling off the target. Each Huey is equipped with several smoke and white phosphorus grenades for marking or burning purposes. The pilots carry individual hand guns and have a choice of a Smith and Wesson .38, a six cylinder revolver, or a magazine loaded Colt .45 that holds nine rounds that can be fired either in a single-shot or semiautomatic configuration. The squadron also has a number of Thompson automatic submachine "burp" guns that shoot pistol ammunition and a few single shot M-79 grenade launchers that are optional to carry on certain missions. We were not trained in the use of these shoulder held weapons, but the crew practices with them during dull flights over the jungle. There are a few M-2 carbines with automatic selectors with several banana clips available for certain missions. We carry survival kits, charts, and C-rations for the entire crew for the day. We have personal bulletproof vests that we zip on prior to each mission. Some of the pilots sit on their vests, fearing a round from underneath the plane more than a front or side shot. Each pilot carries a survival knife with a sharpening stone in the sheath.

I carry a .38 pistol, the weapon I used to qualify during weapons training. I keep only five rounds in the chamber. The sixth cylinder sits directly underneath the firing pin and is intentionally left empty in the event of a clumsy accident. We all have acquired personal leather holsters, and those with .45's keep their magazines in a separate pouch, so they can be loaded quickly. The .45 would be a better choice for me. It has more firepower, packs a bigger punch, and is safer to carry than a loaded .38 revolver.

4 March, 1966

Gary Hebert's forewarning that we would hit the ground running proved prophetic. Yesterday, I rode shotgun on 24 hour medevac standby with Major Cliff Reese, a crusty Old Salt who really didn't need a copilot. There were a couple of times I wished he didn't have one because my sphincter was taking big chunks out of the foam seat cushions on some of his maneuvers, especially during one of our night-time extractions.

Not every medevac is a hair-raiser; some are routine things like a heat stroke or just plain exhaustion. Last night, one of the missions involved a kid with appendicitis. This is one more thing that can be life-threatening when you're stuck in the middle of the jungle. Our midnight trip to pick up that kid will forever be etched in my memory. We almost *"bought the farm,"* an expression we use in the states when a military aircraft crashes into a farm, and the government has to settle with the farmer.

Goldfinger, as we call Major Reese, has been wounded before, and he's as nervous as a cat in some of those landing zones. He tends to be a little jerky on the controls when he's antsy. This mission didn't have any live fire, but we don't always know those things in advance. Since it was pitch black and there are no street lights in those neighborhoods, Goldfinger didn't want the ground troops to bring attention to our landing by using any kind of flare or bright light. We have a landing light on the plane that would light up a football field, but we only use it as a last resort since white light causes night blindness. Once you turn it on, you have to leave it on.

After we made radio contact with the ground unit and Goldfinger knew our patient wasn't bleeding to death, he tried to take his time and play it safe by asking the radio operator to signal us with two blinks of a flashlight straight up in the air. This was real close to a village where people are burning candles and God knows what; so everything down there looked as if it were blinking back at us. After several blinking attempts and a couple of low passes, Goldfinger finally says he's *"got it"* and heads down to where he thinks he saw the blinks. We go down in a rice paddy beside the village, and the guy on the radio tells us we missed him by 200 yards. Goldfinger decides to taxi over there to stay low and dark rather than climb up and start the process all over again. The radioman is directing us as if we were blindfolded, which basically we are. When we were about 100 yards from the ground troops, Goldfinger becomes disoriented and tells me to hit the landing light rather than shift his focus. Suddenly, it's daylight, and instead of taxiing at five knots, we're sailing through that rice paddy at about 40 knots, and the first thing we see is a big tree directly in front of us. Goldfinger horses the plane to the right, and the tree limbs slap my side of the plane. The rotor blades get a taste of the rice paddy on the pilot's side. Somehow, the airplane manages to find a hover, and there stand five or six silhouetted Marines with our appendectomy candidate. We could have killed ourselves and every one of those Marines.

We landed and took the poor kid to the hospital.

Goldfinger never let me touch the stick until we were well out of the area. Then, he bellowed, *"You got it!"* I looked over at him, and he just put his head down and hollered, *"SHIT!"* He didn't need to use the intercom system for that word to be clearly heard over the noise of the engine and rotor blades. I think he meant it as an expletive, but it could have been a *verb*. Whatever it was, I knew exactly what he meant.

After pulling an all-nighter like that, they normally give you a short break, so I'm not on today's flight schedule. I could take the bus to town today and try to get organized, but for the first time since I've been here, I'm too busy loving just lying around the hootch in my skivvies, doing nothing. *"Laying sorry,"* as we call it back home in Tennessee. After last night with Major Reese, I'm practically a seasoned veteran. We flew seven missions, two of them in near total darkness. I could use a little down time.

I see some guys are playing volleyball on the beach today, but my unconditioned pink skin and the broiling sun don't make a good combination. No sense walking down to check the mail because I haven't been here long enough for the five day delivery period. Besides, I have too much homework ... learning about code names, landing zones, names of towns and landmarks, radio frequencies, names of different ground units in our area, and how to find my way out to those places in pitch black darkness -- something we didn't train for in North Carolina. Basically, I need to memorize the entire map of our TAOR. In addition to all that, I just came off a thirty day leave in preparation for coming here, so I have more to think about in the cockpit than where I'm going and what frequency to contact. I'm a little rusty. Aviation may be like riding a bicycle, but when it's a life or death matter, you need time in the saddle to give yourself every advantage. We will be working with dozens of units, and each one has its own radio frequency and call sign. I will fly as a copilot a few more times and then find myself out there calling my own shots.

Just as I was beginning to feel comfortable and safe in our cozy beach community, I had to hear the epic tale about the night a VC sapper (suicide) unit broke through our perimeter and blew up the flight line. Five months ago, just after midnight on 28 October, 1965, suicide sappers infiltrated our perimeter and used satchel charges and hand grenades to destroy most of the Hueys on the flight line. The pilots and crew chiefs were forced into the action as the VC were all among them, and bullets were flying through the VMO ready room. There were many heroes that night, and among them was a First Lieutenant Jennings, who owns the filthy bed I've been sleeping in.

As the legendary story was told to me, Jennings and another pilot, John Masters, were in the ready room when the attack began. The sappers had penetrated the barbed wire, and all hell broke loose. Ron was on the bed asleep when a bullet passed right over the top of him, grazing his flight suit. Masters took a position behind a three drawer metal filing cabinet with his trusty government-issue six shooter, the .38 pistol. The sappers were tossing charges into the parked choppers, and one of the explosive packages was thrown into a parked UH-34 where movie star Tab Hunter's brother, a corpsman, was hunkered down. He was killed when the helicopter exploded.

Only Masters was left in the ready room as the others had scrambled for cover in the sandbag bunker just outside the ready room. Masters was still behind the steel filing cabinet when a sapper appeared in the doorway with an AK 47 Russian rifle. When the VC raised his weapon, Masters aimed and dropped him in the doorway with one round. Immediately, a second sapper appeared and made the mistake of standing where Masters could see him. Masters shoots him, too. One of the sappers fired a round that hit the metal file cabinet, where the charts were stored. When the raid was over, Jennings was slightly injured, and all of the sappers were either killed or captured. One of them was identified as the barber who gave haircuts to Marble Mountain personnel. They suspected that he gathered the intelligence and also led the mission. It was clearly a one-way mission because none of the VC escaped alive, and several prisoners were taken.

I went over to the filing cabinet to find the hole and put my finger in it. These are not the kinds of stories that a green rookie needs to take to bed with him on a rubber mattress. The CO at Chu Lai doesn't allow locals on base, and after hearing the saga of "The Barber of Marble Mountain," I don't know why our CO would allow it either. It's part of a program to win the *hearts and minds of the people*." Our irreverent but lovable grunts came up with their own sarcastic version of that civil action program: *"When you've got 'em by the balls, their hearts and minds will follow."*

When you find yourself in the hooch during the day, there is a downside in that you have to share the space with the Vietnamese maid. She does laundry chores for five or six people in the unit, and your socks and underwear had better be clearly marked if you ever want to see them again. They come at 0800 and leave at 1500, and it's difficult to tell the difference when they leave. They sit and chat with the other maids -- an activity that takes all of them out of commission. We have a small refrigerator with a couple of tiny ice trays which she takes over completely. She combs her hair while singing her favorite song, *"Ling ting tong bong"* or something to that effect.

2200 hours

There is something about laying your life on the line that makes you appreciate a beautiful moonlit night like tonight. A cold shower and a cold shave and the cool breeze off the Gulf of Tonkin are good reminders that peace is a wonderful luxury even in its simplicity. The moon isn't full, but it's up there competing with an occasional night flare or distant artillery round flashing its report from the mountains. All this tranquility is in marked contrast to my trip into the city earlier tonight. I just decided to go for it and see what all the fuss was about. So after dinner I wandered down to the bus shuttle for the ride to town with a busload of people I've never met. This was a terrible mistake, and one I will never repeat again.

Starting with the bus ride past the hovels and make-shift shelters, some of which were only 10 or 12 feet square housing families of six or eight people, to the water buffalos standing in the street, and the rag-tag kids begging the bus to stop and give them a handout, it only grew worse. As our bus sped past these squatters, living literally on the road, we blew heavy clouds of red dust into their crude shelters while they tried to cook their rice. After about 15 minutes of this, the bus mercifully came to a stop across from an orphanage near town, not far from what I assumed was a popular bar. Jose Melendez was going to *"try"* to meet me at the bus, but he wasn't there. I waited for him beside the road while the others dispersed.

Standing alone on those dark streets in front of that orphanage and watching soldiers trade piasters with the locals sent an icy chill through me. Everybody looked suspicious. The Vietnamese men passing by, chewing and spitting their betel nut and smiling their black smiles, made me feel out of place and insecure. Where was my .38 pistol when I needed it? These men were like the ones in the sapper story. I have been on some back streets in Juarez, Mexico, where I had that same queasy apprehension and swore I'd never go back there again.

On the corner, I could see that the bus had not gone back to the base and was waiting there for a return trip. There was a military guard, and several orphanage kids had gathered around the bus. I decided to take my chances with the kids. Wild horses could not have dragged me into that town. I entertained some of the kids for a while with my limited repertoire of magic tricks and tried to talk to them about their orphanage, but they couldn't converse. Adults came around selling candy and gum, and I bought some and gave it to the kids. A cute little girl about six years old tugged at my pocket and said, *"Beaucoup money."* I told her she was *number one,* a phrase that means *great* to them. She said, *no ...* that *I* was *numba one,* and she was *numba ten,* meaning the lowest because she was Vietnamese.

I counted the seconds, not the minutes, until that bus took us back to Marble Mountain. As I stared out the window of the bus, I knew then that there were at least two wars being fought in Vietnam, and I could handle only one of them.

There was a lone sentry at the barbed wire entrance to the base with hundreds of yards of nothing but darkness surrounding his phone-booth-sized shelter. Surely, this was not our perimeter defense.

7 March, 1966. . .(written on 8 Mar)

Several Hueys were sent down to Chu Lai early this morning to support a large operation. I was included. A massive maneuver has kicked up a hornet's nest about 60 miles south of here. The joint operation of Marines, Army, and the infamous Army of the Republic of South Vietnam (ARVN) has claimed anywhere from 580 to over 900 VC, depending on who's counting. Weapons and people were captured.

Our airplane made a small contribution by calling in an air strike on two VC "strongholds." They looked like sleepy little villages with thatched roofs to me. Heavily armed fixed wing jets, F-4's and A-4's, loaded with 500 pound bombs and a variety of other weapons are on station to rain hell on any target that the chopper pilots designate. We do this by giving the jet jocks a set of grid co-ordinates or map directions. Then, the Hueys make it easy for them to see by marking the target with a red smoke grenade. Once they've obliterated the targets, the Hueys swoop down and shoot a few of our small rockets into what's left of it and spray it with our M-60 machine guns for good measure. That seems to be the standard operating procedure or SOP as we like to call anything that's standard. Including the five hour convoy escort at Chu Lai, I was in the saddle all day and logged nine hours of flight time. A standard rule of thumb is that every hour of actual flight time represents two hours spent with the airplane. Briefing, debriefing, loading, refueling, rearming, and waiting constitute all the extra things that take time. We returned home at 2230, well after lights out. I fell into bed and dreamed in full color of red smoke and red tracers.

TONY'S FIRST FLIGHT

I had a quick lunch at Chu Lai yesterday, but not dinner. I saw several of my old friends there in the mess hall, including Tony. He, too, had been snapped-in, and he told me the amazing story of his first flight. He was a different person, and after he told me about his first 24 hours at Chu Lai, it was easy to understand why. Since our plane ride from Okinawa a few days ago, I could tell that both of us had made "the conversion."

Tony's First Flight in his own words:

"After they told me that I would be assigned to VMO-6 in MAG 36 at Chu Lai, near Ke Ha, they directed me to a helo pad where a chopper would fly us down there. In a few minutes, I was joined by Major Plamondon.

A Huey landed beside the pad and out stepped our old friend Bill Kirby. This was like old home week, I thought. Kirby asked the major to ride with him to Marble Mountain. He said that someone had pulled some strings for him to go to VMO-1 with Plum and Willis. Hearing this gave my stomach a crank. What was going on?

Whether he was ribbing me or not, Kirby told Plamondon, 'Believe me, you don't want to go where Tony's going, there's a real war going on down there.' After they left, I tried to process Kirby's wisecrack. I had worked as hard as anyone to be a proud Marine aviator, and I trusted the system to be as faithful as I had been. So what was this? I'm not part of the clique? I had no idea where I was going, what to expect, or what we would be doing.

When our UH-34 landed at Chu Lai, I saw the familiar Hueys on the flight line and two men who were swordsmen in my wedding, Mike Bartley and Jerry Fraioli. They took me for a short orientation and showed me my hooch. At dinner I met some of the people I trained with, as well as another close friend, Stan Johnson, who was also a swordsman in my wedding. Stan is a low profile, "stand-up Marine" and a great guy. He arrived at Chu Lai exactly one hour after I did but was attached to a 34 squadron. In this friendly atmosphere, I had completely dismissed Kirby's bad joke.

After dinner they announced an all-pilot meeting in the ready room at 1900. I went a few minutes early, introduced myself to the other pilots, and took a seat in the back for the briefing, which I had no idea would include me. When our CO, Colonel Zitnick, entered the room, we all stood for the most senior officer and took our seats when asked.

He disclosed a top secret mission codenamed "Utah." A massive insertion of Marines would take place near Quang Ngai. This all meant absolutely nothing to me. I didn't know Quang Ngai from Saigon. They discussed the strategy and a launch time of 0500. We all went to our hooches, wrote letters, and went to bed. I slept like a stone and woke to people stirring in the hooch. We ate breakfast at the mess hall and reported to the ready room for the final briefing. Wow! I guess I will be involved after all. My name was not only on the flight schedule, I was the copilot to the flight leader, our executive officer, Major Purcell. We would be leading the entire mission.

I looked at my watch and noticed I had been at Chu Lai for about 14 hours. We would be the first chopper in the strike zone. The Hueys were to soften up the resistance for the 34's to make the troop insertion. I copied down all the frequencies and call signs, figuring that I would mostly be tuning in radios and paying close attention if Purcell needed to check a map or something. I hadn't touched a plane in six weeks.

Eight Huey gunships headed south toward the strike zone. We broke off into two flights of four in a scouting line formation. Suddenly, holy shit! The sky went black with helicopters, filled with 34's with their bellies full of Marines. They sandwiched in between the Hueys in flights of four, and the show was on. The major signaled me to arm the machine guns. Then, he spoke the first words to break the radio silence …"Klondike Six, rolling in hot with guns."

We went straight in. In my life, I never thought I would ever see anything like what happened next. Red tracers were streaming from every chopper. Fire balls the size of golf balls were zipping past us. They had to be fifty calibers. All I could hear on the radio were the transmissions from the other pilots: "I'm taking fire!" "I'm hit!" "Mayday!"

A 34 went down like a rock and exploded like a bomb. Suddenly, we were hit. It came through the floor, hit the door gunner's hand, took a chunk out of the roof, and put a hole completely through our rotor blade. The Huey started bucking like an old car hitting pot holes. We were headed right into those tracers, and I thought the rotor head might separate from the plane, and we would turn into a baby grand piano at any moment. We managed to pull off the run and find a place to land, so the crew chief could assess the damage. We called for a medevac for our door gunner, and he was taken to Bravo medical. The crew chief said he thought the plane could make it back to Chu Lai, and he was right. We managed to land safely. Wow! This was my first day, and I had 13 months of this to go.

Kirby's words haunted me that night as I watched them load body bags of Marines into six-by's. Later, I learned that Stan Johnson was the co-pilot of the plane that had exploded in front of my eyes. One of my best friends had not even made it through 24 hours in Vietnam.

Welcome to Chu Lai, Tony.

A couple of days later, I saw the nature of the enemy first hand. We went back to that site after the Marines had secured the captured area and landed for a look-around. A gunnery sergeant treated us as if we were VIP's and gave us a tour. He showed us a large cave entrance. He pointed to the shallow grave of an NVA general killed in the gunfire and said they had already dug him up to show a colonel who wanted to see the man's uniform. The gunny was chewing tobacco and spit a stream of brown juice on the fresh mound of dirt.

There was a heavy caliber automatic weapon unlike any that I'd seen. It was mounted on wheels that had wooden spokes like something out of the Confederate War. This primitive apparatus had been rolled hundreds of miles to this spot. There were chains near the tree attached to the weapon. I was told that the gunners who were killed in the conflict were chained, so they couldn't run and had to stay and fight to the end. This was the type enemy I would be fighting in this war, and it made a tremendous impression. We were also told that they had used mortars that were set to explode in the air, and that was how they were able to knock down some of the choppers that day. It occurred to me that these were ingenious and determined warriors.

How could people with wooden-spoke wheels possibly compete with a powerful country with B-52 Bombers and satellites orbiting the earth? Did they really expect to win? And why would they even try?"

(Told to Bud Willis by Tony Pecoraro.)

[When Kirby made the comment to Tony that there was a real war going on at Chu Lai, he had no clue about what was happening down there. Utah was a top secret mission. As Kirby told Tony and me years later when we asked him about it, *"I was probably just being a smartass. That sounds like me."*]

The culture of Chu Lai is much different than Marble Mountain. Part of the reason may be the living conditions there. The place looked like a concentration camp compared to our beach front property. Their mess hall was so huge they had to put picnic tables outside to accommodate all the men. Instead of sand, like we have at the "beach resort," they walked on hard-packed dirt, having stomped it clean of every living thing. With all

92

those choppers flying around, the whole place had a red dust cloud over it. That same knot in my stomach that I felt when I took the bus into Danang paid me another short visit. This felt like the middle of the jungle. I wanted to get back in the plane and fly up where the air was clean and fresh. After seeing Chu Lai and hearing the story of Tony's first flight, I consider myself lucky to be at Marble Mountain.

8 March 1966

If we can believe the reports, Tony's Utah operation had much success. Hundreds of North Vietnamese soldiers were killed. A huge concentration of the enemy was dispersed. Whatever they were plotting, the Marines certainly disrupted it. This was the first known contact between the North Vietnamese Army (NVA) and the Marines.

We wondered how so many of them managed to walk all the way from North Vietnam without being detected. Small bands of NVA have been recruiting villagers for years. Since 1960 they have supposedly increased the number of these VC recruits from 10,000 to 65,000. They also extort rice from the farmers. Every village that we fly over has a couple of huge burlap bags of rice, presumably left there to buy protection. Viet Cong literally means Vietnamese Communist, and the Communists preach the convenient doctrine of *community* to anyone who has something they want.

There is only one person who really needs to be recruited in each village, and that would be the *village chief.* Whatever he says becomes law. Ironically, every time we shoot-up one of their villages, we make it that much easier for them to recruit another VC village. All those villages are connected through blood kin.

A system of tunnels and hidden ammo supplies has prepared these people with an almost perfect system of warfare. They are also experts in several guerrilla tactics, including a variety of ambush techniques, escape, and evasion. They have used these methods for decades against the French. There probably wasn't a single person in those houses we hit yesterday. They were all safely underground or had fled to a spider hole in the nearest tree line. It may cost us a hundred thousand dollars to inflict a single enemy casualty while the VC might be able to do the same thing with 25 cents worth of junk and a well placed booby trap. Bamboo punji sticks with razor sharp tips laced with poison have taken more than a few good soldiers out of commission.

For us chopper pilots, the most feared weapons are the .50 caliber machine guns supplied by China or Russia via Hanoi. The weapon is so big it usually needs to be mounted on a vehicle. The "fifty" fires a projectile larger than a man's middle finger and has a red tail of fire that makes it look like a flaming Coke bottle. It can hit a target as far up as 5,000 feet, according to the book. The choppers don't need to be more than a couple of thousand feet, but we sometimes "cruise" at 3000 for added insurance and because it's a few degrees cooler up there.

Three of the weapons destroyed during the Chu Lai

operation, including the ones that Tony saw, were anti-aircraft weapons. Their presence represented months of backbreaking labor dragging them through the jungles for hundreds of miles on foot and under cover of darkness. This was a chilling discovery since there had been no evidence of anti-aircraft weapons until then, according to our senior officers. Even so, this is a small threat compared to the situation facing our pilots in North Vietnam. Up there, Air Force and Navy fighter pilots are being shot at by Soviet made surface-to-air missiles and MIG-21 fighters.

The hastily trained VC are poor marksmen. They haven't learned to lead a flying airplane with small arms fire. The Huey gunship presents an easier target when flying straight into them, as Tony's plane was. When we are flying perpendicular to the snipers, they don't know exactly how far to shoot in front of us. They also don't understand the importance of caring for their weapons. Having to drag them through the muck and mire, the gas port and firing mechanism of a rifle need to be properly cleaned every day to prevent jamming. Marines are heavily indoctrinated in the cleaning of their weapons. All this information is in training manuals that are in clear view of the village maids that clean our hooches. I doubt there's much separation between those maids and the men we are fighting. It's only a matter of time before they know everything we know, including all our radio frequencies, our names, and our flight schedules.

Decades of struggle against the French allowed Communist elements to develop well-established and deeply-rooted recruiting methods. Generations of villagers had been exposed to Communist propaganda by the time we arrived in country in 1966. In order to keep them focused and on a task, they were tirelessly brainwashed and incessantly told the reason why they were doing whatever they were asked to do. According to documents we have seen, captured VC revealed that the basis of their training began with a ten point Oath of Honor.

1. Fight to the last breath.

2. Obey all orders wholeheartedly.

3. Fight without fear or complaint and never retreat.

4. Learn to improve fighting skills in order to kill American invaders and their servants.

5. Preserve organizational secrets.

6. Reveal nothing if captured.

7. Love and co-operate with fellow soldiers in your unit.

8. Covet and maintain the weapon assigned to you.

9. Respect, protect, and help the people you are fighting for.

10. Indulge in the practice of self criticism daily.

In addition to this oath, there was also a 12 point code of discipline that the VC were sworn to maintain. All these rules were eerily similar to our Ten Commandments, specifically citing honesty, honor, love, obedience, fairness, and respect. This indoctrination was continually reinforced through daily self-criticism sessions where each member of a three man cell had to explain his own reactions to daily situations, and then publicly confess and criticize his own shortcomings and weaknesses in thought and deeds in the presence of his peers. Eventually, the fear of corporal punishment or death became less important than the fear of humiliation and dishonor that could fall on him or his relatives.

(Source: Department of Defense, *Know Your Enemy: The Viet Cong.* Publication dated 8 March, 1966, Armed Forces Information and Education.)

A new squadron of CH-46's is moving into Marble Mountain. They have been flying their equipment in from the ship for the past couple of days. These are big, tandem rotor choppers for troop transport which can carry up to 20 fully loaded Marines. The 46 is slow and unwieldy, compared to the smaller, jet-powered Huey and is used for large troop insertions. It can haul out a crippled chopper with an external sling if need be. Part of the 46 mission is called Sparrow Hawk, a 24-hour standby strike force that can be dropped in at a moment's notice in case some of our ground troops encounter a concentration of the enemy. The idea is to drop some troops in behind them and sandwich them. The Huey provides gunship escort for those 46 missions.

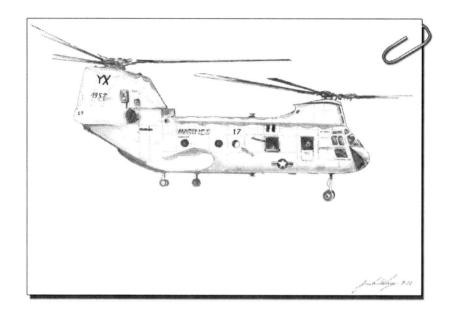

A new squadron of CH-46's is moving into Marble Mountain.

9 Mar, 1966, 2200 hours

I'm tired now - very tired. We have been in every imaginable zone and situation today and tonight picking up casualties, from a cable hoist out of a 200 foot jungle canopy to a Marine sergeant who was drunk and accidentally shot himself. We picked up sick ARVN soldiers and other very seriously wounded Marines. The adrenaline rush that keeps you pumped up for these flights also gives you a crash landing afterwards, almost like a strong drug. I'll have a day off tomorrow and might be able to lift a pencil by then.

MEDEVAC

I developed a habit of going over in my mind the types of missions that I was seeing and how I might be able to do them more efficiently, similar to debriefing myself. At night, especially, I would go over them in detail and sometimes dream about the ones that made the biggest impression on me. The following story is an example of a typical medevac and subsequent dream.

The operations duty officer is busy sorting maps in a file cabinet in the VMO-2 ready room when he's interrupted by the dull rattle of the military hotline. A half dozen men in flight suits accustomed to the chattering phone barely shift their focus from their paperback novels as the duty officer handles another call from group operations.

"Deadlock Three, Lt. Bailey speaking, sir.

"Ah, Roger, I have an emergency medevac for you."

Bailey covers the mouthpiece of the two-pound field phone receiver by holding it against his chest and alerts the pilots in a booming voice, *"MEDEVAC!"*

Two copilots gather their kneeboards and scatter out the door across the metal matted surface of the parking lot heading for two Hueys not fifty yards away. A corpsman, two crew chiefs, and a door gunner from the maintenance shack next door sprint ahead of them. Back in the ready room, the two pilots gather near the phone to collect the details of the mission while Bailey copies the incoming message.

EMER ... 3 US WIA ... at 955 595 ... LZ not secure ... Green K ... WH LP 3 47.8 FM

He repeats the information in a clear voice while the pilots transfer his words onto their knee boards.

"Emergency medevac ... three us wounded in action ... coordinates alpha tango niner five five ... five niner five ... landing zone is not secure ... zone will be marked with green smoke ... contact warehouse lima papa three on four seven point eight fox mike."

The pilots locate the coordinates on a five by eight foot area map permanently pasted to the ready room wall. Using a string, they are able to determine the compass heading and distance to the LZ. They each locate the corresponding smaller map in the pockets of their flight suits and scurry to the Hueys, turned up and waiting. Before they can buckle up, the crew closes the cargo doors, and the Huey lifts off the mat.

"Marble tower, this is Deadlock Medevac, taxi for two, over.

"Roger Deadlock, you are cleared for immediate take-off, taxi runway one seven, winds one five zero at eight knots, altimeter zero two niner niner. All other aircraft hold your positions."

The two planes bear down the runway in close formation. Turning toward the general heading of the pickup area, the lead pilot climbs toward 1500 feet while the co-pilot dials in the radio frequency. The copilot keys the intercom button on the flight control and reads the mission details to the pilot and the crew.

Within minutes, the two Hueys are nearing the area of the pickup zone, and the pilot keys the radio transmitter, already tuned to 47.8 FM.

"Warehouse Lima Papa Three, this is Deadlock Medevac, over."

"Deadlock Medevac, this is Warehouse, go ahead."

"Roger, Medevac is three minutes north of your zone... pop your smoke."

"Roger, Medevac...smoke going down."

After a few seconds, a thick cloud of green smoke rises from a small clearing marking the exact location of the landing zone and the direction of the wind.

"Warehouse, this is medevac, tally-ho your smoke, are there any enemy near the zone at this time? Over."

"This is Warehouse, that's negative sir, however, you may expect fire from the village 500 yards south of our smoke. Request you approach from the north."

"Roger north. What are the locations of your friendly units?"

"This is Warehouse. We have no friendly units outside the 50 meter perimeter of our zone."

"This is Medevac, roger. My escort will make a rocket run on that village. Escort, copy?"

"Warehouse, roger, we would appreciate that."

"This is escort. We copy."

"Okay, Escort, make your runs east to west and watch the friendlies."

"Escort, Wilco."

The pilot of the medevac slick decreases his power and begins losing altitude as he visualizes the approach in his head. He photographs the obstacles around the landing area in his mind, visually memorizing every detail. Zagging from side to side, he tries to create an elusive target while examining the terrain around the smoke. Then, he makes his sudden commitment and plunges rapidly downward. The plane appears to be falling out of the sky until the Huey's nose lurches skyward about fifty feet above the waiting Marines and somehow rights itself just before touchdown, making a hard landing in the center of the troops. A stout volley of small arms fire rings out from the village, as promised, kicking up dirt around both the chopper and the Marines guarding the perimeter. From prone positions on the ground, the Marines answer in unison with a stout volley from their M-14's. The incoming fire becomes less intense.

"Escort's rolling in hot!"

The gunship dives for the village with white trails of smoke from its rockets and a relentless hailstorm from six M-60 machine guns. The door gunner adds traversing cover as his spent, hot cartridges shower the floor of the chopper. The   gunship startles the Marine riflemen who pause to admire its firepower. The thumping of the rockets and the racking of the machine guns silences the village.

The crew chief and corpsman of the medevac slick, undaunted by the gunfire, scramble to deliver stretchers to the three wounded Marines and to help load them into the "ambulance." The two pilots can only sit and wait as the acrid stench of   burnt gunpowder and green smoke swirl inside their cockpit.

The corpsman evaluates the medical priorities and administers emergency aid to the three men, none of them over twenty years old. The crew chief secures them on the stretchers, then tethers himself to an overhead strap to prepare for whatever takeoff might be necessary. The corpsman administers plasma and morphine, bracing his legs against the stretchers for support. Slamming the cargo doors shut, the crew chief taps the pilot's shoulder, signaling the all clear.

"Medevac is lifting off."

Exiting in the opposite direction of the hostile village, the pilot executes his get-away, disregarding any advantage of wind direction to avoid the risks of snipers. The stripped down Huey is fast and responsive, banking sharply out of the hot zone to treetop level, heading for the U.S. medical center that services Danang. A mile away from the hot zone, he ascends rapidly, distancing the plane from small arms fire. The voice of the infantry radio operator crackles inside the earphones of his flight helmet.

"Deadlock Medevac, this is Warehouse, thanks for a nice job; we sure appreciate it."

"This is Medevac. Warehouse, we should be thanking you. Don't worry about these guys. We'll have them at the hospital in no time. If you need anything else, give us a call."

"Wilco, Deadlock. Thanks again."

10 March 1966, 1400 hours

Our ground troops must think that the Huey pilots are either lunatics or gods who can do anything. There is a Johnson's Wax commercial on TV that shows bullets bouncing off an airplane windshield when the wax is applied. Our windshield is a thin layer of Plexiglas that wouldn't stop a carrier pigeon. Why don't we have any Johnson's Wax?

Last night they called us to evacuate a sick Arvin (our nickname for ARVN soldiers). Could that extraction not wait until morning? To make matters worse, he had to be hoisted out with a sling in a basket between tall trees. This is about as spooky as a night mission can be because you have to turn the landing light on in order to have a visual reference to hold a steady hover long enough to pull the basket straight up to keep him from rattling around in the treetops like a pinball. There is a guillotine system that will cut the hoisting cable in case the basket gets hung up in the trees, but Arvin doesn't have to know about these things. During that nerve-wracking process, which took about 40 minutes, we were sitting ducks with a bright light for a target.

In the middle of that hoisting job, we received an *emergency* call to evacuate a wounded Marine. This new mission was more urgent than the sick Arvin, but we already had Arvin in the basket on the end of our cable. Now we have a decision to make, a moment of triage. Which one of these assignments is more important?

Should we abort Arvin to go pick up the wounded Marine, or do we finish what we are doing first? Since we were already committed, we went ahead and hoisted the basket with the Arvin. This took about 10 more minutes. Since we were already in the air, we saved the time it would have taken to launch, so we were that far ahead of the game. But now we had to take Arvin to the hospital. Instead, I suggested that we take the sick Arvin along with us to evacuate the Marine. There are times when we have to make it up as we go along. But I can tell you that if we had not been that far along with Arvin's extraction, he might have spent a long night in the bush while we rescued that Marine.

One thing that is becoming clear to me is how important it is to fly as often as possible. There is so much happening out there that it's much easier to know what's going on today if you know what happened the day before, if that makes sense. The idea that it's less dangerous to *avoid* exposure is not necessarily true over here and may even be the opposite. Confidence is the key, and the only way to get it is to have as much information and experience as you can. Lady Luck doesn't hang out with the unprepared. Armed with experience, you can make better decisions and also justify your actions if necessary. One thing is sure; ignorance isn't the answer to anything in these situations. Some of the pilots who have been here for a few months are trying to minimize their flying time, which seems a foolish choice. I don't know how they do it, but I see them on the beach instead of the flight schedule. Any horse who hangs around the paddock would be a risky bet in a horse race. I have a feeling that the men who fill out that flight schedule and the crew chiefs who have to fly with them feel the same way.

I received a big stack of mail today, one of the benefits of having eight brothers and sisters and a wife who writes every day. We have a runner who brings our mail to the ready room. A real popular guy! Plamondon and Plum have not received their first letter and when they saw my stack of mail they were visibly pissed. I also gave some direction to the maid, instructing her to put some of my things in order, and I finally found some sunscreen. Too lazy to go to the mess hall, I had a can of peaches and some peanut M&Ms for lunch.

One of my temporary roommates, Captain Perry James, is into vocabulary books. We have that in common. He didn't complete his college degree, and he's maybe 10 years older than me. When he saw my books, he wanted to pick my brain, etymologically speaking. We grilled each other from a long list of archaic words that nobody ever uses. He became fascinated with the word *vindictive* and adopted it as his "word-o-the-day." He likes to find a way to use his new word around the ready room a few times, which amuses the hell out of both of us.

The sand finds its way into everything: our ears, our shoes, our watchbands, our food, our teeth, and our "you-name-it." Sea water is not warm in the morning for bathing, and a bar of soap in salt water is like bathing with a piece of sandstone. A mouthful of the South China Sea tastes similar to alum. A beach without females is no beach at all. This tropical sun is relentless, but useful for telling time by sticking a pole in the sand and observing its shadow. These are just a few of the things I learned during a one hour visit to the beach this morning.

11 March, 1966

The Utah operation that took place all last week in the Quang Ngai area has ground to a halt. Unfortunately, there were plenty of casualties on our side. It was probably on TV. I participated in one of the last days of it. More villages had to go. The term *VC* applies to men, women, children, and even babies, but I guess we are not supposed to look at it that way. After you've picked up a few dead Marines, everything fades into an assignment. The Marines are a family, and we have to look after our own. We have all heard stories about eight-year-old kids tossing live hand grenades into helicopters, so they all seem suspicious after a while.

We have four of our aircraft about 60 miles north of Marble Mountain in a place called Ashau. This is an ARVN outpost stocked with American advisors about three clicks (kilometers) from the border of Laos. It was over-run last night by North Vietnamese Regulars (NVA). Marines were sent in to "fix it," and some of our pilots flew up there late last night. We don't know when they might come back. One of them was Gus Plum.

I saw Tony yesterday when he stopped by our ready room. He was bringing a general from Chu Lai to meet with another general. He is the same wide-eyed Tony, taking it all in, with stories of blood and guts and Buddhist Monks. He was excited about purchasing a silk pillow for his son Tyrone, with the words, *"Chu Lai-1966"* embroidered on it. He had dinner with us and asked if we had a beach, which you could see clearly from the window of the mess hall, and he had just flown over it in a helicopter. Guess he missed it! Later, we took a short walk out to the beach together, and I asked him to re-tell the hair-raising story of his first flight and his subsequent visit back to the strike zone, so I could record it in my journal accurately. I worry about Tony down there at Chu Lai, but he claims to like it. He has a handful of buddies who are skilled at finding humor in just about anything -- a favorite outlet for frustration!

Operation Utah began as a joint operation with one battalion from the 7th Marines and one from the 2ND ARVN Division based on intelligence that the 21st NVA Regiment had recently moved into a region seven miles northwest of Quang Ngai City... the first known USMC contact with the NVA. Allied forces claimed to have killed nearly 600 and captured five along with many weapons and mortars. The Marine casualties were 98 dead, 278 wounded, while the ARVN had 30 killed and 120 wounded. At least one F-4 and several helicopters were shot down. Three 12.7 millimeter antiaircraft weapons were captured.

12 March, 1966 Saturday 2100 hours

On Thursday, March 10, the government of the Republic of Vietnam decided that it no longer needed one of its highest officials, Lieutenant General Nguyen Chanh Thi, commander of the South Vietnamese Army in Danang. The popular general was relieved by Nguyen Cao Ky with the full support of the RVN government, and I suppose, ours.

Its effect shook Danang, especially the Buddhist monks. The tremor reached Marble Mountain, only a couple of miles away. Last night, on the 11th, there were 2500 to 5000 civilians demonstrating in protest of this decision (Hanoi radio said 10,000). Our squadron was placed on a 24 hour alert, and all pilots were ordered to stand by and to conduct visual recon missions of our TAOR from Hoi An to Monkey Mountain about six miles north of us, observing and reporting any suspicious behavior of the Popular Forces (civilian fighters for the RVN) and even the Army of the Republic.

Suddenly, nobody is being trusted. There's speculation that Arvin (the "good guys" that we have been pulling out of the weeds day and night) might turn against Saigon and begin a civil war, as if we didn't have one already.

Danang is so far away from Saigon that it's almost like a separate war up here in the I Corps. And, we might soon have a third war because there is a delicate situation brewing between the South Vietnamese Army, which is more loyal to Thi, and their Air Force, which is more loyal to Ky. Thi is a popular general with a loyal following. With these two factions at odds, this could spin off in any direction. This is a strange place we have come to.

Captain Perry James has a shortwave radio that can pick up Hanoi Radio and Peking. We tried to hear some tidbits about all this from their point of view. Their female broadcasters are blatant propaganda specialists whom we refer to as Hanoi Hannah and Peking Polly. On a broadcast from Peking, Polly reported that the many "*U.S. atrocities being committed in Vietnam*" were the root cause of the political problems. She closed out the broadcast with a children's choir singing *Chairman Mao is the Sunshine of our Hearts.*

In the meantime, VMO-2 is busying itself with preemptive flyovers, observing and receiving an occasional sniper shot. We see a random muzzle flash, otherwise nothing that unusual. I did see a gaggle of 40 or 50 locals marching into Danang, but they were unarmed and seemed peaceful enough. We spooked one or two snipers by tossing smoke grenades at them, and they probably ran back into their mole holes. We can't just fly around in gunships leveling every village that takes a pot shot at us. We find ourselves in a state of quasi-diligence until told otherwise.

After one of those uneventful flyovers, we were summoned to escort two 34's to an ARVN outpost to pick up some casualties. When we arrived, snipers were shooting at the 34's from a nearby village. They apparently didn't see our gunships coming in behind the 34's. When the 34 driver reported two hits in his fuselage, we rolled in with our little rocket package while our crew chief and gunner fired the M-60 machine guns out the doors. We fired all the rockets we had and saw secondary explosions, which usually means we hit an ammo dump or something. Who knows, it could have been a can of cooking oil. Anyway, we were all over that village, and when we left the area, there wasn't anything down there that wasn't smoking. The wounded 34 was able to pick up the injured and take them to a special hospital for ARVN soldiers. Vietnamese girls are trained to be nurses there as part of our civil action program. We try to *help them*. They try to *shoot us*. Quite a party!

Snipers are more confident about shooting at a 34 because it isn't as well armed as a Huey gunship. The enemy knows to expect a fight from a Huey. In its defense, the 34 has something that the Hueys don't: a massive engine that sits directly in front of the pilots and provides a convenient shield.

All trips by U.S. military personnel into the city of Danang have been terminated until further notice. No kidding? No more *liberty* as we call it. Despite all this chaos, morale at VMO-2 is quite high, and that is extremely important. Some of that can be attributed to the enormous amount of comic material being supplied from the ridiculous situation we find ourselves in.

When the VMO-2 pilots returned from Ashau, they brought with them incredible stories of the overrun Special Forces camp. The outpost was manned by 10 Green Berets and a couple hundred Arvin's. The Huey pilots had to land to try to evacuate the wounded while the camp was under attack. Two Hueys succeeded in landing even after a 34 was shot down trying. The Arvins stormed the Huey, stepping on and over the wounded to scramble onto the plane while the crew chief and door gunner were assisting the wounded. It was a complete panic that threatened to overload the capacity of the chopper and jeopardize everyone. The crew chief and the door gunner had to literally kick the stowaways out of the plane. Once outside, they began desperately hanging onto the skids.

The pilots ordered the gunner to shoot the men off the skids if necessary. Warning shots were fired as the Huey struggled to lift off while the crew kicked the panicked Arvins off the plane. As the overloaded plane reached the end of the outpost clearing with no more than three feet of altitude and no more power left to give, the pilot had to milk a few extra beats from the rotors by lowering the nose and executing a dive toward the bottom of the hill. The Huey was flying downhill now and was falling more than flying, taking off small limbs from the surrounding trees. As the terrain dropped off, allowing the heavily overloaded plane to gather some critically needed translational lift, the Huey grabbed a last second gust of wind and picked up enough airspeed and rotor rpm to barely clear the trees at the bottom of the valley. They somehow found the right side of the power envelope, and the bird started flying again. They made it. One of the pilots on that aircraft was Captain Harold E. "Gus" Plum. The other plane that landed and took off successfully was piloted by Captain Perry James, my hoochmate and vocabulary study partner. Meritorious, gentlemen! A couple of genuine heroes! This is one more tale that their grandchildren will never hear because real heroes never tell these kinds of stories about themselves.

POLITICAL CHAOS IN DANANG

The Buddhists in South Vietnam were deeply intertwined in the politics of their government. Premier Ky was a Buddhist himself, who ran the Vietnamese government from Saigon. Danang is a long way from Saigon, and General Thi's philosophy differed from Ky's in that he favored negotiations over military action, openly criticizing Ky's war tactics. Even though the two men were friends, Thi was a straight talker and accused his friend Ky of being an American puppet. In a government famous for corruption, the Buddhist monks considered Thi one of the few honest men. A *TIME magazine* story had managed to fan this fire by suggesting that the more popular Thi could take power whenever he chose. In Ky's eyes, Thi was now a serious rival.

On Feb 6-9, 1966, Ky met with President Johnson in Honolulu, and whatever secret promises were made to Ky, this meeting must have bolstered Ky's ego. In the next two years, American spending on the war increased from 1 billion dollars to 20.6 billion dollars. On Ky's return from his meeting with Johnson, he was committed to ridding himself of anyone opposing his military solution. After all, money was pouring into the country, and he was large and in charge. One month later, on March 10, Ky announced the firing of his friend Thi as commander of the I Corps, accusing him of using government funds for anti-government activities (a favorite accusation). This triggered mass demonstrations on the 11th of March in and around Danang, a stone's throw from our perimeter at Marble Mountain.

Lieutenant General Lew Walt commanded the U.S. Marine operations from his compound on China Beach in the Northeast corner of the city of Danang and had a strong relationship with Thi. On March 12, the Buddhists called for the return of Thi and his overthrown generals. Thi's replacement, Major General Chuan vowed not to confront peaceful demonstrators, and by March 15 the city was paralyzed by a citywide strike. One thousand ARVN soldiers joined in the demonstrations.

These events were also triggering unrest in the cities of Saigon and Hue as political squabbling spilled onto the streets. Being in the middle of all this was both exciting and scary. We either had the best seat in the house or the worst depending on how it would turn out. We weren't sure if we were involved in a comedy, history, or a tragedy. The reality that we could be killed in the middle of this ridiculous tumult was not lost on any of us.

13 March, 1966 12:30

Actress Ann-Margaret is in Danang for a few days and will be putting on a show today at Hill 327, a Marine outpost nearby. I will be flying at a comfortable distance around the show to provide the audience an illusion of security.

Danang is still under political stress and several factions are attempting to sort themselves out. Our squadron usually provides transportation (and security) for celebrities visiting Danang, as well as for dignitaries, high brass, and politicians when they visit the I Corps. Everybody wants to ride in the Huey. It seems ludicrous to me that we would be flying celebrities around during one of the biggest political challenges of the war. Shouldn't we be working on our master disaster plan or an exit strategy?

15 March, 1966 1700 hours

I'm flying with Bill Kirby today. We're escorting General Lew Walt's personal pilot, who's carrying Miss Ann-Margaret and her entourage. Our squadron CO felt it necessary to volunteer himself to go along on that assignment as a copilot. Kirby and I stayed at the Danang "Hilton" last night, and the actress was in the room next door. The *"Hilton,"* as we call it, is really a rundown hotel in Danang that has been converted to a rundown officer's quarters. There was no air conditioning for us or for the actress. Each room had a ceiling fan. I slept on an actual bed with a mattress, a few feet away from a celebrity sex symbol. (I'm not talking about Kirby.)

She visited the troops at the hospital and departed the area around noon. Kirby and I were impressed that she would come all the way over here to do that, pro bono. The balance of the day was set aside to take generals back to wherever they wanted to go. Even if we're only taxi drivers, it's pretty exciting to be surrounded by big shots. The gentleman who sat in my co-pilot's seat this afternoon was none other than the man who is replacing General Thi. His name is General Chuan, at least according to the name somebody sewed above his shirt pocket. They could be using doubles for all I know. He was a very polite man and the only person on the plane to thank me when they exited.

Being a VIP pilot is not a dangerous job, but it feels like ten tons of compressed responsibility, and I was wondering why they would allow a rookie like me to handle this assignment. Kirby has done it before and seems comfortable with it. Captain Tim Common, who only has two weeks left on his tour, is Walt's permanently assigned pilot.

I was in the midst of a dozen high ranking Vietnamese officers today who weren't speaking English, and I heard more than my share of strange conversation. There was whispered dialogue and side bars among the generals. It would be scary to know what they are really saying to each other. Even though they knew I didn't understand a word, they weren't taking any chances by letting me overhear too much. I'm wondering if I will ever learn any of their strange language. Their language is littered with tongue popping, and my mouth won't make that sound. When they speak to us they use pigeon English.

"We go now." "Tank you."

The general acted like a little kid when I offered to let him hold the stick when the plane was straight and level. I pictured him going home and telling his wife, *"I fly airplane today."*

16 March, 1966 1630

Our maid, Nguyen Thi-Toc, didn't come to work yesterday. The Vietnamese were on strike because of General Thi's ouster. We heard they had a picket line and wouldn't let the maids into the compound. They came in this morning, so maybe the strike is over. No sense asking her what's going on because I would only hear more tongue popping. I did ask her if she thought General Thi was "numba one," trying to find a clue as to which side she might lean toward. Not much response. It could be that she isn't politically oriented one way or another. They learn to say *"numba one"* and *"I like you too much,"* out of necessity because it results in more tips.

I received a letter from my mother yesterday asking

if the military censored our mail. I haven't seen any evidence of it. As long as President Johnson has Bobby Kennedy and Jane Fonda breathing down his neck, our sarcasm isn't likely to grab anyone's attention. Besides, we know less than anybody. As one of the crew chiefs said, we are like mushrooms; they keep us in the dark, covered up with manure.

At the moment, I am on Sparrow Hawk standby, a strike force, ready to go on a moment's notice. It's rarely launched, so the guys in the ready room have nicknamed it *"Chicken Hawk"* because some of the pilots that like to fly the safer missions will volunteer for it. You can't put anything over on these Old Salts. They don't miss a trick, and they don't suffer fools.

Any time we receive a call to evacuate a casualty from a combat zone, we can be airborne in a couple of minutes. We use a "slick" for the pick-up plane and strip it of its armament for more maneuverability. We keep about a half tank of fuel in it for the same reason. In addition to the co-pilot, the slick carries a Navy corpsman to give medical attention to the wounded, and there is a crew chief to assist with whatever is needed.

We always travel in pairs on medevac. The armed escort is called the *gunship*, and it packs enough firepower to help suppress enemy small arms fire although it doesn't have anything in the way of protective armor. The gunship carries a crew of four, including a crew chief. A door gunner operates an M-60 machine gun on a swivel. The biggest problem with the medevac mission is that where you find a wounded soldier, you usually find the people who wounded him, so the armed wingman is a crucial part of the equation. The VC are especially crafty when it comes to setting up a helicopter ambush. But because the Huey gunship packs plenty of heat, they know there could be a heavy price to pay for firing on a Huey. At least we like to think that's the case.

A third major mission of VMO-2 is visual recon of our tactical area of responsibility or TAOR. This is also a daylight-till-dark, rotating assignment. Then, there is that VIP taxi service that I was on yesterday, shuttling big shots around. VIP's will rarely ride in anything but a Huey. We don't always have enough airplanes for all that, mainly because we are always banging them up on those medevacs.

If a plane is in an incident, it has to be written up, and then it goes into a "down" status. Those problems, plus normal repairs or new parts, have to be checked out by a qualified maintenance (test) pilot before going back into an "up" status. All this takes time, and the war doesn't wait.

In addition to those assignments above, we do practically anything they ask us to do, especially if it has to be executed *quickly* and is the least bit dangerous. We are often asked to do certain jobs because the Hueys are a newer and more versatile aircraft. The 34's are bigger, older model helicopters that are far more difficult and temperamental. The engine rpm and the rotor rpm need to be kept in a certain range for the chopper to respond properly. We all had to learn to fly these cumbersome contraptions in training, and it takes incredible skill to keep those needles synchronized. It also has to be properly warmed up and babied. If you find yourself behind the eight ball with the UH-34, it can become stubborn, and it will sink like a stone. My hat goes off to those pilots. If the truth were known, and it rarely is, those guys who can fly those choppers are the better pilots. The Huey is much more forgiving, and can take all kinds of punishment and pilot screw ups. It doesn't need to be warmed up and coddled. We just "*kick the tire and light the fire,*" and we're off.

The most critical thing about a turbine engine (the jet that powers the Huey) is its engine temperature. Since we're pumping raw fuel into the turbine every time we kick the spurs to it, we have to make constant adjustments to fine tune the engine rpm for cooling purposes. If you overheat the engine's burner basket during peak performance, you could be sitting in front of a time bomb. Hueys have skids for landing gear instead of wheels. The skids aren't as sensitive to a hard landing. They just spread out a little if you happen to have poor depth perception after a rough night at the officer's club. Most of the time we semi-crash in those hot zones, and the skids absorb our lack of pilot finesse. Maneuvering in and out of a hot zone quickly is key to a successful medevac, and those skids take a beating.

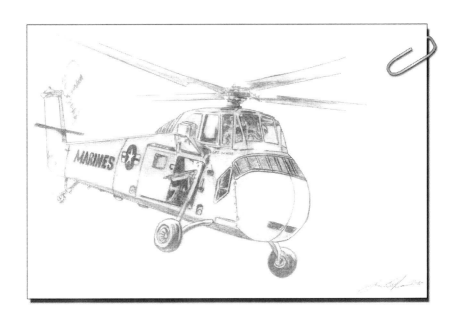

If you find yourself behind the eight ball with the UH-34, it can become stubborn, and it will sink like a stone.

Once in a while, a pilot actually sees the results of his efforts. I was the Sparrow Hawk pilot when we received a call to drop a re-enforcement squad into a known infested area to serve as a blocking force for a sweep already in progress. This is similar to a deer hunt in Mississippi where one group drives the animals into the waiting hunters. The VC had somehow managed to become trapped against a horseshoe-shaped river. We dropped some Marines in behind them and circled overhead to watch the action. We saw a cluster of suspects in a village about 400 yards southwest. When we dropped a red smoke near them, they went bonkers, heading for a large bunker they had previously dug for that purpose. They have a cockroach mentality and almost always prepare an underground escape route

before exposing their position. We own the skies, and they own the underground.

When we relayed this bunker information to the Sparrow Hawk unit, they asked us to make a strafing run on it. That may have scared them, but it was otherwise ineffective because they were well entrenched. As the Marines approached the bunker, one of the VC popped up to toss a hand grenade. That was not a good idea. Those grunts are trained for the pop-up. The Marines then dynamited the tunnel, and about 15 VC came scrambling out with their hands up. Six others were not so lucky. The Sparrow Hawk ground troops became the heroes and were jubilant that none of their buddies were injured. They also found and destroyed a sizable store of ammunition. The Huey crew felt as if we had made a small contribution, and we were all part of a real-time war drama.

We received word this evening that the airbase at Saigon had been heavily attacked with mortars. In addition to the loss of lives and airplanes, this could also disrupt some of our supplies since most everything comes to Danang via Saigon, especially our mail. Danang is slowly returning to normal, and the roads are open again. There was a rumor that they had mined the bridge into town, and this had the entire population in an uproar until the local mayor walked across the bridge and personally directed traffic. After that, things settled down.

Doc Zimpher is our squadron flight surgeon. The senior squid (Navy)! He doesn't really perform surgery -- maybe a stitch or two, but he's our go-to-guy for minor medical issues. Some people must have time to be sick over here because Doc has a small cadre of followers that keep him busy for a couple of hours every day. It also gives him someone to talk to since he doesn't fly. If he can figure out a way to get four hours of passenger time in an aircraft each month, he can earn a couple hundred more dollars of flight pay. Any pilot coming to him complaining of an allergy, a cold or an "ear block" will receive an automatic medical grounding chit for a couple of days. I don't know exactly what an ear block is, but they're popular.

Doc entertains his followers with tales of penicillin and sexually transmitted diseases. He said that when Americans first started coming over here, it took 6000 units of penicillin to knock out gonorrhea, but now it takes 160,000 units to do the job because the strain has become much more resistant. He also keeps a journal, and I guess that's the kind of stuff he writes in it. Aren't you glad you're reading this one?

There is a pecking order among the pilots that has nothing to do with rank. Competence and experience trump rank, and everyone accepts this unwritten rule. When I have the time to look around and observe these subtleties, I can feel the confidence in the pilots on the top of the ladder. I can also sense the uncertainty of those who don't seem to have or want that responsibility. It isn't difficult for me to know which one of these clubs I'd rather join, but as with any club, there are dues to pay. The cost of hanging around on the beach with Doc Zimpher, feigning nebulous maladies and the constant uncertainty that comes with fear, are a high price to pay. I'll take my chances behind the wheel (or the stick in this case).

So far, other than flying, bathing, sleeping, and writing these letters, I haven't had much one-on-one time with any of these guys to validate my observations. Our conversations are short, shallow, and infrequent. Most pilots are busy coming and going and carrying out their assignments, and we seem to be always one or two airplanes short or one or two pilots short.

17 March, 1966 1330

Lieutenant John Chizinne inherited a pet monkey from one of his hooch- mates who transferred home. They adopted the monkey after its mother was killed when a military truck ran over her. The monkey's name is Justin Case, and they walk him around on a leash like a puppy. The biggest problem with Justin, other than being a wild animal, is that nobody has bothered to try to house-train him. Instead, when he's introduced to someone new, he crawls up on their shoulder and takes a pee. This act receives howls of laughter, which only makes Justin want to continue being the squadron piss artist. Witnessing this act first-hand saved me from falling victim to this hazing gag. I don't want Justin near me, period. Sometimes, he's left in the ready room when the joint owners are on an assignment, and he's likely to do anything from crapping on the maps to crawling all over the medevac pilot while he's trying to take a nap. Justin is only worth mentioning because he's a symbol of the chaos that surrounds us. There has been a serious discussion about putting Justin on the next medevac run and returning him to the wild. We'll see how it plays out.

Captain Kurt Mason, one of my hoochmates, collected a few bucks from everyone in our hooch to keep some beer in our reefer (fridge). He calls it a beer cartel. If we want a beer, we have to pay a dime to keep the beer fund going. Friends who are not members of the cartel would pay 15 cents. This was sold to me as an investment, basically a way for other people to pay for our beer. Someone has to go all the way into Danang to purchase the beer when it runs out. If he had not been a senior captain, I might have pointed out some of the inherent flaws in the beer cartel, the first one being that I don't care for warm beer. I can drink beer if it's ice cold and with a pizza, but neither of those things exist here. This fridge only works when the generator is running, which is half the time. If the cartel lasts more than a month, I'd be surprised.

I have already logged more flight time than anybody else in the squadron this month. The political situation has slowed our operations, and our little war has turned into a confusing free-for-all. Until the dust settles, we're just making sure our perimeter is secure and that we don't have another suicide sapper attack on our base.

Almost every day we receive a call to evacuate a soldier with "heat stroke" caused from hauling 80 pounds of gear through those steaming jungles. Heat exhaustion may not sound serious, but it is. The medics don't have any ice in the boonies to cool a man down. Once we have the heat victim in the medevac slick, the corpsman strips him to the waist and pours all the water we have over him. Then, we take him up to about 3000 feet with the doors open. The evaporation of the water sucks the heat out of him. By the time we land at the hospital, he's already talking and smiling again. They do have ice at the hospital at Danang which is called Charlie Med. I use the word *we*, but I'm talking about the corpsman and the crew chief ... the ones who have to jump out of the plane, sometimes under fire, to help put them onto the stretchers. All the pilots do is remain comfortably in their armor plated seats making sure those skids are barely touching the ground in case all hell breaks loose.

Doc had a long come-to-Jesus meeting with the interpreter who supervises the maids. Our maid, Miss Nguyen Thi-Toc, was chewed-out for not performing her duties satisfactorily. She improved a little that day, but she won't make eye contact with Doc Zimpher anymore. When I asked her to polish my boots, she polished everybody's boots. We'll see how long her new burst of energy lasts. We give the girls a small gratuity for just about everything they do, so their monthly pay could be doubled or tripled with a little effort. Some of the younger ones know how to work that system very well. Others, not so much.

The maids' schedules have been interrupted by political squabbles that cause erratic transportation issues. When they do show up, they sit in a circle in that familiar "hunkered down" position with only their feet touching the ground and their knees under their chins. The older gals chew betel nut which makes their teeth turn black and produces a red juice which they dribble and spit all over the place. One story that accompanies this nasty habit involves their long period of occupation by the French. Young, pretty Vietnamese girls would chew this vile concoction to make themselves less attractive, and therefore less susceptible to being raped by French soldiers.

The maids cook their lunch on the floor of the hooch and use a jar of fermented fish parts as a condiment. When the lid comes off that nouc mam jar, it will strip the hair out of your nose. Sometimes, when I see them drinking out of my favorite glass, it reminds me to keep my shot records up to date. They all use the same latrine; a one-holer down by the officer's club, which we try to avoid at all cost. They don't shake hands but prefer a polite nod. They take their shoes off in the hootch, considering the soles of their shoes unclean. They leave their sandals in the doorway with the toes pointing out. In their culture, pointing your feet at anyone is considered extremely rude.

I have two alarm clocks. Neither really works. One tells the correct time, but the alarm isn't dependable, and the other has a good alarm but never has the right time. If Miss Thi-Toc ever does anything spectacular, like clean my sheets, I'm going to make her a gift of those two clocks -- tick tocks for Thi-Toc. She won't know they don't work. I don't really need an alarm clock because I sold newspapers when I was a kid and developed an internal alarm clock. Besides, most of us sleep with one eye open anyway.

The problem with Justin, other than being a wild animal, is nobody bothered to house-train him.

That same night, 2000 hours

Only a few minutes before lights out! Everything is quiet, and the guys in the hooch are fiddling with their gear and preparing for whatever tomorrow brings. It's good to have everything laid out in case you're called out in the dark and have to dress by flashlight. The flight schedule is being circulated. They bring it around just before lights out. I'm the medevac escort tomorrow beginning at 0700.

Two days later, 19 March, 1966 Saturday 2200

What a wild day! An unmerciful wind from the South China Sea has whipped this camp to its knees. Blowing dirt and sand have found their way into every nook and cranny of MMAF. Clouds of speeding grit pushed by 35 knot winds have sandblasted our hooch and everything in it. Because we are located on the corner with no protection, it has been especially brutal for us. I wonder how this is affecting the aircraft. We don't need the additional concern of our choppers being fouled with all this dirt, for the same reason you wouldn't want a bucket of sand dumped onto your car engine. It's a performance issue.

I have a well deserved Saturday off, earned by having only one hour of sleep during yesterday's marathon medevac duty. We were called out a half dozen times during the daylight hours on routine medevacs, if you can call picking up pieces of people routine. Then during the night, a group of Marines were pinned down about 10 miles south of here by VC mortar and small arms fire. Our first call came in just before dark. Two casualties were square in the middle of a fire fight. We could see the flaming tracers flying back and forth across the landing zone that they had chosen for us. Not sure who the biggest lunatics are, the medevac pilots or the bush Marines. That would be a close call.

We managed the pick-up without a mortar round landing on the slick. I was in the overhead plane flying escort and making precautionary runs firing into virtual nothingness, while scanning for muzzle flashes or a mortar flash in the dark. Clearly, the slick pilot saved those two guy's lives and risked his own.

Twenty minutes later, we are called back to the exact same location. Now, it's pitch black, and the zone was still red hot with tracers flying back and forth. This was now a fierce, close-quarter fire fight, and nearly impossible for me to determine how to launch any of our erratic rockets without the risk of hitting our own guys. We made a couple low passes trying to make some noise and were firing machine guns far enough away from the location of the landing zone to be safe. Maybe, it might scare them off. But the nighttime is a friend of the VC, and they have the home field advantage. I called a couple of Air Force fighter jocks (F-4s) who are always on 24 hour airborne standby and asked them to come down and make a couple of low, dry passes. It might cause the VC to hunker down or take cover in their spider holes. The F-4s were there in five minutes and made a couple of treetop swoops that would have scared the daylights out of me if I had been down there. Then, I made several low passes with my lights off. I could see an occasional tracer flying skyward, but they were just shooting at sound. However, we could tell from those tracers just how close the enemy was to the Marine position. *Shit* ... this was bad.

The F-4's made four more low passes right over the zone just as I had been doing, more for effect than anything else. The slick waited overhead, burning precious fuel and waiting for his opportunity. My heart and my head were pumping for the slick crew because I knew he was going to go in there at the first opportunity, come hell or high water. That was his job. I also knew that it was too dangerous to drop that chopper in there right now because it would have only been shot down and would have compounded the situation tenfold. He tried it anyway while I tried to divert with low passes, this time with my lights on to provide a distraction.

Ten times the slick made an attempt. The VC had set a trap for the medevac chopper. They seemed determined to bag a trophy. As the night progressed, the casualties increased, and the situation became more urgent. The slick tried approaching from different angles for over an hour as the casualties swelled, now to more than twenty. Our boys were pinned down, and we were pinned out, but we were determined to stay there until we resolved the crisis. With that many casualties, bigger planes were needed, and two UH-34's were dispatched. The Huey slick went back for more fuel after they arrived.

Just as daylight approached, everything came

together. It was 0530 before we had all the wounded out of there. Two of the men had died during the night. There were bullet holes in all the planes except mine, mainly because I was not expected to land an armed Huey in the zone. As daylight approached, the VC ran out of darkness, courage, and ammunition all at the same time. When they no longer had the advantage, they bugged out ... "dee-deed" as we call it.

There was no information available on VC casualties. It's not our job to keep up with all those types of things. Our job was to go after the wounded, and we wondered if we could not have done it better and saved those two kids who died.

Sleep was hard to come by after that. But when my body finally shut down, I slept until noon and woke up to the slapping of tent flaps pounding the hooch. At first, I thought the room was full of smoke, and perhaps we were under attack. The red dust from the packed clay streets mixed with dusty sand from the beach made it look as though the sky had turned upside down, and the clouds were now on the bottom. Fifty feet above the swirling dust cloud, the sky was clear and blue. I looked down at my bed, and there was an outline of my body on the sheets and of my head on the pillow. My toothbrush was now dirt red, and the condensation on our refrigerator was dripping red mud and running down the door. The whole scene resembled an amateur reproduction of Hell for a high school play. I needed a shower but saw the senselessness of it.

Nobody was around the hooches. I knew that all the talk would center around last night's all-night extraction, so I slipped on my dirty flight suit and boots and headed for the mess hall for some company. After lunch, Doc, Perry James, Jose and I decided to go into the Danang Exchange. This entailed traveling the same route that I had taken into town, but the PX was on the outskirts of town and was heavily guarded. Perry James procured a Jeep from the motor pool for the trip. Broad daylight and a stream of military vehicles, plus what I had been through the night before, made the ride more tolerable than the one I had taken in the dark a couple of weeks ago.

The PX (Post Exchange) was over stocked with customers and under stocked with merchandise. No Cokes, no tape recorders, no radios, no 35 millimeter film, no reading lamps, and no pillows. I purchased some wash cloths, sunglasses, a box of gum, root beer Lifesavers, dental floss, Band-Aids, shoe polish, and a case of Upper 10 (a lemon-lime soft drink, which is all they had). A big spree, but none of those things were on my shopping list.

I was still tired from the night before when we came back to the hooch, but I couldn't sleep anymore. Too many things were swimming in my head. By now the outline of my body on the bed had disappeared. The entire bed was dirt red. I didn't find the outhouse any more inviting either, but there is nothing to compare to a healthy visit to a military latrine to make you grateful for the really important things in life.

Dinner was excellent tonight with all the freshest available seasonal canned products, flavored with just the right amount of red sand.

20 March, 1966 2200   Hue Phu Bai (pronounced way-foo-by)

My crew and I are spending the night in another Marine outpost about 50 miles north of Marble Mountain. We came up here this morning at 0'dark thirty to escort a troop lift 25 miles north of the city of Hue. Our target area is south of the DMZ, or the 17th parallel, which is a line of demarcation that neither side is supposed to penetrate according to the rules of engagement. War does have its rules, you know.

Hue is an ancient and very attractive city from the air with a river winding through the middle of it, much like Paris. There is a military operation in the flatlands north of this area which is a long way east of the mountainous terrain where the NVA usually hide. We will escort 12 CH-46's and 6 UH-34's in dropping 400 troops into two small adjacent villages to find out where all these enemy troops are coming from.

The predawn briefing for this mission was absolutely hilarious. The primary drop zone was about 50 yards from a village called Phouc Mi. The overly serious, thin-lipped major who was leading the 46 flight had only read the name of the village on the map and had never actually spoken it aloud prior to his briefing. When he made the statement that he would be leading the flight that would make the first landing at a place called … ! After a long hesitation, while he stared in disbelief at his map and the words he had already committed to say, upon hearing the words *Phouc Mi* come out of his mouth for the first time, it literally sent the 30 pilots in the packed room into hysterics.

Many of these small Vietnamese villages have a second tiny village nearby that is annexed to the parent village and also named for it. A second flight of 34's, led by another major, would land close to this second village to allow plenty of separation for all those choppers and spread out the 400-man strike force. This major, too, was a little nervous about his role as the flight leader. When he came to the part where he was to disclose his top secret landing zone, we literally came out of our chairs laughing so hard. The name of his LZ was Phouc Mi 2.

When we walked outside that small briefing room to go to our airplanes, it wasn't even daylight yet, and we all had tears streaming from our eyes. No comedy writer could have come up with a funnier script.

Everything became less funny after that. The first two-hour attempt at this coordinated drop was a clusterf***; compounded by bad weather, poor radio discipline on the part of the 46 drivers, and just plain chicken-heartedness on the part of the 34 flight leader who didn't seem to be comfortable with his landing area. The Hueys were there to provide gunship support if needed, but the landings had to be aborted when the pilots couldn't pull the trigger and coordinate the troop drop. Even the A-4's (heavily armed fighter jets) going along for added insurance were confused. At 0900 we tried again, and the weather and a new 34 flight leader managed to let us put the troops in.

The final troop drop was quiet, too quiet, in fact. We had already telegraphed our intent and given the enemy time to prepare a strategy. The element of surprise was now on their side. The gunships had just come in for refueling when we were called right back out there. The Marines were in a fierce fire fight not 200 yards from Phouc Mi 2. An O1-C with an aerial observer on board had already marked the friendly and enemy positions with green and red smoke grenades. (Red, of course, for the bad guys.) We killed about 10 hooches with our rockets and shot every round of everything else we had and came back to the ammo dump to rearm.

By noon there was a real war going on. The medevacs were in progress, but we were in gunships, not slicks, and could not make any pickups. The A-4's were dropping bombs, napalm, and strafing the enemy positions with their 20 mm guns. Our two Hueys shot 10,000 rounds of our little 7.62 mm NATO-approved-full-metal- jacket rounds from our M60's and a total of 116 rockets. I was the co-pilot with Captain Dick Carr who ran the whole battle once it started, and I must say, I was impressed. He was calm and professional, and by observation I learned that a cool head makes a great leader. As the lead gunship, he was the Deadlock-in-Charge, and when his voice broke through the chaos on the crackling radios, everybody shut up and paid attention. They followed his instructions to the letter without question. He gave me, the door gunner, and our crew chief a job to do and made us all feel as though we were each vital to the mission. When it was over, he went back to his bunk, laid down with his boots on, and was sound asleep in less than 10 minutes.

These people near the DMZ were not your standard VC. I had the feeling that we had run into something bigger than a few villages with a bunch of gun-totin' rice farmers. North Vietnamese regulars were operating in and out of that demilitarized zone at will and running truck loads of weapons down through it. We finished the job that we came to do in escorting the lift, but I know we haven't seen the last of Hue Phu Bai.

This was the biggest thing I've been a part of in my 20 days in country, and from the looks of what's pouring through that DMZ, we may be just warming up. I hope those Marines on the ground aren't taking too much of a pounding out there tonight. Can't help but feel for them. When the sun goes down, the pilots normally come back to a fold-up canvas cot and curl up on a comfortable rubber mattress. The grunts don't have that luxury. If I sleep tonight, it will have to be in a stranger's bed. His doesn't look any cleaner than the one I woke up in this morning. His pinups are great though. Another titty man!

The mosquitoes are thick up here. There's no sea breeze like there is at Marble Mountain. It's difficult to believe that a mosquito would come near me after being in this flight suit all day. They have a nice officer's club here, but there will be no rum and Coke tonight. We need all the rest we can get. We are all on five minute standby for the night, and we can't even leave to take a shower.

21 March 1966 2100 hours

We flew back to MMAF this morning at 0800. We were able to sleep through the night last night without being called back out. As soon as we checked in, I saw that I was on the flight schedule for an 1100 flight which sort of pissed me off. I didn't say anything, but there seems to be plenty of guys hanging around the hooches who aren't flying that much. I had time to pick up my mail, take a shower, and grab a bite to eat before I was back in the saddle. The mess hall is open for some kind of snack around the clock to accommodate schedules like this, but the hot food is limited to meal times.

This mission also turned into a powder keg. An outpost south of here was drawing fire from two or three different villages, and we emptied our little packages on them. Shooting up a village is not my favorite thing to do. It takes a long time to build a thatched-roofed house by hand. Those villages were peaceful until they were visited by Ho Chi Minh's recruiters handing out rifles.

When the hop was over, I walked into the ready room to see that I was scheduled to report to Chu Lai in 30 minutes about 56 miles south of Marble Mountain. I felt as though I were being put through some sort of hazing. I'm already leading the squadron in flight time, and I haven't even been here three weeks. I wanted to complain about it, but I figured if I were not doing that, I'd just be doing something else. Might as well stay busy! This experience might come in handy later, and in an odd way, it fit into my strategy of not wanting to be a pansy.

There was some serious action going on around Chu Lai when we arrived, and we were instructed to escort 22 planes headed south to a place near Quang Ngai. They would drop in some Marines where two battalions of VC were supposed to be hemmed in. We were told in the briefing that these VC were the remnants of Operation Utah which I wrote about a couple of weeks ago. Off we went to shoot at designated targets without ever seeing a single living creature. I suspect that these villagers spend most of their time digging hidey-holes when they aren't growing rice. Like us, they probably don't sleep much.

I saw Tony at Chu Lai but didn't have time to speak to him. He looked like a real warrior now and seemed to be all business. Since we arrived in country on the same day, I'd like to ask him how much flight time he has so far to see if he's experiencing the hazing treatment, too.

After every skirmish, we fly out of the jungle and back to our beach camp, isolated from the constant, day-to-day, close-up images of the war. I spend too much time feeling guilty about that. We have hot meals and luke-warm beer from our beer cartel. Compared to the ground troops, it's a country club. I worry about them out there in the jungle for days at a time, fighting off insects, leaches, and immersion foot. When I use my brain to think about something other than myself, it makes my job seem easier. I don't mind going an extra mile for them. I'd rather be doing that than playing volleyball. Soldiers are incredible people when you actually know what they do. They are down in those jungles depending on us to help keep them alive. Other than themselves, there isn't anybody else for them to depend on.

None of us college boys ever thought we'd be over here experiencing anything like this. This war is not like World War II where the average soldier might see a couple of days of combat during the entire war. Here, a kid can be sitting around reading a letter from home one minute, and we might drop his butt in the middle of a firefight before he can finish the letter. This helicopter war is mobile, fluid, and fast. I'm surprised that it gets thrown at us so quickly. I was in the BOQ in Okinawa having soap handed to me, and suddenly, I'm rolling in on a target in some God-forsaken place near the DMZ. We didn't even have an orientation class. The cockpit is the classroom, I guess. Three weeks over here, and I'm practically a veteran. I've already been in on more action that some pilots see in a tour.

The biggest reason not to bitch too much about flight time is that the seasoned pilots are going to be rotating out of here soon, and I'm going to look around and see some other wide-eyed rookie looking to me for answers. Most of my flights so far have been in the co-pilot's seat, and I've had the benefit of seeing how things are done, as well as how they can be botched up. One day I will have to co-ordinate a complicated mission, and I can't afford to be like a Tennessee deer caught in the headlights.

I had a baseball coach pull me out of a game once because I dove for two consecutive fly balls. I caught both of them, and the crowd thought the plays were spectacular, but the coach had a different view. He said if I had reacted sooner and been in the right position in the first place that I could have easily made both catches and been able to make a throw instead of flopping around on the ground. As much as I hate criticism, I had to admit that was excellent advice. If that landing at Phouc Mi had been handled properly the first time, it may have had a completely different outcome. Instead, we wasted valuable time, compromised the advantage of surprise, and found ourselves playing defense instead of offense. Sometimes, a person who appears to be a hero because he had to scramble out of a jam, may actually be just an idiot who didn't make the right decision in the first place. Experienced pilots are extremely keen to these subtleties.

22 March, 1966 Tuesday 1230

Nothing improves officer morale like the promise of a brand new air conditioned Officer's Club. The scuttlebutt (rumor) is that there will be a grand opening on Friday. This is about 150 yards from my hooch on a piece of prime, beach front property. They had to tear down the crab-infested maid's latrine to make room for it. The Phu-Bai club has pictures on the walls, tablecloths, comfortable wicker chairs with cushions, and a long bar, complete with swivel bar stools. Multiple speakers play sexy stereo music, and they even have a separate game room. Everything but a dance floor! I hope our new club can come close to being as nice as theirs.

In a few days, I will be relocating from my temporary living quarters. I have been crammed into a makeshift corner with no motivation to make improvements, knowing I would move. There are five others in my current space, and they are all captains, including Doc Zimpher. I have been invited to join five other first lieutenants (junior officers) who have asked me to fill the space left by Ron Jennings who is rotating home. I'll still be the rookie, but not the lowest in rank.

Rank doesn't come into play often, but it hangs in the air. Some of the older guys have been in the Corps for several years. They're Marine regulars, professionals looking to climb the ladder. Most of the lieutenants are citizen soldiers, reserves, like me. We have no long-term contract, and we're not planning to make this a career. There's pressure on the reserves to make the leap to regular Marine because of the pilot shortage. It does make sense not to have to keep re-training new people for this, but I won't be standing in line for that one. The subtle difference between USMC and USMCR (Reserve) is that the "R's" are passing through for one tour while the career Marines are in competition with other regulars for advancement.

The irreverent atmosphere among the reserve lieutenants in my new hooch fits my sarcastic personality to a tee. These guys can make something funny out of almost anything. Their standard joke is, "*I would rather trade my bar than my R.*" The bar meaning the rank of lieutenant … not the new O Club *bar!* We wouldn't trade that for anything.

I have been standing the Sparrow Hawk duty all morning. If you recall, that's the standby strike force that's hardly ever launched. Well, I've only had it twice, and it was launched both times, including today. I must be the Sparrow Hawk magnet. This one was much tamer, and all we did was oversee the troop insertion and come back home to refuel and wait to see what might happen. Nothing did.

All our outgoing mail is free, which is nice because we don't have to fool with finding and buying stamps all the time. Incoming mail is not free, and some of the packages are a nightmare. God only knows how they find their way over here. Some arrive two or three months late. Maybe, they come by ship. No telling what might crawl out of some of those boxes that arrive two or three months after they left the states. If there is such a thing as a post office I don't know where it is. We have a postal clerk who brings our incoming mail to the ready room. We drop our outgoing mail at the mess hall. In this hazardous environment it would make no sense to buy stamps by the page, or green bananas if we had any.

23 March 1966, Wednesday, 1930 MMAF

After a blistering day that saw the temperature reach 113 degrees, we are now enjoying a cool twilight breeze which is restoring some life into our tropical camp. There is a cloud of insecticide passing through my tent at the moment, and all is right with the world.

I flew my scheduled two-hour visual recon of the Danang area at noon today after sleeping later than usual and taking the first of four cold showers. We found a target south of a place called Hoi An and called the fixed wing jocks in with their napalm, bombs, and rockets. Their rockets seem to shoot a little straighter than these things we have. There are times when ours look like a snake when we fire them, and I wonder if they might turn completely around and come after us. When the jet jocks were finished, we went in like young cowboys and shot our little wad on what was left down there. Ho hum!

The irreverent lieutenants came up with our own solution to this war. Since nobody can tell the good guys from the bad, why not ask all the good guys to meet at the beach where they could be loaded onto boats. When the boats have been taken a safe distance out to sea, we then bring in B-52 Bombers with all the bombs we have. Then in a twist that only a reserve Marine could appreciate, *we bomb the boats.*

Yesterday when I returned from a flight, I saw a commotion around the bulletin board. There were six VMO-2 pilots scheduled to take three Hueys to a helicopter platform ship stationed at an undisclosed location in the South China Sea to support an operation yet to be announced. They would be gone for an indefinite period of time (minimum three weeks) and further details could not be disclosed. My name was the sixth one on the list. Former VMO-1 pilots Shep Spink, Bill Kirby, and Jose Melendez were also on the list. Was this my reward for being a good Boy Scout, or was this going to be the hairiest assignment in the history of this storied squadron? Fear of the unknown has pretty much described my Vietnam experience up until now. But just as quickly as my name appeared on that list, it was decided that only five pilots would go. The CO batted it around and decided to ask only those people who really *wanted* to go. All five said yes, and they seemed excited about it. After all, it would be a change of pace, and they would be sleeping on a comfortable ship at night, watching movies and taking hot showers. So, there were some "bennies" with it (benefits).

I gave Jose some money to buy me a couple of tape recorders at the ship's store, which is better stocked than our PX. I'll know in three weeks if it was a good deal or not. Meanwhile, we are left with five fewer pilots, and good ones at that, to take care of business around here. Ce' la vie!

The maids didn't come today. More problems in the city! I expected her to be here to cover my bed with my vinyl poncho, and now my clean sheets are red with dirt. When I move to my new tent, I won't have Miss Thi-Toc anymore. She hates any kind of work. There is a young girl who works in my new hooch who likes working for the lieutenants, and they reward her well. If we ever liberate these people, she will make a decent capitalist.

My current hooch is quiet when Gus Plum isn't here. Gus is a perfect name for Gus, who can be embarrassingly inappropriate. He can also scare the living daylights out of you if you have to ride with him as his copilot. This is another reason to become as competent as possible, as quickly as possible. That way, you never have to be anybody's co-pilot. I always feel a little safer when I am in control of the plane, as I imagine any pilot would. There is a balance ball in every aircraft that tells the pilot when the aircraft is properly trimmed. If the plane is slipping, yawing, pitching, and crabbing all the time, it can be a very uncomfortable ride. It's the same as trimming the sails on a sailboat. Some pilots never get the hang of this, and it seems as if they run their lives in similar fashion, always slightly askew! Gus is a great guy and will do anything he's asked to do, and he was a hero at Ashau. I want both of us to leave this country alive.

I'm learning more about my true nature. Abstinence has an uncluttered clarity that has great appeal. There is a source of pride in minimalism; shaving with cold water, opening a can of peaches for lunch instead of walking down for a hot meal, or just relishing a few minutes of reflection. After hearing those rotor blades beating in my ears all day, a little peace and quiet is a magnificent luxury. Maybe, nature is preparing me for a situation where my survival disciplines will be tested? Could I hold out a few nights in the jungle if my plane was forced down? God forbid, but I probably could.

26 March, 1966 Saturday 2130

Back on the gerbil wheel again! I'm driving the medevac slick ... the ambulance as we sometimes call it. I've been called out seven times since I came on duty at 0700. More sickening sights that make a tremendous impression on a man with no medical experience! Never mind the details, but some of this can be emotionally overwhelming. I'm simply going to have to rely on the sense of satisfaction that comes from knowing that I may have helped save several lives today. There's honor in it from that perspective. Watching the dedication of the doctors and medical crews is humbling. I can't say enough good things about our own corpsmen and our crew chiefs. The best a pilot can do when these men have finished putting the stretchers in the plane is to get everybody out of there as quickly as possible and fly them to the hospital as safely as possible. Once we're free of the zone, you can sense the relief of the wounded. *"I'm hurt, but I'm not dead. I'm safe now. I'm out of there, and I'm going home."* The morphine helps.

When the lights go out at night, sometimes I lie on my rubber mattress and think about my narrow, selfish life before I knew anything about any of this. I knew I would be exposed to death, but I was not prepared for the sheer volume of daily incidents that we are being exposed to. I think about my quiet little hometown and how I coped with dying and the fear of it as a child.

When I was eight, a derelict man hanged himself

in an abandoned building about 200 yards from our house. One of my classmates claimed he saw him hanging there, and he made up a big story about it. He saw "a *real live dead person*," he told us. Tullahoma was a railroad town, and if you weren't familiar with the train schedule, it was like playing Russian roulette with those poorly marked crossings. After a long 4th of July weekend, we might hear of an unfortunate kid drowning in a few feet of water down by Dement's Bridge on the Duck River. *"The current pulled him under"* was the usual explanation. It was always a boy. No girls were ever killed.

A family member might sit up all night at the funeral home with the corpse, and the whole town would come to a halt for a funeral procession. Automobiles were the popular way to be killed, and every couple of months a mangled Studebaker or Ford would be dragged through town on the way to the junkyard. Safety belts, as they were called, barely existed. Two-lane "thunder roads" through moonshine country were our only link to the rest of civilization. A Saturday night joy ride with a half pint of Lem Motlow could be a one-way ticket to a James Dean adventure.

Airplane travel was another sure-fire way to end up in the obituaries. The entire family would dress up and go to the airport to see their relatives off. They waved at the plane until it was out of sight, as if it might be the last time they would ever see them. I wonder why the FAA never saw the irony of calling those places *Terminals?*

After every spectacular tragedy, there would be a Baptist revival. We always sang, *Bringing in the Sheaves*.

The Baptist preacher explained in graphic detail what happens *after* we died, and that was no picnic either. Apparently, if we had broken certain important moral rules, such as lying, for example, an invisible man who lived in the sky, who loves us very much, would see to it that we were burned in an underground furnace until the end of all time. The harsh punishment didn't seem to fit the crime, and since lying had been the basis of my entire childhood up to that point, this was not good news for me. That was too much to process for an adolescent. I managed to survive Dement's Bridge, and the comments of the Baptist preacher, and somehow I have to find a way to survive all this. If for no other reason than to go back home and help people appreciate the thousands of personal freedoms they enjoy every day. It's not corny to be grateful for them.

Tomorrow is Sunday, and I have a few other things to be thankful for. We have a new shower building and a new officer's club. I missed the grand opening of the club, but I hear it was a blowout. We have some real rowdies in this group, so I hope we can keep the new club looking respectable. We have a new piano in the club. One of our squadron lieutenants is an accomplished pianist. The Pianoman, Dick Drury, provides quality entertainment two or three nights a week.

We also have a new barber shop in the officer's area. A quarter for a trim! If the generator goes out when you are in the chair and the electric clippers don't work, the half haircut is free. What a country! There is a stray dog that hangs out down by the barber shop that may have belonged to that dead VC barber that helped blow up the flight line a few months ago. The dog never barks or makes a sound. Supposedly, there's a breed of dog here that doesn't bark, but my theory is that the dog doesn't want to bring undue attention to itself.

The mail has been erratic since Ky's firing of General Thi. The disruption is playing havoc with air traffic, especially into Danang, which is the focal point of the politics where Buddhist Monks continue to stir the cauldron.

In what little spare time we have, we read from the plethora of paperback books that people send us. The good ones are passed around. Some of the guys receive *Playboy* magazine, which is understandably popular. It has great articles, they say. Some receive letters from people wanting to be pen pals. There *are* military jobs other than aviator, so some people have more time for these types of activities.

I need to be sleeping in case I'm called back out tonight. I'm sending home the pictures I took of Ann-Margaret during her visit to Danang. That's our CO, Colonel Bauman with her. He volunteered himself for the job that day. RHIP... rank has its privileges. You can see her talking to some of the patients there at Charlie Med. Our squadron took all those medevac patients there. Interestingly, Johnny Rivers was a bigger hit with the troops than Ann-Margaret. Spy movies like James Bond are popular with the troops. Rivers has a hit song called *Secret Agent Man.*

28 March 1966 Monday

Monday is malaria pill day. That's the only thing that sets it apart from any other day. That big bowl of orange pills in front of the mess hall line serves as a dual reminder that a new week is beginning, and that none of us is invincible. Nobody in their right mind turns down the weekly malaria pill.

There was some sort of party atmosphere going on at the beach Monday. Marine Air Group 16 was having a change of command ceremony. Colonel Connor was being relieved by Colonel Hunt. They had flown in three Army nurses. American women are in the camp. Round eyes! Guys were caught by surprise running around in their green, jockey-short-makeshift swim suits, making the nurses more of a disturbance than an attraction. Few men care to make their first impression in a pair of wet, green Jockey briefs.

The nurses just wanted to see the beach. Afterwards, they had a more formal ceremony at the helo-pad, and everybody was supposed to attend. About half did, but I wasn't one of them. A day off is a day off. Later, they held a reception at the new club, and *everybody* showed up for that. Free food and drinks, blackjack, and poker in our brand new, decked-to-the-nines club, complete with Army nurses and female Vietnamese bartenders! There are three things in this world that are guaranteed to instantly modify the behavior of men: guns, gambling, and girls. We had the ultimate trifecta (all three). I won more than a hundred dollars that night, mostly because the testosterone level in the club was out of control. I played poker until 2200 and would have stayed longer if I hadn't seen tomorrow's flight schedule. Looks like I'm headed back to Hue Phu Bai at 0500 in the morning.

Next day

It was still dark when we landed at Phu Bai. They were already briefing the mission. By daybreak we were escorting four UH-34's with a hatchet force that was being sent in to recover an Army Special Forces recon team whose mission had gone awry. There were six members of the recon team, two were dead, two were wounded, and two were healthy. Green Beret's are like Marines in that they leave no man behind, so everybody knew exactly what the job required.

The LZ was not big enough to land a chopper, so the 34 had to hover at tree top level and lower a hoist and chair to pluck them out one at the time. The gunships tried to shoot up everything around them during the painstaking process. We could shoot at will and did. That 34 was a sitting duck for 40 minutes, but the pilot and his crew hung in there without a whimper and finally flew those men to the hospital. Later that afternoon, we flew escort for another 21-man Special Forces recon drop that was quick, quiet, and efficient. The Special Forces guys are 100% crazy. I have no idea where we find these people.

We flew our stinky selves back to Marble Mountain around 2000, and I looked at the flight schedule to find that I was the Chicken Hawk pilot tomorrow from noon to seven p.m. Chicken Hawk had been anything but Chicken Hawk for me, but at least the morning is mine, and I'll gladly take the short break.

29 March, 1966 Tuesday 1705 Marble Mountain

I managed to find a private corner in the ready room to jot down a note before I'm relieved from Sparrow Hawk duty at 1900. I came on duty at noon, and at 1215 sharp they called for Sparrow Hawk. Just like clockwork. Three or four snipers were taking pot shots at some rice pickers. A group of Marines happened to be in that area. Three CH-46's and a bus load of troops were standing by to fix the problem. The VC intimidate the villagers with terror tactics to make them cough up a few bags of rice, a couple fresh teenagers, or whatever. The troops were inserted without incident and swept through the area for a couple of hours. I flew in circles with my co-pilot waiting to be directed to a target. The Marines rounded up some suspects, and the 46's landed again to gather up the troops and a couple of questionable prisoners. End of show.

Scuttlebutt that the government might make officer's combat pay completely tax exempt has us all abuzz. Something to talk about! Enlisted military already enjoy that benefit, but officers only receive a modest deduction. They let us shoot up 100,000 dollars worth of munitions on one of these missions, but Congress is having a devil of a time wrestling with that $200 a month deduction. Sorry, I detected cynicism there for a second.

Another one of our ready room discussions centers around how many military jobs could be performed by civilians. In Vietnam, only about 10% of the military is actually doing any fighting. The administrative, non- combat jobs are as safe as any job in the states, their biggest complaint being bad coffee. Supply people, recreation people, carpenters, PX employees, and club managers are only a few of the jobs that don't require weapons.

Some of the carpenters on that list installed a new latrine down at the officer's quarters today, a brand new, "modern" plywood outhouse that accommodates six officers, three on each side facing each other. It's an engineering masterpiece, but bring along something to read. It's strictly business in there -- not much chit chat. The new location is about 50 steps upwind from the old one, which has been torn down and hopefully burned. The new "hot shower" building hasn't opened yet. Like the tax exemption, and the shorter tours, we're keeping our fingers crossed.

31 March, 1966   Thursday 1500 hours

Today, I'm the Operations Duty Officer. My primary responsibility is to co-ordinate the flight schedule by assigning planes to the pilots and putting up with all the bitching. I didn't write the flight schedule. That was done sometime last night. But I have to make sure it's executed in case somebody stubs a toe. Hopefully, the biggest problem I will have is finding someone to stand in for me for dinner. It's a phone watch if everything goes smoothly, which it has so far. Running the daily operations of a squadron, instead of just flying a small part of it, has allowed me to learn things that I wouldn't know otherwise: how things are accomplished, who's hiding out and where, who wants to step up, and who just likes to shoot off his mouth. Ordinarily, I wouldn't bother to involve myself with those issues.

From the duty officer's perspective, it's easy to see why the new guys might be taken advantage of. Some of the Old Salts push back if they don't like an assignment and that might intimidate a lower ranking schedules officer. The fact that I have done my share up to this point helps my credibility for this rotating duty assignment.

Right now, we have 21 planes, and only half of them are flyable. This limits our flight schedule and the number of sorties by that same percentage. The "down" birds are gradually coming "up" but need to be tested by a qualified test pilot. That's handled in the maintenance shack. The enlisted men handle the crew chief and door gunner assignments for each flight. I can only imagine the jostling that must go on there and how they must rank the pilots. There is a pecking order among the crew chiefs the same as the pilots.

This is all sorted out in due course. Everyone eventually receives a label. They quickly fall into one of two categories, and a ladder starts to form. Only one person can be the "man" and lead the parade, and there is also one that is destined to be the last person whom any of us would chose in a clutch situation. This grading system is based purely on behavior with no man being expected to perform a mission that might be beyond his perceived level of experience and competency. We would all have to be stupid not to realize that the fear factor is the main catalyst driving this behavior. Men seem to choose early where they want to fit on this ladder.

I just received a call from a routine medevac for a heat casualty. He isn't bleeding to death, and the zone isn't hot. Some of the ground troops just arriving haven't adjusted to this heat. They aren't conditioned to packing 80 pounds of gear through a steaming jungle. For a well-trimmed 160 pound Marine, this is half his weight. After a night in a cool hospital bed and plenty of fluids, he'll be ready to go back to his buddies and do it all over again.

There is a big operation kicking off tomorrow. Really big, we're told! They won't reveal details yet, but they say it will last eight days. It's very close to our TAOR, so maybe we can root out some local bad guys.

That night . . .

Back in the tent, my operations duty is over. Things went well. I'm out of stuff to write about. This new operation may supply some material. We heard that the Marines told one of the village chiefs about the operation and asked for his co-operation. This must be some sort of new tactic, to tell a village chief, but not tell us. There is no security among those people. The Vietnamese are all related to each other, and blood is thicker than water. Even I know that! We don't have any real facts on this rumor, but we all wondered about the strategy of soliciting the help of a village chief.

I will be escorting the medevac plane tomorrow, which is not part of the not-so-secret operation, but I could be called into it. I have over 80 hours and four air medals so far, and this is the last day of my first month.

No maids today. It's some sort of Vietnamese holiday. The barmaids at the new club came to work anyway. The tips are good when the alcohol and the funny money start flying around, and money speaks any language and transcends holidays. The new bartenders don't speak English, but are phenomenal at imitating sounds. I had a "lum and koh" last night that tasted exactly like rum and Coke.

Tomorrow, the first day of the month, we'll see what April fool's day brings to Marble Mountain.

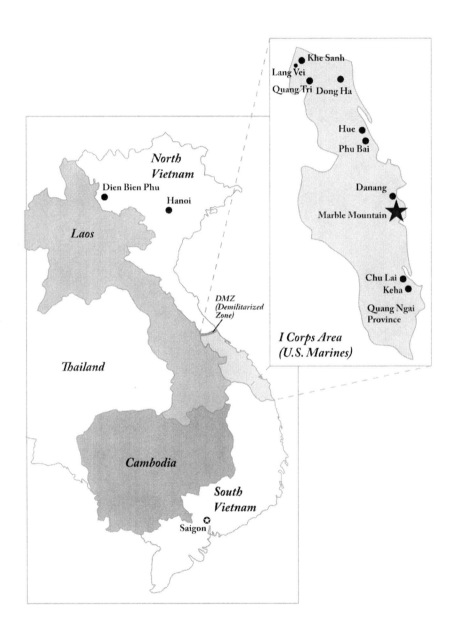

Khe Sanh
Lang Vei
Quang Tri Dong Ha
Hue
Phu Bai
Danang
Marble Mountain
Chu Lai
Keha
Quang Ngai
Province

*I Corps Area
(U.S. Marines)*

Dien Bien Phu
Hanoi

*North
Vietnam*

Laos

DMZ
*(Demilitarized
Zone)*

Thailand

Cambodia

*South
Vietnam*

Saigon

CHAPTER FOUR

APRIL FOOLS

1 April, 1966 Friday at midnight

Our secret new project is called Operation Orange, and it has turned up zilch. So far we are the April fools. Someone must have leaked the surprise. DUH!

The enemy is not stupid. They don't like surprises and rarely stand and fight when the odds and the circumstances are not in their favor. They are like a slot machine that we keep putting quarters into, but nothing ever comes out. They prefer a carefully planned ambush on their terms. A favorite tactic is to attack with a small group and then retreat into an area where they have set up an ambush with well organized escape routes. They will almost always carry away their dead and wounded. They have done this for many years, and they are not in this war for a one-year tour. They don't have to be in a big hurry to kill us, and they don't seem to have a timetable for doing it. We know that they are out there in large numbers because they keep causing mischief. Brer Rabbitts in the briar patch -- the consummate tricksters!

I haven't participated in this new operation today and even my medevac watch is quiet. From 0700 to 1900 we only had one call. Then at 1930 we were called to pick up a wounded VC. You can probably guess what that's about. They need some information from him. He won't be the first person to rat on his buddies after a long ride to the hospital in a Marine helicopter. The VC aren't exactly elite, professional soldiers. Most of them are part-time rice farmers receiving on-the-job training. But we are more like the British soldiers during the Revolutionary War, fighting on their turf and on their terms.

We're hoping the rest of the evening will be quiet. Some guys are organizing a poker game in the ready room to make the night go faster. There are only two beds down here, and I'm watching the game from one of them, pondering whether to give up a coveted bed for poker. We fight over these bunk beds because they are the alternative to a sore tailbone from those wooden-benched picnic tables that serve as our operations "conference room."

3 April, 1966 Sunday night

Couldn't resist the poker game last night -- they were having way too much fun. Some of these guys are a little reckless and don't like being left out of a hand. If you don't mind folding bad hands and being a little patient your odds of winning improve considerably. On some of these missions we have to play the hand we're dealt, but in a poker game we have the luxury of folding a bad hand. Watching their foolishness lured me in. It may *look* like monopoly money, but it still spends. One of them snagged my bed immediately, of course. I traded needed rest for a sweaty little handful of funny money.

Operation Orange is picking up momentum. VMO-2 gunships struck a village full of bad guys with automatic weapons. You may know more about this than we do if you watch television. Every skirmish seems to turn up on the nightly news showing a village in flames and a few "innocent" looking farmers with Marines pointing rifles at them. I was involved in a different mission. While I was airborne, I could see the action and heard most of the radio transmissions.

We had a drill tonight simulating an attack on the base. These exercises are being precipitated by demonstrations in Danang. The sky was filled with illumination flares attached to small parachutes to keep the area well-lit, which makes you wonder which side the flares help. We were supposed to take cover in the bunkers, but we all stood around as if it were the 4th of July, watching the lazy candles float to earth.

Tomorrow, there is a squadron farewell cookout for several pilots rotating home. Half of us will be given the day off to attend while the other half totes the load. The following day, we flip-flop. I'm scheduled to attend the first one. I hope we grill steaks for the party, but most likely it will be dead chickens.

5 April, 1966 1700 hours

I was awakened by a tall shadow beside my cot in the middle of the night repeating my name. When the apparition finally vanished, I realized it was 0355, and he had just informed me that the entire squadron was to report to the flight line ASAP. I woke the others and told them, but they were slow to react. Being rookies, Gus Plum and I were the first two pilots to report to the ready room. We actually took it seriously. Nobody else seemed to be in a big hurry.

Action in Danang had reached a state of alarm. A large number of people had been converging on the city all night long in trucks, tanks, and on foot. Road blocks had been set up at every intersection. We were told to prepare for the worst. Our ops officer needed two pilots immediately to fly an Army Huey from the Army detachment located at the south end of Danang airport over to Danang. The Army Huey was to be completely stripped of its markings and repainted with Vietnamese markings. This plane, we were told, would be for the personal use of Premier Nguyen Cao Ky.

Now, your first question would probably be the same as mine. Why doesn't the Army fly its own Huey over to Danang? The answer is wonderfully military. All the Army pilots live in the city and drive to work every day. The roads are blocked off, and they can't make it to their planes. Eye-yi –yi! A force in readiness, indeed!

Anyway, Gus and I were available, and we were taken over in a Huey to be dropped off to fly the clandestine Army Huey to some location that would be determined by whomever we would now be working for.

When we were dropped off around 0430, several men were in the process of re-marking Ky's new Huey. Gus and I were told to stand by. We pictured ourselves being Ky's pilot and being at the forefront of something historic, like a revolution. At 0700 dignitaries started coming out of the woodwork with heavily armed guards accompanying them. I didn't recognize anyone from my previous VIP taxi-work, and I'm pretty sure they didn't know who *I* was. They were all ushered into another building. In about 30 minutes an Air Force colonel came out of the building and told us we would no longer be needed. The sort of thing they might say just before they shoot you.

We used the radio to call VMO-2 to come back for us, since our Army transportation had been commandeered. Oddly enough, I was disappointed that it all fizzled into nothing because the drama had true potential for a legendary story. I told Gus that we must be turning into adrenaline junkies. He, too, was disillusioned that the whole episode turned out to be a dud. We were both pumped for some action.

I arrived at the ready room just in time to fly 24 hours of medevac duty. Since that time we have had nine medevacs, so I had my adrenaline fix. All the pickups were singles (one person), and were routine (not serious), and most of them were civilians (Vietnamese). The political tension has shifted the fighting away from the military and into the civilian population. Marines are having some time off while the civilians shove each other around.

Part of our squadron master disaster plan calls for the choppers to be prepared to evacuate all U.S. personnel out of Danang if necessary. All pilots are on a five minute alert. I'm already on medevac standby anyway, so none of this would alter my standard of living.

After lunch they delivered the April 5 issue of the *Stars and Stripes* newspaper. The four inch headline read as follows:

TROOPS TO LIBERATE DANANG, KY SAYS.

Ky said the city was in the hands of the enemy (VC, I suppose he meant), and that his government soon would launch military operations to get it back into government hands.

"Either the Mayor of Danang is shot or the government falls."

Ky also moved to placate demonstrators by declaring that the government would call a political congress to draft a constitution. Danang was a city of about 600,000 people (in the aggregate, but only 100,000 in the city itself), and it was the center of the U.S. Marine effort in the I Corps area. The demonstrators were demanding a return to a civilian government. Ky charged that Danang's mayor, Nguyen Van Man, *"has been using government funds to stage anti - government demonstrations."* Ky declared Danang a rebel city and one that needed to be liberated. In the same newspaper, buried in a small column, the Associated Press issued a response from Washington quoting General Wallace M. Greene, Marine Corps Commandant.

"This problem, if there is one there at this time, will have to be handled by the Vietnamese, and I am sure they are quite capable of taking care of the situation." The Marines will not interfere, the general vowed.

There are 50,000 Marines in the Danang area, not to mention Army, Air Force, and all the supporting U.S. personnel. This is more than half the population of the city. If push came to shove, we didn't have enough planes in our squadron to evacuate our own men. Ky was making a statement to the mayor that he meant business and was trying to force him to turn tail and head for the hills to *"join his fellow insurgents."* We, on the other hand, have no choice but to follow our commandant's orders to stay out of it and keep our shoulders to the proverbial wheel.

Meanwhile, the food quality has gone from A rations (fresh food) to B rations (canned food) because problems in Saigon and Danang have restricted aircraft traffic and resupply. This affects Huey parts and everything else. The tropical heat isn't helping matters, but complaining only makes things worse. We hear plenty of that during normal times. So we laugh at everything to ease the stress.

EPIPHANY

That first month was literally a trial by fire for me. Except for a gunship escort of a convoy or medevac, a chicken hawk or VIP taxi service, I was a tag-along co-pilot, watching and learning. All that changed on the 26th of March. I was both proud and scared the first day I saw my name on the flight schedule as the pilot of the medevac slick. As I said before, one becomes addicted to the feeling of excitement. The right seat (pilot's side) of the *ambulance* is the ultimate test on a busy day. I would be responsible for landing and picking up the evacuees for the next 24 hours. I was also the flight leader, and I would be directing both my gunship-wingman and any fixed wing that might be needed. Thank God, I had sweated through some of these things and had seen the good, the bad, and the ugly way to do them. I will not lie to you: I was scared to death.

We were called out four or five times that morning. The zones were not hot, and everything went fine. The afternoon was not eventful until about 1900. We received an emergency call to evacuate three wounded Marines just before dark. Anything coded as an emergency, we consider a life or death situation. When there are more than one or two, it usually means there is a live fire fight. The landing zone they chose for us was a bomb crater on the side of a hill, and the enemy, whoever they were, was shooting down on them. This made calling in an airstrike impossible because any bomb debris would be falling directly down on our Marines.

I wanted to secure the zone before I took the plane in, or possibly have them move to another location, so that we could neutralize the enemy fire and avoid hurting any good guys. Side-hill landings are difficult enough without gunfire. Alternate pickup areas were too far away, and wounded men don't need the additional stress of being dragged around in the jungle. The best solution that I could come up with was to ask the gunship to have its door gunner shoot the M-60 over the top of the zone and in the direction of the well-concealed VC while I tried to sneak underneath his layer of machine gun fire. None of this was working, and the men were hunkered down in that zone still taking fire. The clock was ticking. I was circling and stalling, trying to think of something, all the while wishing this were just a bad dream.

There was an atmosphere of electricity in the cockpit. It had formed a thin wall that was pressing against my face. I could feel the tension of the three men in the plane with me. We all knew that sooner or later we were going to have to go down where all the shooting was, or somebody else would have to. We also knew that if I procrastinated any longer that it would be dark. The situation would only be more complicated. I knew my wingman was feeling all the same things for me because we had all been there. Nobody envies the manager of a shit sandwich. Only one man could make this decision.

Suddenly, I made the call. No words were spoken. Not a single thing changed except that I leaned forward in my seat. As soon as I committed, all the pressure was replaced by perfect clarity. The cockpit tension and indecision were gone. On the other side of that thin membrane, the world was in focus. My thoughts were clear. I had stepped through an imaginary wall of fear. Unconsciously, I had "split the needles" and separated the engine power from the rotor mast. We were dropping like a stone toward the landing zone. All my focus shifted to the crater and tiny openings between tree stumps on the side of that hill. It was a moment I will never forget and a defining one for me.

I asked the wingman to keep pressure on the high ground while the crew loaded the boys onto the stretchers. Half a dozen Marines swarmed the door to load the bleeding cargo. If we were taking fire, I didn't know it. My mind was on flying that Huey and nothing else. I looked straight ahead to keep a reference point as I tried to hold a steady hover two feet above the uneven terrain. The rotor tips were inches away from a pile of rocks on the co-pilot's side. My wingman had adjusted his strategy and was in a hover a couple of hundred feet above me. He distracted the enemy and poured lead into the side of the hill. His spent shells fell all around us, littering the landing zone. Our corpsman had the casualties racked in stretchers and hooked to plasma bags by the time the crew chief squeezed my arm to signal all-clear. I did a wingover down the hill away from high ground, and we were quickly out of there.

By the time we landed at the hospital pad, the sun was setting, and darkness, our other enemy, had stolen what was left of the day. The window had closed. I looked at the clock on the instrument panel. The entire mission took less than 25 minutes from the time the call came until we landed at Bravo Medical. The decision that seemed like an hour for me to make took only a few seconds, probably the most important few seconds of my adult life.

It took years of reflection for me to understand what happened to me on that flight. Fear was the real enemy. I had been swimming upstream against it until that very day. There came a time when no amount of swimming would overcome whatever force it was that pulled me into the powerful current that is the Marine Corps. I had read somewhere that fear exists only to the extent that we give sanction to it. I understood the bravery of some of those grunts on the ground and the corpsmen and crew chiefs. I wasn't about to let them down. A year ago, some of those kids who were too lazy to make their beds back home were now humping 100 pounds of gear through the bush, cooking their own meals, and sleeping on the ground with a tree root for a pillow. I went down in that zone because I respected those young Marines. We came *out* of that zone because my wingman took extraordinary measures to make himself a target and to take care of us. We were a brotherhood. That was the day that I became a member of their club.

7 April, 1966 Thursday night

The planes that flew south the other day were supporting Operation Orange, several miles southwest. It's still grinding on. I have yet to be involved or to hear any details.

The previously mentioned all-squadron farewell party for the departing pilots was a huge success. We consumed a few cases of beer, colas, and the better part of a chicken farm. There was no steak, but burgers cooked over charcoal are hard to beat.

The big news continues to be the uprising in Danang. The town has been closed to all military traffic. The demonstrators have issued a statement that any U.S. helicopter landing at the I Corps headquarters would be fired upon. (That's where I landed with General Chuan.) Each day becomes more ludicrous. We can't even fly over the city we were sent to protect in the center of our own tactical area of responsibility.

To make things even more skittish for us, because of truck transportation issues, we now have to refuel in Danang after each flight just a few hundred yards from where all this chaos is taking place. We mask all our frustration with constant humor almost as though we welcome the next flaming hoop we're asked to leap through. Even the most serious career military tight-ass would have to crack a little smile at some of the absurdity. The war is something that we all have in common.

We know we are all going to need each other to survive it.

Today, I was part of a two plane detachment to Chu Lai to deliver some generals for a briefing on Operation Orange. We had to wait down there for several hours, so I went over to see some of my buddies from VMO-1 in New River, who had just arrived in country. I felt like a crusty old veteran. They all had a million questions, but I mostly steered the conversation toward what they did on their respective 30 day leave times and kept things light-hearted. We have some really great guys in both these VMO squadrons - no sense scaring the holy crap out of them on their first day in country. They would find out soon enough. They were eager for advice. All I could think to tell them was to fly as often as they could.

Tomorrow, I am scheduled to go north again to Hue Phu Bai for a couple of days.

Lt. Col. Barden takes rein over the 'perfect' squadron

DA NANG — LtCol. George Bauman, commanding officer of Marine Observation Squadron (VMO)-2, relinquished command to his successor, LtCol. Arnold W. Barden at a change of command ceremony held at the Marble Mountain Air Facility.

As the new squadron commander of VMO-2 addressed his officers and men, he said, "I know this is a perfect squadron. I don't know, how I can improve upon it."

LtCol. Bauman brought the squadron to Vietnam April 29, 1965. In the beginning, the squadron was quartered in the southwest corner of the Da Nang airstrip, in three big general purpose tents. From here the squadron began its first operations in assisting the Vietnamese people in their struggle for peace.

LtCol. Bauman can look back on his squadron's first year in combat with great pride. He, his men and their aircraft, had flown well over 10,000 hours in combat for a total of 10,000 combat sorties. On 600 medical evacuations (med evacs), their UH1E's evacuated 1,300 wounded and sick. Officers and men from the squadrons have been recommended for many awards including 1 Navy Cross, 1 Legion of Merit, 3 Silver Stars, 16 Distinguished Flying Crosses, 12 Bronze Stars, 7 Navy and Marine Corps Medals, 16 Navy Commendation Medals, 31 Purple Hearts and over 1,000 Air ⁴als.

only be known by the officers and men who lived it. It is one of which they can be proud.

LtCol. George Bauman knows the story well. He helped write it.

[Source: Copied directly from the May 17, 1966 issue of the Sea Tiger newspaper, published each Tuesday by the III Marine Amphibious Force.]

SQUADRON PERSONNEL

The officers in the VMO-2 squadron in April 66 were Lt. Col. Arnold W. Barden (CO), Major Cliff Reese (S-3), Major Bob (R.E.) Brown (Maintenance Officer), Major Bob Plamondon, Shep Spink, Charlie (Black Cloud) Plunkett, Jack Enockson, Jim (Puff) Sweeney, Doug (Windy) Page, Doug (Profile) Devine, Tim (Mr. Poop) Ashbaugh, Bob (Beetle) Bailey, Orlando (Lanny) Ingvoldstad III, Norm (N.E.) Ehlert, Steve Waltrip, Dick Lewer, Bill Kirby, Ben (Secondary Benny) Meharg, Kurt (Smoke) Mason, Perry James, (Big Al) Barbour, Bud (Beasley) Willis, Harold (Gus) Plum, Terry Hines, Jose A. Melendez, Warrant Officer Robert (Wimpy) Norton, and flight surgeon Doctor Fletcher Zimpher.

Some of the others that joined later were Jim Lattimer, Maj. V. Wayne Hazelbaker, Buck Buchanan, Ron Corley, Tony Costa, Lew Larsen, Gerry Smith, Dave Baccitich, Joe Healy, Chris Bradley, Dick (Pianoman) Drury, (Little Al) Mumford, Kerry Massari, Jack Nolan, Ron Osborne, Jerry Ringenberg, Bob Keefe, Jack Owens and flight surgeon Curtis Baker.

Our squadron skipper, Lieutenant Colonel Arnold Barden, was nicknamed *The Governor* by Bill Kirby, although nobody dared call him that to his face. He had a habit of wearing a blue western bandana around his neck. It took one letter to Shep Spink's wife, Isobel, to initiate a shipment of enough bandanas for each member of the squadron. Al Mumford provided the first resupply at a later date. We took quite a bit of heat from the other squadron pilots for differentiating our uniform on the flight line and at the officers club. After all, the word *uniform* means just that. As time went on, they didn't seem to mind so much after we covered their butts a few times with those "kamikaze" gun runs.

Contributed by Al Barbour

Some of the men on the flight line: crew chiefs, corpsmen, and gunners.

Walters, "Wallygater," crew chief; SGT O'Dell, Jerry "Digger" ; SGT Hankins, Don "Hank", crew chief; S/SGT Lazeration, John, line chief; G/SGT Gantz, Bill, night shift gunner; NCOIC Buckholdt, L., crew chief; PFC Mell, Frank, crew chief; G/SGT Fraker, A., gunner; S/SGT Pfeiffer, Frank, gunner; S/SGT Revier, C., crew chief; S/SGT Abshire, Bob, crew chief; CPL Brewczynski (deceased, Navy Cross), crew chief; S/SGT Alger, D. "Duffy," crew chief; SGT Long, Dale, crew chief; SGT Doc Mayton, corpsman (deceased, Navy Cross); Doyle, T. J., crew chief; SGT Scruggs, Tracy.

Scruggs, Tracy, Sgt.

Contributed by Don Hankins

9 April 1966 2105

Last night, on the 8ᵗʰ of April, Danang was evacuated. When I returned from Phu Bai, I barely recognized Marble Mountain. The streets are crowded with civilians and others in strange looking military uniforms. I had to kick some Air Force guy out of my bed who'd slept in it last night. The mess hall was filled, and cots were brought into any available spaces to accommodate all these people. A few women were roaming around the area. The decision to evacuate Americans from Danang had been made at 0200 in the morning. Anyone employed by the Americans, Army, and Air Force personnel, and all American civilians were told to leave Danang. Not because the situation was deteriorating. It just wasn't improving. This was a preemptive move in case the stuff hit the fan.

Communists everywhere are literally partying in the streets. Ordinary citizens called Populist Forces, the Buddhist Monks, anti-American factions, Communist elements, Struggle Forces, student groups, and many of the ARVN are all fanning the flames, some protesting Thi's ouster, and some just taking advantage of a good melee. China has always claimed that America is a paper tiger, and now they are swinging it by the tail. Marines are caught in the middle and being told to stay out of it. It's a "civil problem" we're told. Ky was an air force general before he was president and usually flies his own personal plane. His air force backs him wholeheartedly, but as for his army - not so much. This morning a convoy of ARVN converged on the VN Air Force and were said to be firing on them. Two rockets were fired by an A1 Skyraider to warn the convoy to halt. It did, and no further action followed. Bizarre!

What does all this mean to us? On one extreme it could be a disaster for Ky and the South Vietnamese government; on another extreme, it could bring some closure to our purpose for being here. If the demonstrators are strong enough to force an election that led to Ky's ouster, maybe that would provide a solution. If the situation erupts into a broad civil war, it would certainly be an end of Ky's government, which, according to Thi, is a puppet government. What would Johnson do if that happened? That outcome would be a tough situation for the US, but it could be a good chance for us to "make our bird." (Pilot slang for *"let's get out of here."*)

One of our biggest challenges is that we are not exactly sure who we are fighting, or may be fighting next, so if everybody will pick a side, then we can proceed with real purpose, Marine Corps style. In its present state, it may go on indefinitely. In the meantime, we have to do what we have to do, and tonight I had to wash my clothes. The maids haven't been here for more than a week, and they represent our laundry service. I scooped everything I had together and put it in a big tub with some soap, took it to the shower, and jumped in with both feet. I stomped on it for 10 minutes. Right now, I have everything hanging on the line behind my hooch, and I am sitting here admiring my handiwork along with a dazzling clean pair of feet. At least for tomorrow, I will have clean underwear and a fresh flight suit.

My flight activity has slowed down with all this chaos. I haven't had to arm the machine guns in a few days, and I'm not even on the flight schedule tomorrow. Today, I took a VIP hop to Chu Lai and then went to Phu Bai to help insert a 12 man recon team. In the 15 hours I spent there, I only logged 1.5 hours of flight time.

We received a published order today that we could no longer play poker or gamble in our clubs. It seems that some people were gambling as if there's no tomorrow. *Imagine that!* Some idiot supposedly lost several thousand dollars, and his wife wrote a letter to his commanding officer complaining about it. Too bad, I was winning 40 or 50 bucks a night the few times I sat in on those poker games. One of the reasons I like poker is that it gives me something to do at the club other than drink. I don't care for the taste of hard liquor unless it has something sweet in it, like 7 Up or Coke, and beer has to be ice cold for me to drink a whole one. I usually end up drinking rum and Coke, and they don't skimp on the rum.

VMO-2 pilots were told very little about the details of the political chaos taking place in Danang, but none of us were completely stupid. Whatever progress we had made in taming our tactical area of responsibility was totally undone by Premier Ky. He was the Communist's best recruiting tool. Peking, Moscow, and Hanoi were like sharks smelling blood, and they were literally moving in for the kill.

The relentless US bombing of North Vietnam had only strengthened the resolve of the Ho Chi Minh faithful, and a tidal wave of NVA regulars were pouring across the DMZ. Secret routes through Laos and Cambodia, augmented by a well-planned, concrete-reinforced tunnel that ran for miles, allowed trucks and heavy equipment to travel unnoticed day and night. All our sophisticated satellites could do was snap a few pictures from outer space. VMO-2 heard none of the details about this Ho Chi Minh Trail. We weren't being told much of anything. But we knew that the mortar attack on Saigon was the result of months of planning by someone other than rice farmers. Those mortars had to be hand carried hundreds of miles through tunnels and dense jungles on foot. This kind of effort could only be accomplished by a fanatically dedicated opponent. The soldiers were not hearing this information. All we were hearing was the ringing of the medevac and Sparrow Hawk field phones, the high-pitched whining of the Huey turbine engines, and the "whop-whop-whop" of our rotor blades. One of our pilots came up with a name for the spot we had found ourselves in, and we used it often. We were in a classic *shit sandwich*. The political confusion in Washington and a fledgling, inexperienced South Vietnamese government had been shattered into a dozen different factions. VMO-2 pilots were caught between our compassion for the troops on the ground and the bifurcated world of geo-politics. Ho Chi Minh, reinforced by Russia and China, was taking advantage of every moment, streaming men and war supplies over, under, and around the DMZ.

Westmoreland and the Air Force were turning the Laotian jungles brown with a powerful defoliant called Agent Orange in an attempt to target the supply routes. But most of the supplies were hidden underground. We were still calling these people VC, but they were looking more and more like a well-trained and highly-organized Army, which he continued to underestimate.

[Hundreds of thousands of vets have applied for VA benefits because of health complications resulting from exposure to Agent Orange. Any serviceman who spent as little as one day in that country from 1962 to 1974 may be eligible for compensation. Diabetes has emerged as the most common ailment linked to the sinister defoliant, but the list of illnesses is still growing, and includes several kinds of cancer, hepatitis, heart disease, and others. More recently, hearing loss and erectile dysfunction are two new issues that have been added to the long list of Orange ailments. As I approach my 70th birthday in 2011, it would be difficult to find a peer who doesn't suffer from at least one of those common problems. The melanoma that I was treated for 25 years ago I assumed was caused by overexposure to the sun. The four stents in my heart, I attributed to my not being able to pass up a charbroiled steak, and every Huey pilot still alive today is deaf because he refused to wear the ear plugs that he was assigned and were "mandatory" on every flight. While I begrudge no man for collecting what he is entitled, especially some of the ground troops that actually had the stuff sprayed directly on them, as a pilot, I could never in good conscience claim that I was a victim of Agent Orange.]

10 April 1966 Easter Sunday 2130 hours

For the past few days, we have been supporting Operation Orange about 25 miles Southwest of Danang along the Vu Gia River in the Quang Nam Province, near Thuong Guc. This is a search and destroy mission which doesn't require much explanation, but we have been doing more searching than destroying. Resistance has been light, and the operation is in its second week. During much of that time, I was up north helping Special Forces recon teams try to find out what all the NVA regulars are doing concentrated in the DMZ.

We insert small teams of five or more people, sometimes with a trained dog with a sense of smell 2000 times greater than a man's. The recon team tries to maneuver close enough to capture a lone sentry or a straggler and then drag him off to a "safe" location where we can fly back out there and haul them out with their prized intelligence package. If anything goes wrong with this risky snatch-and-grab plan, the ensuing scramble can become very complicated.

At 0130 this morning, I was awaked by someone shaking my bed and the words *"mount up."* The 12 man team that we had inserted two days ago south of the DMZ near Phu Bai was in deep doo doo. We were headed back up there to rescue them. I knew we would not attempt this until daylight, but when you're in the military, you don't question why they want you up there four hours early. Sure enough, as soon as we arrived, the special ops guys told us we would launch at first light or 0615. We had to find a place to grab three hours sleep. The mosquitoes and a nearby artillery unit that cranked off a round every 15 minutes kept me from doing more than closing my eyes. I was glad to hear the duty officer call for us and had visions of finishing this off quickly and flying back home for some shuteye. As soon as dawn broke, a huge fog bank rolled over the mountain and completely obscured the landing zone. After we were airborne, we had to abort this first attempt. So much for our Easter sunrise service!

Our second attempt, around 0900, met with the same result. By 1100 the fog burned off, and we made a routine, uneventful pickup after saturating the free-fire area around the zone with machine gun fire. When we had the boys in the plane, they pinpointed the area where the enemy was hiding. We did our cowboy thing and came back to Phu Bai for refueling.

The isolation of Danang has changed some things for us at Marble Mountain. The jet fuel that we have trucked over from Danang has been exhausted. Now, we must refuel in Danang after every hop. Jet fuel may sound like a high grade of gasoline but it's really a low grade of kerosene.

Some of our other supplies are running low. We haven't had any fresh food for a few weeks. The canned stuff is tolerable if you aren't too picky. I grew up on that stuff. Canned green beans and mashed potatoes are staples, although we suspect those potatoes are rehydrated. Powdered eggs are barely edible, and our Easter meal consisted of spaghetti with beef hash pored over it. A creative concoction!

Every organization eventually develops its own culture. Our squadron is being influenced by half a dozen or so irreverent lieutenants who have decided to make fun of anything that moves. The veterans have been around long enough to become genuinely cynical, so they haven't been a hell of a lot of fun. As they rotate home, the squadron is receiving a whole new face lift. This new group holds much promise for me, and their sarcastic style suits me. The first thing they do is label everybody with a nickname. Some of the senior officers don't even know their nicknames, for obvious reasons. We have Leghorn Red, Black Cloud, Vacuum Cleaner, Boom-Boom, Junior Hog, Goldfinger, Windy, Liver Lips, Howdy Doody, The Disciple, Disciple in Training, Profile, Dickie Deadlock, Dobie Gillis, Smiling Bob, Piano Mouth, Johnny Rifle, Pianoman, Poop, Puff, and on and on. As soon as anyone finds out my real name, they can never move past it, so I will have to be Beasley until they can come up with something more derogatory.

22 April 1966 Friday Phu Bai

I escorted a five-hour Marine truck convoy to Phu Bai. It's slow-going by vehicle on Highway One. Land mines and ambushes are popular surprises, and even the Marine vehicles themselves are unpredictable. It isn't uncommon to see a broke-down six-by having to be towed. The next day we left for a Special Forces outpost called Khe Sahn just south of the DMZ and five miles from the border of Laos. There was a two battalion operation in progress searching for "infiltrators" along a well-traveled NVA infiltration route. During the 30 hours that I spent there, we flew some low level visual recon, but saw nothing but wild, beautiful, breathtaking mountains and tropical jungle. The waterfalls were spectacular. We even saw elephants roaming around. One of them was white. That night while we slept under the stars we heard a tiger.

Some US Air Force planes were spraying an area with a defoliant that I assumed would kill the foliage and make it easier to spot some of the activity on the well camouflaged roads down there. We could see that some areas had already turned burnt umber from previous drenching. I know now why they aren't serving the local rice in the mess hall.

Despite eating canned rations and sleeping out in the boonies with real Marines, I managed to have a great day. Something, however, didn't agree with me because the next morning I had a terrible case of gastro enteritis complemented by a condition known as the green-apple-quickstep. I didn't shake that off until I returned to Marble Mountain, and Doc Zimpher had to earn his salary. He gave me four different colored pills which I think he gives to everybody for everything. I felt better in a matter of hours. Doc grounded me for the rest of that day (his favorite thing to do). I went out on the beach and ran into a bunch of other goof-offs, and we walked three and a half miles up the beach to a place called China Beach, a public beach serving Danang that someone said had hotdogs and lemonade. The MP's turned us back because Danang is still off limits. So we walked the three and a half miles back. I think if I could do all that, I didn't need to be grounded.

Toward the end of this month (28th?), I am scheduled to go to the Philippines for jungle survival training. We will spend three days in a tropical jungle like the one I flew over at Khe Sahn and will supposedly learn how to stay alive in case our plane is ever forced down over the jungle. It occurred to me that this would have been handy information to have a little earlier in my deployment.

A good example of the need for that training would be the day that my fellow wordsmith, Captain Perry James, came over to me at Phu Bai and asked if I wanted to fly co-pilot with him on a secret mission that had just been given to him. Perry is the only pilot I ever knew who went to test pilot school at Pax River. He's not the kind of person you could easily refuse. On the way to the plane, he said they had given us a firing mission but would not disclose the target coordinates until we were airborne. This whole thing had an uncomfortable feel to it. When we finally arrived at the target, a small village in the middle of nowhere, I knew it was someplace we were not supposed to be. I may not be a Pax River test pilot, but I can read a map.

I had never flown with Perry and didn't know his style. He never let me touch the stick. We passed over the target at about 1200 feet and circled back. He entered into his gun run without saying a word. When he banked hard to the left to pull off his run, the chopper rolled into a dangerous 60 degree bank. The plane went into a violent shutter. I instinctively gabbed on to anything that was available. Then, it just kept rolling over. I saw the horizon turn upside down, and I knew we were dead. There is no way a helicopter can recover from an inverted position, and we were hanging in our shoulder harnesses at low altitude. I literally saw old, dead relatives. I wanted to go down fighting, so I grabbed the stick, and it felt as if I was holding onto a horse's hind leg while it was having a seizure. Suddenly, the plane righted itself. I assure you it was nothing we did. The Huey had flown itself through that entire maneuver.

My heart was thumping in my earphones as we climbed up to a safe altitude and aborted the mission. The rest of my body felt as if it were made of pure oxygen. When the blood returned to our brains, Perry and the crew chief said the hydraulic servo on the rotor head *"went out."* This clever device helps stabilize and dampen the horrendous force on the highly stressed rotor head during steep turns. Once we were in friendly environs, Perry "tested" the plane in shallow 15 degree turns on the way home. He gave me a complicated explanation of hydraulic servos -- the kind of information I like to store in other people's heads. I don't remember a word he said. I asked him how the plane recovered from an inverted position at that altitude. He said he had no idea. We lived to fight another day and so did that little North Vietnamese village.

My third month begins with a fresh new start in my new quarters. I have been promised a used short-wave radio. Perry James couldn't bring himself to *give* it to me, but it was cheap. It was an apology, of sorts, for encouraging Justin, the deranged squadron monkey, to sit on my face while I was taking a nap in the ready room. He was surprised by what he called my "vindictive" reaction to his prank. We also formed somewhat of a bond after he flipped our gunship over, and we were both resurrected from the dead.

My new quarters will receive exciting newly acquired amenities; a new pillow, a new bed from departing Doc Zimpher, reading lamp, bookcase, and my excellent short wave radio. I have decided that minimalism is for monks. Military truck traffic has reopened into town, and all the evacuees went back to Danang. Maybe the fresh food will come back in soon. Marines are running big sweeps of our TAOR hoping to return to normal after Mr. Ky stirred the pot. Things are gradually returning to the same old same old.

I received a bad break on the 8th of this month when someone finally figured out that I had been to embarkation school. All pilots are assigned at least one secondary squadron duty in addition to flying. I held this collateral duty at New River, and I've been dreading this assignment. The embarkation officer is responsible for "mount-out readiness." He is supposed to know the location of, and be responsible for, every piece of equipment in the unit. He has to maintain a complete manifest in case of rapid deployment (which seems odd since we are already deployed) with a complete set of ship loading plans. In addition, he has to supervise both the loading and the landing. I was also assigned some other smaller jobs like Camp Maintenance Officer, Ground Safety Officer, and Awards Board Member. We have non-commissioned officers and enlisted men to help with all this. It isn't as ominous as it sounds -- just a big pain in the butt. However, sooner or later the CO is going to want to see my embarkation manifest.

Along with the bad news, there was a list of places that are available for R&R, namely, Bankok, Hong Kong, Japan, and Okinawa. Hawaii isn't on the list yet, but is being considered. Being in the states, it would not be out of the question for girlfriends, wives, and family members to meet in Hawaii, and the pilot's are salivating over Honolulu being added to the list. There are only a few slots for each destination, and the waiting list is long for the most desirable ones.

I went to the admin office to check on the embarkation files. They didn't have any embarkation manifest or files. I will have to start from scratch.

SURVIVAL TRAINING IN THE PHILIPPINES

24 April, 1966 Sunday night Medevac Standby

Tomorrow at 1400, I will be reporting to Danang Air Freight to be manifested for a three-hour flight to the Philippine Islands for Escape and Evasion School at Cubi Point. They advised me yesterday that the original date they had given me, the 28th, was incorrect, so I will be packing my bags as soon as I am relieved from medevac duty at 0700 in the morning. There isn't much to pack to spend a couple of days in the jungle. Basically, we will wear jungle utilities, simulating minimalism.

Not every day will be spent in the boonies, so I plan to take full advantage of the luxuries of civilization. The first thing I intend to do when I check into my quarters at Cubi Point is take a 45 minute (hot) shower. Then, I'm going to buy one of those tacky tropical shirts with hula dancers on it and find a place for lunch that serves a good salad, a club sandwich, and a glass of cold fresh milk. That may not sound like a luxury, but I haven't had any of those things for a while. We have no fresh milk, no salads and the only sandwiches are cold, dry

Spam. After the first couple of weeks, our food sources started drying up. Our mess hall has been a pretty humble place ever since.

I was standing in for the medevac pilot yesterday in order for him to grab some lunch when we received a call that sharks were terrorizing the swimmers on China Beach. They wanted me to take a chopper out there and shoot them. *Really?* Four sharks were spotted about three miles up the beach, so we launched the gunship to go have a look. I was thinking they meant for us go out there and scare them off because there were a couple hundred locals hanging out enjoying the beach. When we burst on their scene, buzzing around and doing our shark-stalker imitation, we saw all kinds of sea life but nothing that looked like a shark. Finally, we saw a giant thing about 300 yards off the beach that was big enough to be a baby whale. The crew chief said it was not only a shark but a *"whale shark,"* the largest one in the shark family. I had never heard of a whale shark and wasn't about to unleash six machine guns on a baby whale -- or any fish for that matter. I flew in a tight spiral around the big monster that looked to be 50 feet long in that clear, turquoise water.

Our guns were mounted in the front, and I would have to make a straight run at a shallow angle. People were standing on the beach in complete oblivion of what we were sent out there to do. If we shot those guns anywhere near that "whale shark," the bullets could bounce off that water and go anywhere. I finally settled on letting the door gunner shoot a few rounds far out to sea and well in front of it to see if it would leave. We couldn't tell if it was three feet under water or 25 feet. Anyway, nobody wanted to murder that fish or whatever it was just because it was being a fish. It has as much right to be there as anyone, if not more. So we fooled around out there for about 15 minutes looking for sting rays and came home. I filled out a report as we have to do with every mission.

I wrote: *"Flew shark patrol to China Beach. Saw VC shark. Shot said same shark."* Because there were gunshots, it counted as a strike, and we all received two points toward a 20 point air medal. Is this a great country, or what?

All of that nonsense happened yesterday. Today, I flew real medevac, and from 0700 until 1100 we logged 11 missions. I don't know if anyone has ever earned a full air medal in a single day under the flight/strike system, but if we keep this up, my copilot and crew are on track. There is such a thing as a single mission air medal, but most of them require 20 flights.

The next entry into this journal will be made after I've had a hot shower and a club sandwich in the Philippines.

29 April, 1966 1200   Luzon Island in the Philippines

I boarded a C-130 at 1600 yesterday afternoon. Three hours later we were 900 miles east of Danang. Our wheels touched down at Cubi Point on the island of

Luzon in the Philippines. At the moment, I'm sipping a Singapore Sling at the officer's club swimming pool. A group of fighter pilots are rounding up their buddies and throwing them into the pool. So far they've shown no interest in me. In a matter of hours, I have gone from the ridiculous to the sublime.

My 16 ounce strip steak dinner last night was not a US prime cut, but by Marble Mountain standards, it may as well have been Kobe beef. I can't remember when I was more excited to see a piece of burnt dead cow. After dinner and a few American songs in broken English from the female entertainer and her six piece band, I was so sleepy I could hardly move my arms and legs. *Medevac*! Twenty four hours of flying the day before we left, plus the waiting and the anticipation of the trip, deprived me of any sleep. When the adrenalin wore off, I was toast.

I looked for a tropical shirt, but discovered something far more interesting about Filipino customs. They wear white flimsy cotton or linen shirts for formal evening wear instead of jackets and ties. The shirts can be plain and simple or beautifully embroidered in the front. These *barongs* can be slipped over the head or buttoned down the front. This attire is pocketless and worn untucked, like a dress, as *baro* means *dress*. The custom carries a legend that goes back to the Spanish occupation of the Philippines, alleging that the flimsy, transparent shirts were required by the Spaniards to prevent the locals from concealing weapons. The unassuming Filipinos had worn similar garb for centuries. They just decided to adopt the concept for formal evening wear. The officer's club had a number of these "barong

Tagalog" loaners on hand for neophytes like me, who were unaware of any of these wonderful customs.

Tomorrow morning, we begin our jungle survival training. After that, I plan to stretch this boondoggle out for as long as I can. In the afternoon, we toured Cubi Point and Subic Bay. The O Club sits on a high hill overlooking the runway and the bay. One side of the dining room is all glass that faces the water, creating a beautiful panorama. Watching the jets land down below on that runway with the blue water in the background and the baseboard air conditioning vent blowing cold air up the right leg of my trousers, I could hardly keep my eyes on my lunch. A Bacardi cocktail, a chef's salad, a shrimp cocktail, a BLT sandwich, two glasses of iced tea, and a scoop of chocolate ice cream might hold me 'til dinner

Major Clifford Reese, aka Goldfinger, from Greensboro, N.C., is also here. He came over to pick up a Huey for VMO-2 that has been through an extensive overhaul. Many of our planes have to *"go back to the factory"* occasionally because they can be banged up pretty badly. When his Huey arrives, he will test it, fly it aboard a helicopter ship (probably the USS Princeton), and sail for Vietnam. He told me last night that the Princeton may not arrive here until the 5th of May, and may not be able to depart for Danang until the 15th of May. If that happened he said he would test the bird and then take a flight back to Danang right away, leaving me to take the Huey back home.

Let me absorb this. My hand is shaking over the possibility of spending two or three weeks over here eating steak and drinking Mai Tais. This can't be happening to me. I'm in the Marine Corps, and the first thing we learn in the Corps is to never believe the first thing you hear. This would be my first documented miracle if it actually happened.

Goldfinger is one of the funniest guys in our squadron. He has red hair, a ruddy complexion, and a stocky build like the character in the Bond movie. He's two ranks ahead of me, but doesn't flaunt it like some. Whenever I see him, I'm reminded of two incidents that I personally witnessed. I was his co-pilot on a medevac flight one day when we made a clean pickup and were leaving the zone. He thought he saw muzzle flashes as we cleared the tree tops, and he may have, but it isn't uncommon in the heat of a mission for people to be overly stimulated. He was shot in the leg once and is a little skittish. Anyway, he keyed his transmitter and bellowed, *"We're taking fire from the east."* The ground troops responded right away and told us, *"Those are friendly positions to the east"* -- meaning, our own men! Goldfinger looked over at me and gave a little shrug of his shoulders. By now we were pretty clear of the zone and well on our way. He keyed the mic again and said, *"Okay, then, we're taking friendly fire from the east."*

He is fun to be around, but scary as hell to ride with.

The other incident happened early one morning in that horrible little six-holer officer's latrine. We had a full house, and Goldfinger was perched in the middle seat directly across from me. The supply of paper had run dangerously low and a line was forming outside. The major hollered for somebody in the line to find the man in charge of the latrine to fetch some paper over there quick. After a couple of minutes of nervous waiting, an old Vietnamese man opened the plywood door and stuck the handle of a long broom between the six "business men." There were 10 rolls of paper stacked on the broom like a kabob. The old man's face was disturbingly grotesque, and when he broke out his black betel nut smile, the shock of it took away what little breath we had left. We all wanted to make a comment, but no words would come. When the door finally closed, Goldfinger broke the silence with a perfectly timed one-liner, *"Well, I guess you don't have to be too good looking to work in a shithouse."*

30 April 1966 1115 Saturday

If I want time to pass more pleasantly it seems to work for me to have a special event to look forward to. Right now, that is not possible. I don't want any of this to go away. I've been soaking both R's out of R&R since I've been here.

Tuesday, after I finished that letter beside the pool, I went with a friend to the officer's club for dinner. It wasn't much different from the night before. We ate well and came home early because we had the survival school early the following morning. The room at the BOQ is not air conditioned, and it's just as hot here as it is at Marble Mountain. We're on the third floor with four people in the room and only one fan. I was sunburned and woke up several times in a heavy sweat. I walked across the room and pointed the fan toward my bed. Each time I woke up, the fan was pointing toward someone else's bed. I was relieved when I woke up at 0600 for the final time. But it wasn't early enough. By the time we dressed and made it down to the officer's mess for breakfast, it was time to board the bus. The day one leaves for jungle survival school is not a good day to miss breakfast. I managed to down a couple of glasses of cold milk and grab a sweet roll before the bus left for the classroom.

We had three hours of jungle indoctrination and a few demonstrations of craftsmanship and cunning from the Negrito guides. The Negritos are descendents from the "original" Philippine aborigines, and most of those tribes are still wild and primitive. None of them were more than five feet tall. The 10 guides were quite civilized and spoke fair English. Each guide took five or six people in his group. They were going to show us how to live exclusively from what the jungle provides. Our group walked about two miles into the boonies to set up a survival camp. Along the way we found a mango tree and a lush wild grape vine, similar to scuppernongs. The ever resourceful guide set out snares along pathways frequented by small animals. We had nothing but the clothes we wore and a bolo knife (machete) that the guides had crafted out of scrap steel automobile springs. They sold us these "required" knives for four dollars each -- an entrepreneurial, sideline profit center. Each guide carried a small bag of rice, a little salt, and a pair of goggles. We were told they received rice as payment for their services.

We rested from the trek to the campsite and then gathered a supply of green and dry bamboo sections with our sharp new bolo blades. Here, we learned the priceless value of bamboo in the wilderness. You can eat the green shoots, drink the water stored in the green sections, start a fire with the splinters from the dry bamboo, make a cup, a plate, a spoon, weapons, a bed, a shelter, furniture, and generally set up light housekeeping. We did *all* that.

We each made a fire without matches in about 10 minutes from our guide's instructions. We had been divided into smaller groups, so we all had plenty to do. We cut a thick section of green bamboo about 15 inches long that served as a pot because it was hollow inside. We cut a plug in the side which could be replaced like a watermelon plug. The hollow section was then half filled with fresh water from a pristine stream. He added the rice and some salt, locked the plug back in, and threw it in the roaring fire. The 20 year old Negrito then put on his goggles and slipped into the chilly, six foot deep pool of water in the stream. He had a little cloth pouch and a short stick. He emerged a full five minutes later with two small fish, about 15 snails, and a couple of crawfish in his pouch. He cooked it all in another bamboo "pod pot" seasoned with sections of a hard, green mango. Ingenious! We each made a drinking cup out of dry bamboo, prepared our beds for the night, and waited for lunch.

The crawfish tasted like shrimp, and the snails tasted like rotten oysters. We each took five or six small pinches of these unseasoned jungle delicacies. The gourmet presentation of the afternoon was his rice dish. The guide instructed one of the officers to pull the blackened rice pod out of the fire and chop it open with his machete. The white rice, now swollen to several times its size inside the pod, burst out of its bamboo prison like it was giving birth to quintuplets. *Voila! The piece de resistance!* We were all amazed and couldn't help but reward our guide with a cheer and a standing ovation. We ate the rice with our hands. Plain rice is similar to lumpy wallpaper paste, and we weren't that hungry yet. Most of it stayed in the pod. The water from the stream was cold and delicious, and we each drank a couple of gallons of it.

After lunch we took a nature hike, and the guide showed us several edible plants. Another round of applause came when he selected a vine from a tall tree and severed it with his machete. Water began dripping from the vine, slowly at first, then a pencil sized steady stream followed by a two-inch diameter deluge. This was more water than we showered with at Marble Mountain. He asked us all to drink from it, and it was still leaking fresh water when we left the area. Another memorable plant produced a milky, sticky medicinal goo that would stop bleeding, disinfect, and seal a wound with a plastic-like coating. Can't remember the name of it! We all needed some of that because we had small cuts on our hands from misusing our bolo knives. After the sweaty tour, we came back and went for a dip in the frigid stream. Some of the guys borrowed the goggles to see if they could find some more crawfish in the swimming hole. All they found were some more of those "delicious" rotten oysters.

I passed on supper because I wasn't hungry enough for leftover paste, fish heads, and snails. Our guide finished those off. We didn't have any tigers, lions, or elephants visit the camp that night. Nobody had much sleep on those hard bamboo beds covered with palm and banana leaves. The Negrito didn't seem to have any trouble sleeping on the ground, however. Someone told us that those guides have a keen sense of smell and can track a snake by its smell. The rest of us mostly stayed awake discussing snakes. We also discussed why this survival information wouldn't have been more appropriate *before* we started flying in Vietnam.

At 0700 the next morning, we walked out of the jungle. Along the way, the guide captured a wild bird the size of a small chicken that was caught in one of his snares. He stuffed it into his pouch and took it home to mama. The rest of us boarded the bus back to the BOQ. We only spent one night in the jungle.

After a shower, a shave, and a good breakfast, Bob Howerton and I shopped in the exchange for about an hour. We decided to go sightseeing in Manila. Being total greenhorns, we first tried to see if we could hitch a ride on a military plane going that way. We tried to rent a vehicle from Special Services, but we were a day late and a dollar short. They had all been taken. Too bad, the rental was seven bucks for 24 hours. That left us with the bus station at Olongapo, a one-horse town one mile east of the base. We missed the air conditioned bus by just minutes and had to choose between a miserable two and a half hour ride in a broken down bus with the local peasants for an air conditioned room in Manila or go back to the one-fan BOQ sauna. We decided to take our chances with the peasants for the 127 kilometer adventure and the air conditioned hotel in Manila.

We took a cab to the main gate and walked the mile

into Olongapo carrying only our shaving kits and cameras. The cab was halted by a bike-a-thon (a 140 km bicycle race) in the streets. The sidewalks were full of people watching the riders. We had no place to walk except in the middle of the road. Between the bikers and the begging kids, we had plenty to dodge, but it was all worth it when we got into town where the prostitutes hang out. One of the girls serenaded Howerton with an original seductive song. *"You are the King walking through the Kingdom."* Riotous! He had to put up with my singing that song to him for the rest of the day.

At the station there was a 20 minute wait for the next bus. When the red painted "school-bus" finally showed up, the first person off the bus was a young girl about eight years old. She walked about four steps and vomited right in the middle of the terminal. A sick little girl isn't funny, but we knew this had set the tone for our bus ride. Had the incident happened on the bus, we wouldn't have bothered to board the *Victory Liner.*

There were several stops to disembark and to take on new passengers. We tried to upgrade our seats with each stop but couldn't make it all the way to the front. One lady had a wooden crate with two chickens in it. A little girl in front of me, about two or three years old, was standing backwards in her seat and smiling intently at me. The seats were open in the back, and just when I thought I was making a new friend, I felt something warm on my trouser leg. She was having a happy little pee all over her seat, and it was collecting in the cuff of my trousers.

There was a herd of teenage boys in Manila hustling tips for hailing cabs. We could see the cabs lined up on the street, but we rewarded one of them anyway. We needed a 45 minute cab ride to the Mabuhay Hotel. The cabby talked us into an afternoon tour of the city with him the next day. There is something about the enthusiasm of a good salesman that makes me want to reward the effort.

After I rinsed the right leg of my only trousers and showered that little girl out of my life, we took a cab to the American Embassy and stumbled onto a champagne dinner. Back at the hotel we watched part of a Mickey Rooney movie on TV called *Drive a Crooked Road*. We put the air conditioner on full blast and slept like babies while my peed-on trousers paid a visit to the hotel valet.

At 0900 the next morning, Jake, the cab driver, was in the lobby eager for our 30 peso agreement (3.58 pesos to one US dollar), less than 10 bucks for a 3 ½ hour tour of Manila. He was good. He took us to the Chinese cemetery, the Manila-American Monument, the Jose Rigal National Monument, and a tour of the wealthy section of town. Jake poked fun at Philippine President Ferdinand Marcos when we stopped by the presidential mansion and described him as a genius lawyer who had weaseled himself out of a murder charge and a rape charge on his way to the presidency. Jake asked us how we got to Manila from Olongapo and warned us to be careful because some of those Negrito tribes in the mountains come down into the villages near the road to fulfill wedding customs. Some Negrito fathers require the groom-to-be to collect two heads to show their manhood before they will allow the marriage to their daughter. They dance around the heads at the wedding. We believed all this, of course, because now Jake was like a trusted friend and family member.

We took the nicer, express bus back to Olongapo at 1600. A quick dip in the pool, happy hour, a nice dinner and American floor show was about all we had left in us. There was a gal on stage who weighed about 175 pounds. She reminded me that I had never seen an overweight Vietnamese. She sang a dozen songs that sounded exactly like Barbara Streisand. Amazing! Then we went back to our sleeping quarters and played the fan game all night.

This morning I slept until 0900, and then looked for Goldfinger to see if my miracle had materialized. No news yet. Oh, well! Howerton has to fly back to the war tomorrow, while I stay to wait for news of Goldfinger's airplane. I plan to go into Olongapo to a cockfight to see what that's all about.

Author's note:

The Ford and Rockefeller Foundations had established a well-funded institute in the Philippines in 1962 to address the problem of world hunger. The project was named The International Rice Research Institute, or IRRI, based on the premise that rampant population growth was exceeding our capacity to feed it. Rice was clearly identified as the most vital food crop, providing 80% of the total calories consumed by nearly three billion Asians, the fastest growing population in the world, comprising nearly half the people on the planet. Luzon is the geographic center of Asia and the site of the International Rice Research Institute. A new rice hybrid seed had been developed by 1966. This *miracle rice* helped launch what is now known as the Green Revolution.

IR8 was more resistant to bugs and disease and could produce more than twice the yields of ordinary rice. In 1967, the new seed was smuggled into the Mekong Delta by a Filipino agronomist named Jose Ano. Later, these hybrids became known to the Vietnamese famers as *Honda Rice* because one good crop could produce enough excess profit to purchase a motorbike. Luzon Negrito survival guides were paid by our government with a stipend of rice.

In 1966, LBJ, a Texan who understood farming, accompanied by his Philippine counterpart Ferdinand Marcos, visited the IRRI experimental fields to see the new miracle rice hybrid, IR8. Later that day, he paid a visit to Cam Ranh Bay, Vietnam, *"to visit the troops."* He still had his cowboy boots on when he arrived at Cam Rahn Bay. It's interesting that LBJ visited the rice *first,* then the troops.

Source: *Of Rice and Men*, Richard Galli

2 May 1966 1100 Sunday

It's been a pleasant week, but it looks as if my gravy train is coming to an end. Goldfinger is not forthcoming with information about taking that plane back for him, which leads me to believe that I have two chances of that happening -- slim and none. With the delay of the Princeton, they have decided to use the USS Kitty Hawk to take the Huey back to Danang. The Kitty arrived a few days ago. I have been admiring it from the O Club window. It is supposed to leave on the 6th and would take a day or so to "sail" to Danang. I guess

Goldfinger has decided that he will take that ride. I'm manifested on a C130 to fly back tomorrow. Too bad! My younger brother joined the Navy out of high school and was stationed on this carrier for 18 months as an electronic technician. It would be nice to tell him that I spent a couple of days on his ship.

Yesterday after lunch, I took a cab into Olongapo to watch a spectacle called a cockfight. I'd heard stories about these illegal activities taking place in the hills of Tennessee, but I had never seen one. These things aren't allowed in the civilized world, but then, neither is moon shining. There are two cockfight arenas in town, and this national pastime is a major part of their weekend entertainment, if not their economy. Even though I went alone, there were plenty of other Americans milling around."Pregame" rituals were taking place outside the arena so I took a peek into the theater. The crude arena seated about 300 people in a tiered semi-circle about 12 rows deep. Just enough engineering had gone into this crude structure to prevent bad weather from canceling the fights. All of that was wasted on this sunny day. The fighting pit was a 15 foot diameter dirt pad with a two foot high wall around it to give some separation from the enthusiastic spectators. This was clearly a money thing, and I could tell that it represented a significant source of income for many of the locals.

Outside, there were 40 or 50 men with their colorful prized fighting cocks tucked under their arms engaging in curious negotiations prior to "tipoff." They squatted in circles displaying and discussing their birds with each other. Local hustlers who purported to have inside knowledge of the favorites were soliciting the Americans to be their betting brokers for a cut of the winnings. There were several crap tables, and other gambling venues where moneys were being exchanged by the Filipino regulars. The atmosphere was charged with anticipation and somewhat intimidating. The few, and only, females there were selling items such as bananas or fresh mangoes. None of these able-bodied Filipinos showed the slightest concern that their lifestyle was under the ominous threat of Communism or that I had been sent there to protect them from it.

One of the male venders was peddling coconut milk, presumably to mix with alcohol. He had a huge stack of green coconuts which he decapitated one by one with a bolo knife. Every time I heard the "WHUMP" of that machete, I thought of Jake's story of those Negrito boys gathering heads for their wedding night. One of the gambling hustlers glued himself to me so tenaciously that he scolded anyone who came near me. He wasn't even five feet tall. The idea was to give him a stipend that he could manage during the cockfights. Until it was all gone, I thought. There was no admission charge, and I had come to be entertained, so I rewarded yet another persistent salesman. He was also an excellent body guard because once I partnered with him everybody else left me alone. Perhaps this was part of their code of ethics.

When the cockfight started there was pandemonium. Two men were in the center of the ring, each with a fighting rooster. There was a sign above the favored rooster with the word *LLamado* which I assumed meant *favorite*. The sign was on a wire that could slide back and forth depending on the handicapper's interpretation of the mood of each rooster. If one of the birds lost its focus, the sign would be shifted to the other. The crowd would go wild with any movement of that sign. Each of the handlers held his rooster's neck and gave the other rooster a free peck. This further roiled the fighting juices. The ritual of rooster-taunting in the ring and loud fist-shaking in the audience rose to a fevered pitch. I wondered if the red rooster might have been a Communist rooster.

My gambling pimp had taken the 10 pesos I gave him and bet it all with some other con man about 20 feet away and six rows removed. People were screaming and waving like the New York Stock Exchange on Black Friday. At some magical, exact moment the men in the ring took their chickens to their respective corners and attached a four inch long, razor sharp spur to the right leg of each rooster. I was not aware of this part of the program. Then, just to make sure the two cocks were thoroughly annoyed with each other, the men let the chickens peck each other one last time and held them down on a white line facing each other. When the official starter in the white shirt gave a signal, they let go of the birds. The feathers literally flew. It took only five or six lunges until one of the birds was crippled, giving the other one a free shot. The idea was to fight to the death, and if one of the birds lost heart and quit, the other was declared the winner immediately. Its owner then held the losing bird while the victor delivered the "coup de grace." This literally means the *rap of death*, a blow of mercy to a badly wounded creature. This sent a charge of electricity through the winners and a sharp yelp that echoed off the metal roof of the building.

When the two roosters were carried from the ring, an amazing thing happened. All the betters began exchanging money, sometimes allowing two or three middle men to pass it along to the winner, like a bag of peanuts at Wrigley Field. The bets were all settled civilly and within seconds. My pimp was ecstatic. He now had 20 pesos to bet. It was more like six bucks, and he was going to bet it all, of course. I had to wrestle my original 10 pesos back from him, but when I told him he could keep the 10 he had won and all future winnings, he finally understood and relented. I didn't want to win any amount of money from the genocide of a living creature.

After that, we became buddies. He no longer saw me as a mark. He was his own man with his own money. I watched, reluctantly, while he won the next two bets and finally went bust on the fourth. He was suddenly broke and wanted to do it again. But I had had enough of blood sport. These people had both a barbaric nature and a hopelessness about them that didn't allow me to share in their revelry. I had way too much empathy for the roosters and too little for a man who didn't know how to quit when he was ahead. Even though I had seen my grandmother wring a chicken's neck for Sunday dinner, this had an entirely different feel to it. I took some pictures outside, which was more crowded than the inside, and made my retreat back to civilization. I knew that this would be my one and only cockfight. When I returned to the BOQ, there was a note that Goldfinger was looking for me.

8 May 1966 Sunday 2200

It's been nearly a week since I've written, but I have much to report. Major Reese took me to dinner Monday night and explained the procedures for taking the Huey back to Danang. He said he needed to head back to the war. He's a professional Marine, not a citizen soldier like me, and therefore, more sensitive to his evaluation reports. His superiors would not take kindly to his mysterious absence much longer. He was already a week past schedule.

The Kitty Hawk (CV-63), an aircraft super carrier, was leaving Subic Bay in four days, headed for Yankee Station in the Tonkin Gulf to support bombing operations in North Vietnam. He was going to process the plane out of Overhaul and Repair, test it, and I was to fly it aboard the carrier. There, it would be stowed away until we sailed. He was going to take a C-130 back to Danang immediately, leaving me to make the delivery. A crew chief (mechanic) would accompany me.

Alrighty, then! I could handle this. No problem finding the carrier, it was as big as my hometown. So, the first thing I had to do was figure out how to land a brand new million dollar Huey onto a billion dollar ship (or whatever they cost) without wrecking both of them. The ship's crew would store it on the hangar deck until Thursday, and we would take it from there. There was one other small concern which wasn't explained very well. The ship wasn't actually going to Danang. It would pass along a top secret route that could change as the admiral saw fit, but he would calculate the point where I would launch from the Kitty Hawk, somewhere in the middle of the South China Sea. I could be traversing a couple of hundred miles of open sea with only a crew chief. What if the weather was horrible, and I was unable to have a visual reference with the horizon? We had no instrument flight rules at Marble Mountain, and I was not sure what Danang Tower had or how the political situation might have deteriorated since I had been gone. The major left me a full page of contact names, telephone numbers, radio frequencies, and ship board instructions. He wished me luck and flew back to the war.

The following day I called everybody on the list to make sure there was an actual person on the other end. I went over to look at the plane to make sure it was a Huey that I knew how to fly. I met with the crew chief to see if he had ever done anything like this before. He was clueless but also sensed that I, too, was shooting in the dark. When we boarded the Kitty Hawk, and I met some other pilots from other units that were ferrying aircraft back to different places, I felt more comfortable, although none were going to Danang. That Huey was my only way off that ship, and if I missed our jumping-off point, we would end up at Yankee Station in the Tonkin Gulf. This whole experience was beginning to fall under the heading of *"be careful what you wish for."*

My short life aboard the ship was grand, and the food was even grander. The Navy guys were curious about the Huey. Some had never seen one. Not many helicopters had landed on their carrier. They asked me what we used it for. It was clear that they didn't have a clue about what was going on outside that ship anymore than I knew about what went on aboard the Kitty Hawk. The fixed wing drivers were shooting touch and go's (practice landings) on the ship and arrested landings to shake the rust off. I watched all this from a special observation point on the flight deck. Seeing it from that angle put me in awe of the fact that I had done eight of these arrested landings in a T-28C in our Pensacola training. This pumped up my testosterone, and I stopped worrying about crashing that new Huey into Monkey Mountain on the way back to the base.

Before you could earn your wings of gold in 1964, you had to make eight successful arrested landings in a fixed wing aircraft aboard a Navy carrier. Tailhook is the ultimate rite of passage for a naval aviator. The T-28C trainer was modified with a tail hook, and the USS Lexington was stationed conveniently in the Gulf of Mexico to serve that very purpose. We practiced on a concrete runway, painted to resemble a carrier deck.

The key to sticking the ship-board landing was to manage the airspeed and the glide slope perfectly in order for the tail hook to grab one of the four cables. A seven foot concave mirror was mounted on the left side of the ship. The mirror displayed a green ball in its center when the plane was on the correct glide slope. The ball in the mirror would slip out of sight if you were too high or low. This visual reference allowed the pilot to make small adjustments during his descent. It was similar to a spider sliding down an imaginary web. The landing is violent, as you might imagine. The airspeed goes from about 70 knots to zero when that tail hook grabs the wire. Hydraulic slack is built into the arresting system to provide some elasticity to soften the impact.

The day my cadre of T-28's was scheduled to "hit the boat," the five pilots were "pumped" for our big moment. However, one of the five planes in the preceding flight had crashed into the water. The student pilot had forgotten to lower his flaps, one of the 25 points on the pre-landing check list. The flaps were necessary to change the aerodynamics of the wing to provide the additional lift. Without the flaps the airfoil has a higher stall speed. When a plane stalls, it ceases to fly and falls like a stone. Critical mistake! When we arrived at the ship, a search and rescue mission was being conducted to find the plane and the pilot, and our exercise had to be postponed. We were rescheduled to be first off the next morning.

I lay wide awake that entire night memorizing that check list. When I finally climbed into the pattern for the live run, I ran through the checklist in record time. Then, just for good measure, I went through the procedure one more time, unlocking my harness for a quick double check of each item. As I was wrapping up, the tower radioed to ask if I was ready. Whatever I told him was a lie. He had interrupted the last item on my list.

In an ordinary landing, an unlocked shoulder harness would not be a significant issue. But an arrested landing is not ordinary. It was a perfect landing. Suddenly, I saw a flash of yellow light, felt a sharp pain in my right wrist, and heard a loud explosion in my flight helmet. I found myself in a tight little fetal wad, slumped on the floor of the cockpit. My whole body had been thrown out of the seat and into the instrument panel at roughly 70 knots. I was slammed into the flight controls (the stick), and my flight helmet and visor hit the metal hood over the instrument panel. I slithered to the floor like a rag doll, my right hand having slipped off the stick at impact and slammed into the knobs on the panel.

In the three nanoseconds it took for me to leap back into my seat, my entire flight career flashed through my mind. I expected to look up and see a man on each wing summoning me to open the canopy and step out of the plane, especially after what had happened on their ship the day before. As the feeling slowly began returning to my injured right wrist, it occurred to me that I had overlooked the last item on the check list and forgotten to fasten my seat belt.

I learned many things that day, but nothing more interesting than what I am about to tell you. With all the details that have to be considered during those shipboard landings, not one person is assigned to watch what happens in the cockpit. They must assume that the lunatic in there knows what he's doing. Nobody saw a thing that happened to me. In the few moments that it took for them to remove the cable and ready the crew for the incoming airplane behind me, a crewman with earphones was giving me the wind-up signal. I jammed the throttle forward with my good hand and sped across the deck into a 35 knot wind and climbed back into the pattern for my next seven arrested landings.

The Next Day

A hundred nautical miles isn't that far when you're traveling at 120 knots. The trip should take well under an hour. That is, unless you're launching in about one mile of visibility in a dense cloud with rain showers. That was how far we were from land, and those were the conditions when I had used up my chocolate cake and ice cream time on the USS Kitty Hawk. The take off was cocky enough. We were allowed to fly right down the flight deck just like the big boys do. The tower gave us the compass heading to Danang and bid us farewell. My brand new US government issue, unscratched Huey (one each) made a slight left turn and locked onto that heading.

We were about ten minutes into the process when I sensed anxiety on the crew chief's part that his pilot was becoming overly stressed. I wish I could have comforted him, but he was indeed perceptive. The visibility was steadily deteriorating. I had assumed a strained posture in my seat as though by leaning forward and squinting, I could see through the clouds and the steady rain that was pelting the Plexiglas windshield. It seemed as if we had been flying for an hour into a narrowing tunnel. I wasn't eager to have to make the decision to pull the plane up into the clouds and fly instruments into Danang. There was an 1100 foot mountain about four miles North of Danang. I didn't want to leave an environmental pock mark on it.

I won't keep you in suspense. We lived through it.

But that flight was longer than Amelia Earhart's. Most of the time we were less than 100 feet above the water, and I had to constantly scan the altimeter because I don't like water skiing anymore than I like swimming. The clouds finally broke up a little and we caught a glimpse of land. *Tally Ho, indeed.* My unqualified "co-pilot" started breathing again, and his face changed back to its original color. We both managed a nervous laugh. We landed at Marble Mountain at 1900, and it took about an hour to process the new plane in. I wanted to buy the crew chief a drink, but he was not allowed in the officer's club. One of the biggest problems with the military is that the guys who really know what there're doing are enlisted people, and the young, green officers are not supposed to fraternize with them. Most of us college boys would be lost without the rugged common sense and stamina of the Marine enlisted men. Each one of them has been honed for a particular military occupational specialty. In addition, every one of them, regardless of their specialty, is a skilled rifleman.

I had been gone so long I had forgotten how cozy I had made my newly remodeled corner of the hooch. It was good to see my stuff and all my added creature com-forts. Someone told me that Major Gillis had asked them to put my name on the bottom of the R&R list because I had been gone so long. When I checked the list this morning to see if that had happened, I noticed his name was just below mine on the R&R list. He just wanted to move up another notch. Jealous little bastard!

CHAPTER FIVE

MAYDAY

16 May 1966 Monday 2200

Every waking moment that I haven't been flying I have been fooling with that infernal embarkation report. I finally finished it this afternoon but had to compromise on perfection. If a box was marked to have 156 gas masks, my assistant and I would have to count them all and account for any that were missing. There was always something missing. Corporal Dunwoody would lay everything out on the floor and give me the actual count. In almost every situation, the actual count in the crate was less than what was marked on it, say 13 short. I told him there should be 156 not 143, and to go back and recount them to *make sure* there were 156. That was the number the form said we needed in order to be "mount-up-ready."

At first, he didn't catch my hidden meaning, and he actually recounted them. Eventually, he understood what I meant by *make sure*. After that, he would go around the corner for a minute and come back and say, *"I found a few more in another box, so we're good to go."* We both had to laugh at ourselves but what the hell were we supposed to do? The numbers had to match up, or we were going to be responsible for the deficit, and we were supposed to be fighting a war, not counting gas masks. Anyway, the only thing we were likely to be mounting up for was another medevac mission. Dunwoody is another good Marine with whom I'd love to share a cold beer.

In the week that I have been back from the Philippines, I was in Phu Bai for two and a half days, to Chu Lai for a day and a half, and stood a 24- hour stint as the medevac pilot. Other than that, every other second has been spent on that stupid report.

We've also been looking for VC to start a fight. On one of the days that I was at Phu Bai, they found an entire battalion, estimated at about 400. VMO-2 had a busy day expending expensive ordinance on all those targets with six gunships rolling in two at a time for about a half hour. When the smoke cleared and the Marines mopped up the area, there were 175 fewer VC to rock us to sleep at night with their mortars. I had the feeling that the VC body counts were similar to my embarkation report -- a big number sounded better than a small one. Not many Marines were hurt that day, and I would have to give much of the credit to the Hueys for that.

On the day that I was flying the medevac gunship, Sparrow Hawk was launched again, and they formed a blocking force behind another large group of VC. Many were caught out in the open rice paddies. Sparrow Hawk ran out of gas and ammo, and they had to launch my medevac gunship and another gunship to help out. These men all had on green uniforms like NVA regulars but who knows what they were? Making those gun runs is dangerous because when you pull off the target, you are a sitting duck until you can circle back into position. Because they were running for cover and had little time to set up and shoot back, some had thrown down their weapons.

The medevac plane picked up 20 US WIA's and three KIA's after that battle. A hollow victory!

Last night Marble Mountain went into *"Condition II,"* meaning *attack is probable.* All this is due to increased demonstrations in Danang. One of the airplanes on the ground in Danang took a hit, injuring a crewman. I Corps Headquarters was surrounded by tanks, hopefully ours. For some reason everything is in an uproar again. All of this is beginning to be old-hat. We cope with all the chaos by finding humor in it. Condition II doesn't mean a damn thing to us. Sometimes, we continue our poker games in the midst of a mortar attack, especially when we have a decent hand.

Summer is on us now. We have had two straight days of 125 degree temperatures. There is a point in which you feel you can take just about anything. Bring it on! We keep our .38's and our .45's close at hand. The rookies have been transformed from wide-eyed Boy Scouts to full-fledged cowboys. Our flight suits and underwear are never dry. A normal day involves 12 or 14 hours of profuse sweating followed by a cold, welcomed shower. After what we have seen on some of those medevacs, it's just good to look down and see that your arms and legs are still attached.

The Vietnamese maid is worth her weight in dong when that fresh, dry flight suit is ready for me in the morning. She was not here today because of the heat, of all things. Our new maid is younger, more energetic and more eager to please than Thi-Toc. My new hooch-mates are more fun for her to work for, and we keep her motivated with tips. Charlie Plunkett is one of my hoochmates along with his best friend Steve Waltrip. Charlie is half Cherokee. Steve gave him the nickname Black Cloud because he's a VC magnet. Every mission he goes on turns to crap. Charlie's folks send him sa-lami, deer sausage, and pickled green tomatoes, which he shares with everybody including the maid. When one of the maids reciprocated with some candied baby green bananas, Charlie knew it would hurt her feelings if he didn't eat them. He showed some deep Indian wisdom by turning to me and giving me half of them. They were inedible, of course, but we had no choice.

I flew down to Chu Lai today to escort General Thong (whoever he is) to catch a C-45 to Saigon. Tonight, I will stand the TAOR watch in case we have to chase down any more "Charlies" (VC). This afternoon in the mail I received slides that were developed from a roll of 35 mm film. Some of the pictures on that old roll went back to New River, over six months ago. I had planned to take many pictures on this tour, but there aren't many op-portunities, certainly not on a flight. I once had a copilot take a picture during a medevac, and I had to tell him to leave his camera in the ready room from now on. We don't need the distraction of the camera in the cockpit on a combat mission, and I can't understand why any-one would take a picture of a wounded soldier.

19 May 1966 Thursday night

This afternoon I flew a routine TAOR recon and came back to the hooch for a little fun and sun on the beach. A runner came to flag me down and said that I was wanted down at "Ops" (Operations/ ready room.) Back in my flight suit, I bummed a ride in his Jeep for the half mile down there. This was an ASAP message. I figured my embarkation report had bounced off the ceiling, and somebody had actually counted the gas masks, or worse, they were sending me to Ashau.

There were two messages. Neither was urgent. They wanted a Huey to escort a 34 to Hue Phu Bai, and by the time I showed up, another pilot had volunteered to take it for me. The other message was that Hawaii had been added to the R&R list, and about 12 people had moved their names off the Tokyo, Japan, waiting list to go to Honolulu. This jumped my name to the top of the Tokyo list. They wanted me to make a decision: Tokyo in nine days or Hawaii when my name came up? The fellows whose names were underneath mine were pressing the issue. I had to disappoint the guy below me on the Tokyo list by taking it. This was the big emergency that was so urgent they needed to send a driver for me. *Do you think those R&R's are important?*

The extended trip to the Philippines was like R&R, so I really don't need this trip, but with everybody lining up for Hawaii, my name might never come up for Hawaii. I figured if I took the five days in Tokyo, I could come back and put my name on the bottom of another short list and maybe squeeze three R&R's out of this tour. This wasn't an original idea as there was plenty of coaching strategy available from other goobers who study all the angles.

I was surprised to see that they were playing poker at the club again. They rescinded the restriction on gambling and decided instead to reprimand the idiot who was losing his wife's entire allowance, instead of treating us all like a bunch of kids.

The political situation in town is turning into a bucket of worms again. They've run through a couple more I Corps commanders, the latest of which is a General Cao. Demonstrations have picked up, and the new rumor is that the ARVN's have a .50 caliber machine gun set up at the airport and are firing on their own airplanes.

21 May 1966 Saturday night

Mayday is a universal distress signal used by aircraft pilots or boat captains during dire emergencies. Wouldn't you know, it has a French derivation and comes from the word *m'aidez,* which means *help me.* The word has nothing to do with the actual month the emergency occurs, but yesterday on the 20th of May, 1966, for the second time in my aviation career, I had the opportunity to broadcast the word live on VHF 16, the international radio frequency for aircraft emergencies.

We were called to pick up one US WIA (one wounded

Marine). I was flying copilot with Shep Spink in the medevac slick. Spink was on his final approach into a very tight zone surrounded by tall trees. We were just above the treetops, and I was lightly riding through the controls with him, just in case of, well, *you know what!*

In the final stage of our tricky between-the-trees landing, just when a helicopter is most vulnerable, low and slow, the *you-know-what* happened. VC riflemen opened up on us. One round went through the engine. Another slammed a big hole in the fuel tank. The only way they could have hit us in a worse place is to have drawn blood. The plane jolted like it had been hit by a heavy caliber round rather than small arms fire. We both waved off simultaneously. I wanted my hands on the controls along with his. We were scanning the instrument panel for system failures. Before anything could register in my brain, I heard our gunship escort say, *"You're on fire medevac."*

We pitched the plane forward and looked for a clear place to land. Visions of my jungle survival training were flashing through my mind along with a hundred other things. The only clearing we saw was about three thousand meters away and on top of a hill that had been blasted by bombs from previous battles. We made a beeline for it. Our biggest concern was whether the fire that our wingman had reported would allow us to reach the clearing. Our second biggest concern was whether the fire would allow us time to scramble free if we did manage to land.

On the way in, I told Spink that I would shut the plane down if he would focus on himself and the crew. We didn't want the engine running and no one in it. It might decide to take off on its own. We made a crash landing into the dirt and rocks on the hill trying to avoid the tree stumps. Spink told the crew to stay low and well clear of rotor blades on the way out. We were asses and elbows throwing off our shoulder harnesses and slinging doors open, all thinking the same thing -- a spectacular, James Bond-type explosion. It took about five seconds to shut that engine down and apply the rotor brake. Spink was right there with me. When we both literally dove out of the plane, I had forgotten to unhook the mic wire on my helmet. I felt my head jerk back when the wire snapped. I landed on my hands and knees in a pile of rocks and scrambled as far and as fast as I could. The crew stood far apart from each other in a big semicircle around the "crash site." We were staring back at the smoldering plane as the rotors wound down. It looked as good as new. The fire that our wingman reported was mysteriously gone, but the skin of the plane was smoking in the area of the fuel tank. I looked at Spink, and he shot me a puzzled look. I shrugged back at him. I had just noticed that there were a few ground troops in the zone standing armed and at the ready. They were *really* puzzled because they had much less information than we did about what this was all about.

As Jonathan Winters might have put it, we observed "through heavy lenses" for a few minutes before approaching that plane. When the rotors came to a stop, we closed in cautiously for an examination, figuring if the plane was going to explode it would have done it. The one inch hole in the self-sealing fuel tank was too large to seal itself. The fuel had leaked out and streamlined down the fuselage into the open flame of the engine exhaust, causing the raw fuel to ignite. The rotor wash and the air flow from our airspeed held the flame away from the bullet hole and the main fuel source long enough for the fuel in the tank to drain out below the hole. When the fuel leak stopped, the fire was extinguished from fuel starvation. We don't put much fuel in the slick in order to keep it lean and mean. If that Huey had been topped off, we would all be dead. We just surmised all this because we could stick a finger in the hole and feel the level of the fuel.

We didn't know the extent of the damage from the hit to the engine, but the crew chief, Sergeant Terry Scruggs, didn't advise restarting the plane. I think he felt we had used up our miracle for the day. We turned the battery on, and Spink talked to the escort ship on the radio and told him to stay on the scene but to call for someone to pick me up, so I could bring another plane out to finish the medevac. Escort was way ahead of us and had already made that call and was circling overhead diligently. The plan was for Spink and the crew chief to stay with the plane and for me and the Corpsman to go back for a fresh ambulance. We were all perfectly calm.

In a few minutes, a Huey arrived and ordered us all back to the base. In the ready room, the big wigs were in full gear. Everybody had been put on high alert as soon as they heard we were shot down. Colonel Barden, our new CO, and every senior officer were fired up and ready to ride. They launched eight Hueys immediately and went back and laid waste to everything around that zone. After the dust settled, the medevac was completed.

I learned about a rule that you can't fly immediately

after you've been in a plane "incident" for psychological reasons. Spink and I were not supposed to touch a plane for the rest of the day and night. Oddly, we were the calmest people there. Everybody else in the room was in a five foot hover. Doc Zimpher was called down to examine us. He asked a few questions in an uncharacteristically serious tone that we both found humorous, and then he wrote us a medical grounding chit that gave the reason for our being grounded as *"psychological."* Spink and I looked at each other and shook our heads in amusement. Doc was being Doc, trying to do his part.

Spink, whose nickname is *Take Charge*, talked Colonel Barden into letting him fly back out there with the maintenance crew to help install another engine. They took the necessary equipment and a new engine and flew the plane back late that afternoon. The skipper's *okay* easily trumped Zimpher's grounding chit. I would have only been in their way, and furthermore, had no desire to see an engine being changed. Besides, I had to get my helmet fixed. We were unable to complete the balance of our medevac duty, which would have given us the following day off. I had to leave the next morning at 0530 for a two day stint at Phu Bai. That was the funniest part. Losing our day off was our reward for being shot down. Anyway, I figure I've had my incident. We were fortunate. One of those rounds could have easily found flesh.

Danang had been in a revolving door of crises since the beginning of April with a series of Vietnamese I Corps commanders coming and going. After a period of relative calm, the newest Vietnamese commander had planned a social affair on Sunday evening and had invited General Walt to attend. This story is taken directly from Walt's book. It occurred on Sunday the 22st day of May, two days after Spink and I were shot down.

[General Walt's description in his memoir of May 1966.]

"...The Buddhists had now become foremost in the complicated interplay of forces and were carefully solidifying their position, concentrating on control of the Vietnamese Army units in the area and duplicating their command structure with one of their own."

On a quiet Sunday morning, beginning just about dawn, *"This new commander's confidence was smashed by the roar of a massive airlift coming into Danang. With the planes still landing and taking off, the commander came dashing to me by jeep, pursued by Vietnamese tanks. He asked sanctuary. I put him in my quarters and promised him safety. The senior military officer in Vietnam, General Vien, arrived in Danang followed soon after by Premier Ky himself. Somewhat frantically, we used every possible source to find out what was going on. Reports flooded in. The Saigon troops had seized the Danang radio station, the City Hall, and other key buildings and public utilities. Local Vietnamese Army units were on the move toward Danang from the south, and more were headed toward Danang from Hue. The Vietnamese Air Force was attacking Vietnamese Army units outside of Danang. The Chairman of the Joint Chiefs of Staff in Washington, General Earl Wheeler, called to find out what was happening, as did Secretary of State Dean Rusk.*

After things calmed down, the next morning I was notified that the (current commanding) general in my quarters was relieved of his command and a new one would be designated. He arrived the following day, and we provided him with a helicopter and escort to visit the two divisions of his new command. Sensing trouble, I asked one of my senior and most able officers to undertake the task. Brigadier General Jonas M. Platt was a tall, experienced, and very capable officer I had known for many years.

They took off for Hue, General Platt, the Vietnamese commander and his aide, and a Vietnamese photographer. They used the Army advisor's helicopter. The visit was a strange one. There was the usual honor guard, introductions, a briefing and honors again on departure, but all the senior officers of the division were conspicuously absent. As our party was boarding the helicopter to depart, an unruly crowd of civilians and a few soldiers broke into the compound unrestrained by the guards and began milling dangerously around the chopper and its rotating blades. From the crowd, a Vietnamese lieutenant pulled out his .45-caliber pistol and started firing on the helicopter at close range. As the second bullet went ricocheting into the cabin, the Army gunner at the door of the aircraft turned his machine gun on the lieutenant and cut him down with a single burst. Blades whirling, the helicopter took off for safety, the honor guard standing at attention as their commanding general departed. Thereafter, he commanded from the safety of my headquarters until, like his predecessors, he was relieved of his command."

23 May 1966 Tuesday night

In the pragmatic world of aviation, we try to find reasons for everything that happens. It feeds the constant learning process. The reason Spink and I were shot down is really a simple one. It stems from our inability to secure this 25 square mile area south of Danang -- our own TAOR. There wouldn't be a VC or an NVA (North Vietnamese Army Regular) within 50 miles of this place if we were allowed to do our job.

So why do we have to keep doing the same things over and over again, taking one step forward and two steps back? The political situation of the last week might serve to explain some of it. General Thi, is now operating out of Hue and is Premier Ky's most organized political opponent. His followers now call themselves the "*Struggle Forces.*" It isn't as simple as Democrats and Republicans. These people have weapons and military forces at their disposal. Ky has his air force, but his army is split. Thi's loyal army commanders see the futility of a military solution that continues to beat this country down. Money being supplied by the US keeps this candle burning at both ends.

Ho Chi Minh, a most excellent guerrilla tactician, smells blood, and is sending entire regiments of well-trained NVA troops to take advantage of the chaos. The Buddhists leaders, clever opportunists throughout, have tripled their political clout but even they are divided. All this is a recipe for a disastrous civil war with no real leadership.

A few days ago, Premier Ky announced that he would stay in office for only one more year, attempting to calm his dissenters. He outlined his plan for how elections should be conducted and for *whom*. Much of his opposition was conveniently left out of his plan, which caused further hostilities. His I Corps commander, who was Dihn at the time, tossed his hat in the ring with Ky's opposition, throwing Danang into turmoil again.

ARVN forces quit their posts to protest in the city. Forces loyal to Ky tried to block the demonstrations and set up road blocks around Danang. Buddhists in Danang have an active and popular young leader named Tri Quang who has denounced Ky's government as corrupt. In short, just about everybody has something to be pissed about, and most of them have guns. Our little TAOR has become a battleground of the Republic (sic).

Our squadron planes and pilots are committed day and night to the mission of monitoring and observing *"unusual activity"* with orders to use extreme caution not to stir the pot. While we are monitoring all this, our enemies, which seem to be most of these people, are pushing farther and farther into our TAOR, planting booby traps, recruiting new villagers and sniping at Marines. The day before Spink and I were shot out of the sky, our medevacs totaled 87 Marines. In the past six days, many ARVN troops have abandoned their posts. Some left equipment and ammunition behind. The VC moved in on their heels. Where we once flew over quiet little villages, now we attract sniper fire.

All in all, this has been a repulsive week, mainly because we continue to pick up wounded young Americans whose lives will never be the same. So far, I've been fortunate not to be among the wounded.

24 May 1966

I just finished 96 consecutive hours of medevac standby, snatching naps between flights. Any misgivings I may have had about taking that R&R billet to Tokyo have long since evaporated. I'm not ever going to pass up another one. I have only three more days and a "wake-up" before I board that C-130 for the country that bombed Pearl Harbor. Twenty five years later, they seem to like anything that has to do with America. I hope they don't have a problem with me.

THE DAY LEW WALT EARNED HIS MONEY

The lieutenants coped with the chaos by making fun of everything, especially our superiors and the head honcho, General Lew Walt, the top Marine in the I Corps. We should have realized that they had the far more difficult job of senior command. The following incident taken from Walt's personal memoir, *Strange War, Strange Strategy,* shows how little we knew of Walt's true character. It happened in late May, about two kilometers from where I slept at Marble Mountain, on or about the same date that Spink and I were shot down.

Thi's Struggle Forces, led by an ad hoc group of rebels, were trying to wrestle Danang from Ky's government forces when General Walt was forced into a do-or-die standoff. A key bridge connecting the city to supply resources in East Danang had been rigged with explosives by the rebels. The east end of the bridge was being guarded by Struggle Forces led by a Vietnamese warrant officer who had orders to blow up the bridge if government forces on the west side of the bridge threatened any action. Walt's patience with the arrogance of the Struggle Force commanders finally gave out. He personally walked out to the middle of the bridge to attempt to mitigate the standoff.

Walt had already met with an American engineer who thought he might know the rigging of the charges well enough to be able to cut or disconnect the wiring from the detonator and the explosives, but he would need some sort of distraction to permit the engineer to clamor under the bridge.

Here is the spine-tingling story of the bridge incident in Walt's own words from his memoir published in 1970.

"I was the senior in rank, the biggest in stature, and probably the angriest of the group - a combination that made me the most likely distracter. I told the engineer that I would meet with the Vietnamese commander at the center of the bridge, that I wanted the explosives disarmed while we talked, and that I wanted to know when they were safe. Signaling for an interpreter to come along, I started out on the bridge.

The Struggle Force commander on the opposite side, a short, slight warrant officer, came out to meet me. We met about halfway. He was formal, very curt, and spoke only Vietnamese. Through the interpreter I told him my purpose: to prevent destruction of the bridge because it was vital to his own people. I assured him that in keeping with this intent, I would guard the bridge with my own men and keep it intact until the internal troubles of the Vietnamese were resolved. The warrant officer was totally unreceptive. He told me he would not move his troops from the bridge. Looking me straight in the eye and speaking with firm conviction, he said that if I tried force he would blow the bridge up on the spot. Those were his orders, and he was prepared to carry them out.

Playing for time as well as trying to find some kind of reasonable solution, I asked whose orders they were. The minutes ticked by as I tried to get him to bring his commanding officer into the scene. Meanwhile, the Army engineer and a couple of Marines were moving among the trusses beneath us, locating and cutting lead wires. Finally, I spotted the sweat-soaked engineer officer, who gave me the thumbs-up signal. I hoped he had done his hurried job well.

Cutting the palaver short, I told my opponent that he had five minutes to remove his troops and disconnect the detonator. He flatly refused. He had his orders, and he would carry them out. Repeatedly and pointedly, I looked at my watch, and the second hand laboriously crept around the dial.

Everything stood out vividly and unforgettably. The two machine guns at the far end of the bridge with ammunition belts of gleaming brass cartridges clinched into their receivers, manned by stolid, silent Vietnamese ready to open fire in our direction: the detonator, its plunger high, conspicuously out in clear view at the east end of the bridge, two Vietnamese engineers standing by it at the ready; the little officer straight and proud in front of me, determination and defiance obvious in his face. There was a heavily armed Marine Corps company behind me on the west bank ready to cross at my signal. I had gone too far to back down. We would either take the bridge or die fighting for it. Anything less than that and we might as well let the Bamboo Curtain slip down on another 17 million people.

The tedious progression of my watch finally reached the five minute mark, and I signaled the Marines across, at the same time telling the warrant officer, "You give me no choice but to force you and your troops off this bridge."

He glared at me, and suddenly in good English said,

"Gentlemen, we will die on this bridge together," raised his right arm, and swung it sharply down to his side. I saw the plunger go down at the far end of the bridge, and for one heartbeat wondered once again how well the engineer officer had done his work. Instead of an explosion, I only heard the heavy tread of my Marines bearing down on us from the western side. I turned to the warrant officer, not without pity. It is a shame to take such a moment away from a man. He seemed to shrivel right there on the bridge. I gave him one last hard look, he who could have blown my hopes as well as a bridge with that dropping hand of his, yet a man I respected for his courage and will. Then, I walked back across the bridge. My part of this was done."

General Lewis W. Walt, *Strange War, Strange Strategy.*

26 May, 1966

Tonight, I had what was perhaps my most interesting medevac. This was an unusual location about three miles northwest of Danang. The call was for one Marine WIA, and it came in around midnight. When I arrived for the pickup, I could see tracers, and the men had not even selected a place for the chopper to land in the dense foliage. This usually means that there's a rookie in charge, which isn't an ideal situation for anybody, especially the medevac pilot. While I was sorting through my options and chatting with the hyperactive radio operator on the ground and trying to calm him down, I received a second call for another medevac. The co-ordinates of this second medevac were in the same grid square. It took about one minute to figure this out, and it was as plain as day from our vantage point, even though it was pitch-black out there. I tuned to the radio frequency of the second unit and asked them to cease firing. I did the same thing on the radio frequency of the first unit. Sure enough, everything went quiet.

It isn't our job to cast judgment on those kinds of snafus. Honestly, I was relieved, if not ecstatic, that I had two friendly units and could make those pickups without further incident and very close to each other. I shared the call signs and radio frequencies with the two patrol leaders and let them work it out from there. One of our crew members commented that he didn't envy those men for the reports that they would have to file.

27 May, 1966

After Kirby came back from his temporary shipboard deployment, I asked him what they did on their highly secret deployment, and he shared this funny story on himself.

"As it turned out, we didn't really do a heck of a lot other than cruise down to the Mekong Delta aboard the USS Princeton. We put a battalion of Marines and an artillery battery ashore with no resistance. There were some Navy Special Ops guys on board who staged a night ambush or two. They looked too young and too nervous to be Seals.

There wasn't much for the Hueys to do except to fly the battalion CO and the artillery aerial observers around to look for targets. One day when I was flying cover for a Special Ops boat cruising along the beach, I noticed some suspicious "dug in" positions a couple of hundred yards inland. The boat had a 60 mm mortar mounted on the foredeck, and I asked them if they wanted a "fire mission." You betcha they did! These guys were pretty green and probably fresh from Hawaii. Their little boat was bobbing in the water. The first round went straight up in the air and came down about 30 meters from their boat. I was looking at the target area for an impact when I heard them holler on the radio, "INCOMING!" When I looked back at the boat and saw concentric waves of foam rocking their boat, my adrenalin started pumping.

My crew chief was grinning because he figured it out in a few seconds. The damn guys nearly shot themselves. They were all over each other trying to get some more rounds off, thinking they were under attack. They never had a clue where that incoming round came from. We didn't say anything. Why ruin their day? After that, they never got within 75 yards of the target which wasn't more than twice that far. I reported the position as destroyed anyway, just to give them a shot in the arm, which they needed after all that incoming. They probably wrote themselves up for a medal."

28 May 1966 Saturday 1100

My internal alarm clock let me down at 0445 this morning. I woke up an hour late. My first thought was that I had missed the 0530 bus to Danang for my Tokyo flight. I dressed in 15 minutes, hoping it would be late like everything else, but I was wrong. The bus was gone.

It's times like this that it pays to have buddies who fly choppers. I walked down to the flight line, and five minutes later the medevac slick was dropping me off 50 yards from the Pan Am Boeing 707 that would take me to Japan. I had no idea we would be flying to Japan in that kind of luxury. I pictured being strapped into the belly of a C-130 with canvas seats and parachutes for seat cushions.

At 600 knots, the 2,500 mile trip would have taken less time had we not stopped in Taipei, Taiwan. The egg-shaped island of Taiwan is located a couple of hundred miles off the coast of China. You probably know it as Formosa, and it's the midway point between Danang and Tokyo. We used the extra time to squeeze in two big meals. The stewardesses had round eyes, something I haven't seen in a woman for a while. During the flight I read the previous day's edition of the *LA Times* and felt as if I were in a time capsule.

Danang had settled down a little, otherwise Pan Am would not have landed there. Now however, the action was picking up in the North, around Hue, a more sophisticated city about 70 miles north of Danang. Marine and Special Forces outposts are springing up near the DMZ. Names like Dong Ha and Khe Sahn are starting to find their way onto our flight schedule.

TOKYO

29 May 1966 Sunday in Tokyo

I'm checked into the New Japan Hotel after an eight hour flight. We boarded a bus to Camp Zama (Army) for another couple of hours. Add processing, briefing, buying civilian clothing, money changing, and checking into this hotel, and you have my first day of R&R. We changed our Vietnamese monopoly money for green US money before we left. Now, we had to change our US legal tender to Japanese MPC and then into Yen. No more money than I have, none of that was a big problem. It just takes time.

We caught a six o'clock bus for the one-hour ride into Tokyo. The Sanno Hotel was full. They have a contract with the US government to run the hotel for military officers. Everything from food service to valet is run like an officer's club. They even have a spa and shops that resemble the PX. But the main reason for staying there is that the price is right. They put me on a waiting list. I stayed in another hotel about a block away.

Japanese businessmen go home at lunch and spend time with their families during the afternoon. At night, with huge expense accounts, they entertain their clients. The price of poker goes up in the evening as the night life cranks up and prices are "marked to the market" with these high rollers out on the town. Brace yourself if you decide to compete in a nice restaurant with Japanese businessmen on unlimited expense accounts.

I wanted some lobster for dinner, and the hotel restaurant only had Lobster Thermador. This is pieces of lobster baked in a rich sauce. I ate dinner by myself, by choice, because I didn't have much fuel left in my tank and didn't want to use it paying attention. Good thing too, because when the Mai Tai went to my head and my metabolism crashed at the same time, all I could to do was fumble my way to the elevator. But while I was sipping that drink and watching the Japanese hotel staff smiling and waiting on Americans, I thought about how far our relations with the Japanese had come in the last 25 years since Truman dropped those two bombs that killed more than 230,000 of them. I wondered if we would ever be able to rebuild the bridges that we were blowing up in Vietnam.

Overnight, the Sanno found a room for me. By the time I arrived, they had a family-style buffet set up. Most of it was American and Italian food. The lobster dish the night before was too rich for me, and I had slept too late for breakfast. I was hungry for familiar food and devoured the Italian buffet. Then, I mostly walked around in a daze and wondered why I was so tired. I never knew how much stress the body can store. Without the adrenalin, it was difficult to get motivated for a tour of the city. I remember having that same feeling in the Philippines. Whoever came up with the idea of R&R was a genius.

I had dinner with an Air Force major who told me

that Pan Am has a contract with our government to fly those R&R flights for a dollar per flight. He was an air traffic controller and was fascinated by all the things my squadron was doing around Danang.

12 June 1966 Sunday morning Marble Mountain

Since my return from Tokyo, I have been strapped into an airplane. When I'm not flying, all my spare time is taken up with collateral squadron duties. The day I returned, there was a note from our CO, Colonel Barden that he wanted to see me. I always worry about those little notes. I'm not exactly "AJ squared Away" when it comes to details. Sometimes I can't even find my own cover (hat), and I often walk around with no insignia like a buck private. You always think the worst when the skipper wants to see you.

This visit was the exact opposite of that. He wanted to tell me what a good job I was doing. He said that he had heard good things about me from the senior officers and my peers as well. *Alrighty then!* He never mentioned the dreaded embarkation report.

However, he did have an agenda. It seems that other squadrons aren't doing nearly as much flying as we are. Those squadron pilots have been receiving more citations and awards because they're more aggressive in their approach to writing themselves up for medals.

VMO-2 has always taken a lower profile, modest approach to medals. The prevailing attitude being that we are all doing the same thing, so why single out any one person or a particular mission. This was a culture established by the senior men, who felt that a pilot needed to do something extraordinary to receive a medal. Over time, however, the extraordinary had become routine for VMO-2.

Barden thought his men were the most exemplary of all, and that the squadron needed to do a better job of making sure the crew chiefs, door gunners, corpsman, and young pilots received the recognition they deserved. We were not doing ourselves any favors being humble, according to him. He had already held a meeting while I was gone and expressed his sentiments by telling the senior men to make sure we did a better job of this.

Most of the pilots were modest in filling out mission reports but would sometimes comment on the courageous performance of the crew, rarely mentioning themselves. Medals were somewhat competitive, and the Colonel thought that we were letting the pilots in other squadrons grab all the hardware. Barden's boss at group headquarters had brought all this to his attention because he knew what our squadron was experiencing.

"The biggest problem is that we had never assigned anyone the task of aggressively writing, submitting, and following up on these awards. The quality of the writing can be the deciding factor," Barden hinted.

I knew from the outset where this was headed. He had found out that I could construct a sentence. He showed me a handful of award recommendations and asked me to look over them. They were scrawled in bad handwriting and poorly worded.

"Flew out to (location) and picked up (whatever number) and took them to Charlie Med. We received enemy fire going in and out of the zone, and the gunship made a couple of runs to suppress it. Corporal So and So and Corpsman Whatzit had to get out of the plane to load the wounded because the Marines in the zone were pinned down. I would like to recommend them for a bronze or silver star award. Total fight time 1.1 hours."

One of the reports was a flight that Cliff Reese and I did on the 6th of June with a note clipped to it in which he had suggested we both should receive a Distinguished Flying Cross or a Silver Star. Another was a recommendation for Lance Corporal Palmer where I had recommended him for the Navy and Marine Corps Medal for administering mouth to mouth resuscitation and external cardiac massage to a critical Marine on a medevac mission on 4 June. The latter one, that I had written, had been approved immediately and unanimously. Barden stared directly at me to see if I got his point. Finally, I asked him the question to which I already knew the answer.

"What would you like for me to do, Sir?"

He told me to take them and rewrite them and that he would make sure these men received what they deserved. I asked him to take my name off the list for two reasons. First, I would look like a fool writing myself up for a medal, and second, as Major Reese's copilot, all I was doing was hanging on for dear life like a kid on a carnival ride. I sure as heck didn't deserve a medal for nearly peeing my pants. When he laughed at that, I changed the subject and wanted to clear my conscience on the embarkation report.

I told him there were probably some mistakes on that report because some of the items were not where they were supposed to be in all those boxes. At that point, he said something that will make me love that man until the day I die. He said all that crap in those boxes had probably dry-rotted anyway, and if this squadron was ever deployed while he was the CO, he would recommend setting fire to all of it. In other words, don't worry about it.

I walked down to the 34 squadron to see how they submitted their citation requests. The sergeant in their administration office said he typed them, so they looked more official, and he flowered them up a little. We had an old Olivetti typewriter in our admin area, and I asked if someone would type them if I wrote them by hand. One of the corporals seemed delighted to do it. I went home and took out my Thesaurus and my vocabulary books, and by the next day I knew eight different ways to be *"in complete disregard for one's own personal safety while being selflessly exposed to a hail of withering enemy fire."* I also found that it was helpful to say it several different ways in case the review panel missed it the first time. That way it sounded as if they did it several times. I don't know if the awards committee had seen the word *intrepid,* but I wore that one out. Barden was delighted.

The irony of this medal business is the moral dilemma of knowing that there are VMO-2 pilots who have flown dozens of these missions and think nothing of it, while another pilot who hasn't flown very much gets a couple of holes in his plane and thinks he should be awarded the Medal of Honor. This latter group had soured the citation game for some of the pilots, especially the reserves who could care less about a medal. To us, medals had become one more thing to make fun of. *"A Silver Star and 10 cents won't get you a cup of coffee when you get out of here -- you'd still need another nickel," according to Black Cloud.* However, the career Marines wanted those medals for their competitive annual fitness reports. Nothing fuels a promotion faster than a random act of courage.

15 June 1966

The missions are repetitious. Each day is a repeat of yesterday. We did have a "first" the other day in the Phu Bai area. We were called to extract a 17 man patrol that had become entangled so deeply in the jungle that they had no way out. They were trapped against a swollen river with heavy gear. They had tried to cross and underestimated the depth of it. They nearly had a drowning. They couldn't clear a landing zone and were too exhausted to go any farther. The only way to extract them was to perform an over-water extraction close to the bank of that swollen river and dangerously close to the trees.

The pickup chopper would be exposed both up and down the river from several directions, a clear shot for snipers. We were in gunships, and the 34's we were escorting were too big to get close enough to the bank. Their rotors would be in the trees. The water was too treacherous for the exhausted Marines to swim out into to river to them. If we are going to pull those kids out of there before dark, we would have to go down in the smaller gunships, stand on the skids, lean out and drag them into the plane. We made a grand total of eight trips, plucking them out like wet rats, two at the time, and taking them to a larger LZ to be picked up by the 34. Our gross weight was a factor in the jungle heat with the heavy ammo package on the gunships. Otherwise, we could have taken five or six at a time. Those guys didn't need to be out there for another night after what they had been through.

16 June 1966

We have a no-nonsense senior captain named Dick Carr who has been given more than one nickname by the creative lieutenants. Carr is a very efficient, highly competent senior pilot who doesn't waste any motion. When he isn't flying, he's resting flat on his back idling his energy for the next big emergency. The word *laconic* floats to mind. Even when he's upright, he moves slowly and methodically - the epitome of cool. One of his nicknames is *Cougar,* mocking his "cat-like quickness."

Carr shamelessly hogs the space in the coveted ready room bunk beds. His other nickname is Boo Radley because he sleeps all day and sometimes shows up out of nowhere to perform a precision medevac. Boo

Radley was an odd character in *To Kill A Mockingbird* by Harper Lee. He was a batman-type hero who had a mysterious creepiness about him that fascinated the kids in the story. Carr had the same spell on us. We had all been reading Harper Lee's book, and it was on our list of favorites.

While Carr was away on an assignment for three or four days, I was camped out in the cots between medevac flights when they decided I was just like Carr, always hogging the bunk bed. Up until then, I had just been Beasley, but Boo Radley was too good a name to waste on a senior captain, especially when they were afraid to call him anything but Captain Carr. Ergo, I inherited one of his nicknames. When I came back from Tokyo, someone had taken my flight helmet and put my new name on the back of it with florescent tape. I guess they had been dying to stick somebody with that name, and now they could actually call someone Boo Radley.

17 June 1966

When I returned from Phu Bai, I was scheduled to fly Brigadier General Lowell English, assistant division commander, who would then present me with a list of the places to go. These flights are a little unnerving, especially when there's no copilot. Most of these generals are not helo-savvy, and you never know where you'll be going or what they might ask of you.

His aides handed me his itinerary as he strapped

himself into the copilot's seat. A 34 was assigned to escort us in case the unthinkable happened. The first stop was Danang where a British ambassador and the British Minister of Southeast Asian Affairs were waiting for their nickel tour of our TAOR. It was about 120 degrees, and these two Brits were sweating profusely. I could sense that they weren't too interested in what their host was telling them on the intercom. There are two buttons for transmitting and half the time General English was broadcasting on the wrong one. His conversation was being transmitted to the whole world. All the two Brits wanted was to get back on that air conditioned, private jet and grab a couple of cold ones for the ride back to Saigon. The three men shared a couple of hours together, and I took them back to their plane.

The next day I flew Gen Kyle, division commander and second in command under our III MAF Commander, Lew Walt. I was taking him to Phu Bai along Highway One when he said,

"Lt. Radley, I'd like for you to fly down that road at about 500 feet, so I can take a look at those Buddhist booths they've constructed down there."

(He was calling me by the name on the back of my helmet. I knew then I would never be Beasley again.)

The stands on the road were something that the Buddhists had installed up and down the highway, presumably to publicize their politics and hand out propaganda. There might be two or three booths in close proximity, indicating the different factions even in their politics. Five hundred feet was as close as this Boo ever came to any of them.

21 June 1966 0745

I have been assigned for an entire week to fly gunship escort to our illustrious General Lew Walt, whom we have dubbed "Big Dumb Lew." You might ask why we would make fun of the man who might one day be our commandant. We do it for the same reason that we would make fun of the Pope's hat if he showed up over here. It's what we do. We make fun of everything. Besides, it's an honor to have one of our nicknames.

The honor of being Walt's pilot is a dubious one because of the obvious pressure. *Escorting* the General only entails trailing along at a comfortable distance behind his Huey providing guns if needed and carrying any of his lesser entourage. Trailing along behind the main guy is the safer job and one that I am sometimes called to do. General Walt can go anywhere he wants any time he wants, and there is only one absolute; he is going in a Huey. No matter how many medevacs or shot-up planes we have, Lew requires a slick and a gunship every day. Sometimes, Walt takes as many as 10 people with him. Lately, there have been many secret strategy sessions among the generals concerning the influx of NVA swarming through the DMZ.

Some of the generals like to sit in the copilot's seat. They must flip a coin for that, or pass it around, like calling *shotgun* in high school. Walt's new permanently assigned personal pilot is VMO-2's Captain Dick Joiner, so when you fly the general's chase plane, you are at Joiner's beck and call.

Every day starts out with the general's ice run. The escort plane (let's say, me) picks up a 50 gallon drum of crushed ice while Joiner picks up Walt at his beach house on China Beach to bring him to work. From there, anything can happen. Sunday, we flew to Dong Ha, a new Marine outpost near the DMZ, about 40 miles north of Hue. We went to Phu Bai, and latter, all the way back down to Chu Lai with several stops in between. On Monday, we went to Chu Lai and back. Later that night, I returned to Chu Lai (with no copilot) with a full colonel and a major. After dropping them off, I flew back after dark in an empty plane, alone.

There is a standing rule in VMO that you don't fly without an escort, for obvious reasons, and certainly not without a copilot, and never *alone*. We seem to have thrown these rules out the window. We would be in deep trouble if we ever had a forced landing with a "code" on board and no one there to pick us up. These ground generals know surprisingly little about those risks, and this adds to the pressure of flying them. The pilot has to sort through all the what-ifs while the VIP's ride along, "fat, dumb, and happy," as we say. Things that go through your mind during some of these VIP flights are both scary and amusing:

… Is the plane overloaded? Can I pull this heavy gunship straight up out of this confined LZ with four generals aboard and all those people standing 20 feet away, waving? Which one do I tell to get out? Why doesn't that two star fasten his shoulder harness? What if he breaks his nose on the instrument panel? He looks upset about something. Should I ask him to buckle up? I wish the clown in the copilot's seat would stop using the stick as a

lever every time he wants to straighten up in his seat. Uh oh, he's put his feet on the rudder pedals again. Oops, now he wants a flying lesson. Yessir, I'll show you how! Sir, you're talking on the air; this is the intercom button. No sir, that's for the machine guns. Sir, Chu Lai is that way. Sir, they're asking us not to fly over those ammunition dumps. Wonder how long this will take, I haven't had lunch and its supper time...

Waiting for hours on VIP's requires a special brain skill similar to a dolphin. You can only use half your brain for a nap. The other half needs to be alert. These guys expect you to anticipate their moves. After a while, you can tell by their walk and their body language what they want. Walt can dismiss you without saying a word. Just a look will do. The alpha dog doesn't want any eye contact or any conversation from his pilot. You also have to learn their posturing habits, who gets in first, who gets in last: the ever present pecking order.

John Wayne came to Danang Sunday and was the guest of Walt for the day. The Duke wanted his Huey fix, too. Although I didn't get to fly him in my plane, I was the escort plane. The grand old actor looked gaunt and thin but stood tall, bedecked in his jungle utilities and camouflage. He could be my grandfather. In the movies, the Duke was a Marine among Marines and probably the best recruiter the Corps ever had. From the admiring looks of the men around him, you'd think he actually did all those things in his movies. I felt a little twinge as I watched an icon gracefully fill the passenger side of a

6X6 truck and ride off in a cloud of dust to be displayed like a championship stud horse. I heard myself say out loud as he rode away, *"John Wayne is here."* It's funny how perception can become reality. John Wayne never did any of that stuff. The real Marine was standing next to him, unnoticed, with rows of ribbons on his chest -- his host, Lew Walt.

22 June 1966

One day while having lunch at Chu Lai, one of my old flight school buddies came rushing over to me as if he had seen a ghost.

"My God, Willis, we heard you got shot down and went down in a ball of fire. We thought you were dead."

I noticed several people in the mess hall glancing over their shoulders at me and whispering. It gave me the creeps. It would appear that the story of my being shot down had circulated among the pilot fraternity. As with most other Marine communications, by the time it made the rounds, it became slightly garbled.

24 June 1966 Friday afternoon

Yesterday, after taking two high ranking officers to a secret meeting place on the bank of the Hoi An River where generals plot their schemes against teenage guerrilla insurgents, we experienced a cyclonic-type dust storm. I was waiting in a make-shift shelter with only a roof and a wooden floor when my Huey started jumping around in the yard. The rotor blades were slamming back and forth to the point that I thought they might separate from the rotor head. I had to go out there and tie the blade down to the nose of the plane as if I was trying to hobble a wild horse.

The wind and dust storm was followed by a driving monsoon that threatened to wash the chopper into the river. The violent wind was playing havoc with the roof of my shelter. The longer it lasted, the worse it became. The airplane was changing its position on the ground like a restless animal, while I watched helplessly as my chest pounded. I thought it might fly away without me. Runoff water created deep craters around the skids. My imagination was having a field day with what-ifs. The rain was pouring out of the sky in buckets, and the jungle was laid on its side with palm trees kissing the ground all around the landing pad. I expected someone to come out of the building and invite me in from the terror. No such luck! I waited through the peak of it which took about 30 minutes, but seemed like my entire life. The back half of the storm took the rest of the hour. The rain wasn't coming straight down, and I was soaked. Water was squishing inside my flight boots. As soon as the worst of it was over, the brass came storming out of their meeting toward the plane. There was no eye contact -- not a single word to me! The VC would have been friendlier.

I can honestly tell you that I was more terrified during that storm than I had ever been in an aircraft. When you are a pilot, you have a sense of control, even if the engine quits, but when you are at the mercy of Mother Nature, you are a small and insignificant creature. The power of it is humbling. It felt like the Big General in the sky was having a bad day or maybe just wanted to send a message that He is still the boss. Whatever it was, it had my attention. *I believe!*

In marked contrast to yesterday's cyclone, today is beautiful. Except for the war, the tropical jungle after a storm is breathtaking. Despite all the devastation and death of the war, there is a peaceful, calm serenity that dominates the landscape, especially when you're soaring above it. It's just so hard to fathom that between the striking sunrises and glorious sunsets that there are these two conflicting ideologies below that are bent on destroying each other in the name of peace. Peace is right under their noses.

Today is my last day to chase the general. I'm sort of relieved to be relieved, especially after that monsoon incident. Waiting on people who treat you as an inferior irks me a little. Don't know why I would expect otherwise. I'm in the military, and I *am*, by definition, inferior to them. But I miss all the fun and low class games of the squadron and my four irreverent hooch-mates. They're going to ask me how Walt expects to run the whole III MAF if he can't even keep our little

TAOR neighborhood secure. They will expect me to have amusing stories for them when I return, even if I have to make them up.

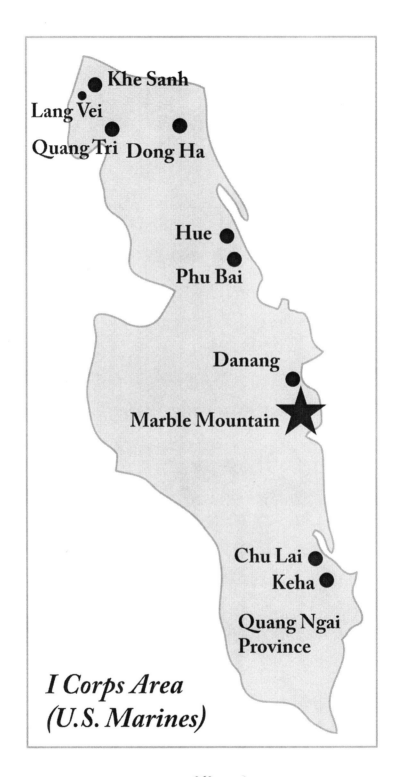

Khe Sanh

Lang Vei

Quang Tri   Dong Ha

Hue

Phu Bai

Danang

Marble Mountain

Chu Lai
Keha

Quang Ngai
Province

*I Corps Area
(U.S. Marines)*

CHAPTER SIX

STEVE CANYON AND THE ROCKPILE

10 July 1966 Sunday evening

Now, I know why those generals were having all those secret meetings. I will have to go back a few days to recount all that has happened.

It began on June 28 or 29. Can't recall exactly! At 0500 I left Marble Mountain in a slick with one crew chief and no copilot to fly 20 miles north of Hue and do whatever the CO of the 4th Marine Battalion wanted me to do. As I flew though Ha Van Pass at sunrise, I was fanaticizing about landing on that peaceful beach and sleeping undisturbed for about two days. Then, I began engineering a special fuel tank that would take me all the way to the Philippines, and from there I could refuel and make it to Hawaii where I would ditch the plane and live happily ever after.

My little luau fantasy was interrupted as I approached the field command center (LSA) and saw a big fire a couple of hundred meters from the LSA on Highway One. This was in an open area with no mountains and very sparse vegetation. I could see in every direction for miles. There was an ARVN convoy of about

15-20 trucks, and three of them were on fire. From the transmissions on the radio, I learned that the convoy was being attacked by an unknown number of VC. The convoy had taken a few casualties already. The VC may have pulled off an ambush, but they didn't know that there was a battle-ready battalion of Marines about 400 yards northeast of them. The Marines began shelling the VC as soon as they figured out what had happened. An aerial observer (AO) in a fixed wing O1-C called in two F-4's that clobbered the enemy positions with bombs and napalm. The Marines then launched a reactionary force (Sparrow Hawk) to trap what was left of them in a vice.

I was watching and listening to all this because I had already reported in by radio and was told to standby. While I was contemplating the role I might be asked to play in all this, they called me to land and report to the command center. I was instructed to shuttle various unit commanders back and forth to assorted outposts that had been established for this operation. Following that, they called me over to the planning table and asked me to relieve the O1-C spotter plane. I reminded them that I was a slick with only a door gunner, sensing that they might not realize the limitations of a slick. The crew chief was eager to operate the door gun since that was not his regular job, but with just two of us in the plane, I wanted him to sit in the copilot's seat, so I could have some company. It feels lonely and unnatural when you're looking over there at an empty copilot's seat.

When we flew into the battle area, there were some Vietnamese pilots flying propeller driven AD-1's that resembled a scene from WW II. They reminded me of the T-28's we flew in training in Pensacola. The AD's had some sort of bomber capability. They were working on a target in tight circles from 1000 feet. An Air Force spotter plane was controlling them. I was trying to stay out of their way and took up a lazy orbit south of their strike zone at 1500 feet. All these unilateral operations were taking place in a wide open, flat area. I could see several different engagements at the same time. It looked like a Steve Canyon action comic strip.

I was just drilling holes in the sky when my crew chief pointed down to a trench line. We saw 20-25 uniformed men walking down a long ditch. They were so bold I thought they might be our guys. They had full military gear and were making no attempt to conceal themselves. I called the control center and asked if they had any friendly troops at those coordinates, and he said negative. It looked as if we had us a target. Two more F-4's showed up, and I asked if I could control them on my target. The crew chief marked the target with red smoke, and I asked him to go back and man the door gun to fire off a couple of bursts near, but not at, those troops. When they started shooting back, it was a good validation that they weren't our guys. I took up a high orbit away from the jet's approach and high enough that I thought I could auto-rotate (emergency land) close to one of those Marine positions in case something squirrely happened. Their first pass put a round of napalm (bomb canisters of congealed gasoline) through the middle of their ditch and just swept right up to the end of it. That should have done it, but they walked the flaming jelly right on up that trench for a couple more passes for good measure. I could smell the napalm from 1500 feet, and it is not something you ever want to smell. After it was over, I didn't care to make a low pass for a visual damage assessment. No thanks!

Later, it was reported that nine NVA were found in the trench and evidence that others were dragged away. The NVA always drag away their dead. Where they would take them, I have no idea. Since the Vietnamese diet consists mostly of rice and very little protein, their bodies decompose rapidly. The sheer volume of these shallow graves, coupled with the millions of explosions over decades of war, has permeated the soil with a chemical concoction that bakes in the stifling sun. The lingering stench of this death cocktail is singular, and the odor lingers in the air on hot summer days like this. A single whiff of it can trigger fears of your own mortality. The smell of death is said to be encoded in our genes. I don't know anything about that, but I know that once you've experienced this particular smell, it is permanently imbedded in your memory bank.

Admin flights with unit commanders rounded out the eight hours of flight time. That afternoon, we watched Marines bring in prisoners and captured weapons. I was offered one of the captured weapons for a souvenir, but I wouldn't have known what to do with it. Somehow, that doesn't seem right -- taking something that belonged to a dead man.

On the 1st of July, I went back to that same LSA with my favorite general, Brigadier General Lowell English, assistant commander of the 3rd Marine Division. We are practically buddies now. This is a man who passed up an invitation to play professional football for the

Chicago Bears in favor of the Marine Corps. He wanted to see just about everything and go everywhere, so we made the rounds: to the LSA (Logistics Support Area), to Dong Ha, Phu Bai, Cam Lo, and all points in between. The following day, I flew Sparrow Hawk at Marble Mountain. When the mission was over, the schedule officer calmly informed me that I would be going to Dong Ha, 40 miles north of Hue, for four days. I packed a shaving kit and left that night. This time we had two pilots, and I had Jim (Puff the Magic Dragon) Sweeney with me in a gunship. We joined another VMO-2 gunship already there. The two gunbirds support a reconnaissance unit. Their mission was to insert small recon teams in strategic areas to gather intelligence. Every suspected infiltration route soon became a confirmed infiltration route. The enemy was all over the place. We could hardly find a clearing that didn't have NVA troops in it. On one occasion, we almost landed right on top of a group of enemy soldiers cooking their breakfast in a clearing. As soon as we inserted a team, we would be called back to extract them 15 minutes later. Some of those extractions became very complicated.

In one village alone, 40 enemy troops were killed. In seven days approximately 15,000 acres of mountainside covered with tall elephant grass was burned. They found anti-aircraft sights and machine gun positions hidden in the grass. It was evident that the enemy was everywhere, and they were definitely not VC. They were well-trained North Vietnamese Regulars (NVA).

On one occasion, we were called to support a local ARVN unit that was pinned down by automatic weapons fire. We made several gun runs and fired rockets until the ARVN could sweep through. The battle damage assessment recorded seven KBA's (killed by air). They captured three automatic weapons. That same evening, an ARVN artillery unit had a short round that landed in the middle of another ARVN unit that was under attack. Thirty five Arvins and a US advisor were wounded. While the wounded US advisor was attempting to control the medevac effort, he reported slightly wounded Arvin soldiers trampling the more seriously wounded to board the medevac chopper. It was a reminder of the Ashau extraction. A heavily overloaded CH-46 barely made it out of there. It required two more trips under fire to rescue the one person who boarded last -- the US advisor. Now, you know why we call the Arvins, the friendly VC.

On the 5th of July, I saw my first NVA prisoner of war. A Marine recon team brought in a captured soldier from a snatch and grab mission. He looked like all other Vietnamese men, small and brown-skinned, but firm and resolute. The faces of the Marine recon team were covered with their trademark black and green paint, and some of them seemed twice the size of their prisoner. The idea was to interrogate the prisoner to gather some details on the size of his unit.

At the end of five days of flying eight hours a day, I was informed that I would not be relieved for two more days. On the day I was scheduled to leave, we engaged the enemy on two different occasions. We caught six in an open field with no place to go. The next morning started quietly, but that night we inserted a recon team that became engaged with the enemy as soon as the Hueys left the area. We had to go back for them, of course. We shot everything the gunships had and called in two fighter jets before the enemy dee-deed. With only 30 minutes of daylight left, the two Huey gunships decided to save some time and go in for the six recon troops and their German Shepherd while the F-8's covered us with low passes. None of the good guys were hurt, but I don't think that recon team would have made it through the night once their position had been compromised.

This all happened on the 8th of July. After we refueled and reloaded the expended ammo, we returned to our small outpost at Dong Ha to bed the planes down for the night. The number two plane, which had been following me all week, finished the refueling task before I did and decided to head back to our confined little makeshift perimeter. I had always taken the front spot in the pad, and he had always taken the one behind it because we always arrived in that order. But this time, he was the first one to arrive and should have taken the front spot. Out of habit, he landed in his familiar place, leaving me to fly directly over the top of him in a dangerous twilight situation. The air temperature was well over 100 degrees, and we had a full load of fuel and rockets, close to max gross weight. His rotor wash and the postage stamp sized landing area created a very unstable and challenging situation. I managed to stabilize the Huey about 20 feet directly above the spot where I wanted it and began to lower it, but it was gasping for more air. It started bucking a little, and the nose was yawing to the left. I had full power and full pitch on the rotor head, and there wasn't anything left in the bird. Every muscle in my body was steering some part of that plane. There was a group of Marines standing and gawking to the left of me, and a five foot tall, French concrete machine gun bunker to my right, dangerously close to my tail rotor. The Marines obviously did not understand the situation, or they would have run for cover.

I managed an uncontrolled landing, plunging the helicopter into the ground abruptly and perilously close to that bunker. When we regained some of our wits, Puff and I both breathed a sigh of relief and decided to move the plane over toward the Marines a few more feet to position the tail away from the concrete structure. The pilot behind me, having just seen this near catastrophe play out live and in color, realized he had screwed up by putting me in that position. He decided to back up to give me some room. When he added power while I was doing the same thing, it kicked my tail rotor into the concrete bunker. There was a sickening clink, and the chopper started to rotate wildly out of control as the tail rotor came apart. I say it started to rotate, but before that could happen, I punched it into the ground immediately, partially collapsing the left skid.

The Marines in the small perimeter, not 50 feet away, were still gawking as I shut the plane down, and we started heading for the exits. Our door gunner in the back, who had unbuckled after the first landing, had fallen in the fracas and bruised his hip against a heavy metal ammo box. Puff forgot to duck as he ran from the left side of the plane, and I saw the rotor, which was lower on that side because of the collapsed skid, take a swipe at Puff's flight helmet, missing it by inches. Once I had shut the engine down and was clear of the plane and realized it wasn't going to blow up, I looked back at the pilot of the other plane, as if to say, *"What the hell were you thinking?"*

The biggest problem was that we had all flown way too many hours and were so far over the limit, and we were all so tired that we just sort of looked at each other and laughed. Then, I called back to home base. I asked if they were going to relieve us, or did they want us to go ahead and crash the other one.

We slept in the planes that night as we had been doing and the next morning purchased bananas, pineapples, and a loaf of bread from two Vietnamese women who walked up from a nearby village and offered them through the concertina razor wire perimeter. The rice flour bread looked like raisin bread when we broke it open. Weevils were baked into it that were the size of houseflies. This doesn't seem to bother the locals, who consider it protein, but we passed on the bread. We cut the pineapple with our K-Bar survival knives and devoured the delicious bananas. It was the first fresh fruit I'd had in months and tasted so good we wanted to call those women back to bring more, but it was too late. They had already disappeared into the village.

Somewhere around 1100, two new planes arrived to take us back to Marble Mountain. All of us received nothing but kudos and apologies from the Skipper and the rest of the guys for not relieving us when they should have.

That was my first aircraft *accident.* Naturally, it was pure pilot error, but it was never reported that way. After Colonel Barden read the details of our mission reports, he just passed it off as another combat related incident, and nothing more was ever said about it. Normally, there would have been some sort of investigation, and the other pilots would never let me hear the end of it. Not a word was said! The next day, a CH-46 flew up and strapped a sling to it and flew it back to Marble Mountain. The maintenance officer would have to scrounge another tail rotor from another busted aircraft and fix the skid. Case closed!

The most valuable thing we learned from all that activity near the DMZ was that Ho Chi Minh was sending thousands of well-trained troops and tons of equipment into South Vietnam on a daily basis to take on whatever we had to throw at them. If Westmoreland wanted a war of attrition, Minh seemed happy to oblige. We could barely find a clear place to land a chopper that wasn't already occupied by enemy troops. It shouldn't take a Rhodes Scholar to figure all this out, which is the primary reason we gave Walt his famous nickname, BDL. Winning the hearts and minds of people who chain themselves to .50 caliber machine guns is going to be a tough sell. Ho Chi Minh isn't interested in Civil Action Programs. He has a game plan of his own, and he is in it to win it. Our squadron is putting in 18 hour days up there. Our pilots averaged 100 hours of flight time in July, and I turned in a record 120.

Authors note:

The Marine Corps seemed to take special pride in the bizarre fact that we could operate out of a scrap pile. We didn't belong to, nor were we supported by, the Army. The Air Force had very little to do with us. Organizationally, the Marines are part of the Navy, under the Secretary of the Navy. After all, the word *marine* means water, but we have none of the Navy's wealth of resources. We use the Navy's left-over planes and have to bum spare parts and equipment that the other branches of service don't even want. The Marines were never intended to be anything other than a strike force that could be sent in quickly to secure an objective and then get back to the ship or to base camp - kick ass, take names, and go home. Suddenly, we find ourselves in a garrison situation, without the benefit of a total support network such as the well-equipped Army, which is designed and trained for garrison duty. Our little VMO squadron might have to wait for two months for a certain Huey part, while the Army was throwing good, used parts in a trash bin down in the II and III Corps. Ironically, when we crashed a plane, we might harvest enough spare parts from it to put three other planes back in the air.

Continuing my tirade, which part of South Vietnam do you think the Marines were assigned to defend? We had *The I Corps,* snuggled right up next to Ho Chi Minh, the DMZ, and his main thrust. We had a handful of airplanes, too much territory to cover, and Marines in the bush screaming for re-supply and support. We didn't have enough choppers to deliver the support they really needed. If intelligence reports indicate that there are three regiments of NVA streaming through the Ho Chi Minh Trail,

Walt might send a company of a couple of hundred Marines up there to *kick their butts.* These issues dominated discussions among the pilots. How long will it take, and how many resources of men and machines will we have to lose before we get our act together and figure out that the Marines can't climb a 100 foot mountain with 10 feet of rope? And why are Corporal Dunwoody and I counting gas masks for a contingent deployment when we are already deployed?

During the early stages of the war, Marine General Victor H. Krulak expressed optimism over the prospects for American and South Vietnamese success. But in the mid-1960s, when he commanded all Marines in the Pacific, he opposed the strategy pursued by Army General William Westmoreland. Westy proposed the use of Marines in large-scale battles. Krulak wanted to emphasize pacification and win over the villagers by assisting in economic projects and protecting them from the enemy. He also advocated the bombing and mining of Haiphong's harbor to cut off supplies to North Vietnam being shuttled down through Laos on the "Trail." He met with President Lyndon B. Johnson in mid-1966 to press those ideas, but as General Krulak later said, "…*as soon as he heard me speak of mining and unrestrained bombing of the ports, Mr. Johnson got to his feet, put his arm around my shoulder, and propelled me firmly toward the door.*"

20 July 1966 2200 MMAF

The attempted recon insertions gathered enough intelligence for General Walt to launch Operation Hastings, the biggest initiative of the war so far. Walt has been convinced that there are NVA operating in that DMZ. A captured prisoner bragged that three divisions were already there and more were on the way. The following incidents provide clues to the reasons that Walt shifted his focus to the problems in the northern portion of the I Corps.

Walt sent almost every chopper in our group to Dong Ha to support Operation Hastings. Two large tents were erected, and cots were brought up to accommodate a large number of pilots and support people. Most of our squadron is there now. There are 30 people in each tent; some literally camped out under the stars. They sleep in shifts around the clock. All the planes are squeezed in next to the tents, jammed against the Dong Ha runway. The barbed wire perimeter is packed with airplanes and an artillery battery that does most of its firing at night. C-130's are bringing in supplies for the Seabees (Navy construction battalion - CB) to create a permanent base at Dong Ha.

The squadron's only casualty so far has been Al Barbour, who was sitting peacefully on his bunk briefing Doc Zimpher's replacement (flight surgeon Curtis Baker), when Al Mumford landed about 30 yards from our tent and turned it into a hot air balloon. The canvas roof rose up about three feet, and the 20' tent poles came loose. One of them fell across Big Al's noggin. It took nine stitches to close him back up, and we debated whether his wounds were Purple Heart worthy. Probably not, since it was friendly fire. Fortunately, Doc Baker was three feet away from him, was able to treat his first casualty and justify a flight surgeon's hazardous duty pay.

On the positive side, because we are all camped so close together, and this is such a break from our normal routine, we are actually having fun with this situation. Our meals consist of canned C rations. We see how real bush Marines live in the boonies. We barter over things like ham and lima beans and caraway cheese and crackers. The ham and lima bean combination is considered almost inedible by some, but my mother used to make me eat that stuff when I was a kid. It reminds me of the school cafeteria where I ate things that the others wouldn't touch. The canned rations need to be heated with sterno cans and a generous dose of Tabasco sauce. The secret is to stop eating when you are no longer hungry … unless you have a love affair with heartburn. There are several different kinds of cigarettes in small packs of four, and most of these end up being tossed into a heap for the smokers along with the unopened cans of lima beans. A can opener which we call a "John Wayne" is less than the size of a quarter and can be worn around the neck attached to the dog tag chain.

One night, I was sent to the USS Princeton to help support a 40 airplane troop lift, and I spent the night aboard ship. A one night R&R! We had a real meal, a hot shower, and clean sheets, and I wondered why I hadn't joined the Navy.

HELICOPTER VALLEY

On the 15th of July, we escorted several flights of 46's for a large troop insertion in a valley west of Dong Ha and northeast of the Rockpile. The disastrous result of this mission was the most horrific experience of my tour to date. So many helicopters were crashed or shot down in the landing zone that the area has been named Helicopter Valley. Our mission was to drop a couple of hundred Marines into LZ Crow, not too far from the DMZ.

The Story of Helicopter Valley, Official USMC Source:

"After Marine jets and artillery prepped two initial assault LZs for operation HASTINGS, 24 CH-46s from MARBLE MOUNTAIN-164 and MARBLE MOUNTAIN-265 brought the first wave of Marines from 3d Battalion, 4th Marines into LZ Crow, about five miles northeast of the Rockpile starting at 0800. The 24 CH-46As were divided into six divisions of four aircraft each since LZ Crow appeared large enough to accommodate four aircraft landing together. Each CH-46 carried 14 troops plus a crew of four. Since numerous automatic weapon positions were located to the northeast, the final approach heading was generally southeast, which caused the terrain to slope downhill to the zone. There was a tailwind of about 5 knots. The first two divisions landed in Crow without incident. MARBLE

MOUNTAIN-265's EP-155, in the third division, overshot the landing point and hit a tree line, causing strike damage plus minor injuries to the crew and passengers. It came to rest to the right, outside the zone, and was smoking. MARBLE MOUNTAIN-164's YT-15, flown by MAJ Tom Reap, was the fifth division leader. The second ship in the fifth division was MARBLE MOUNTAIN-164's YT-18, flown by CPT W.J. Sellers. MARBLE MOUNTAIN-265's EP-160, flown by CPT R.O. Harper, was the third ship and CPT L. Farrell in EP-174 was the last ship in the fifth division which approached the zone in a free-trail formation. In the report of aircraft mishap, MAJ Reap stated he believed he was slightly high and fast on final. Rather than flare and place his wingman in an awkward position, he picked a clear area about 75 feet east of the LZ. He came to a hover, and the crew helped him avoid a small ridge already occupied by Marines. He started losing rotor RPM as he pulled power to move over the ridge. The CH-46 dropped the last 8-10 feet to the ground and landed hard. Sellers was about four rotor diameters behind Reap and a little higher. He flared to about 20 degrees nose up to get rid of this airspeed and moved abeam of the leader as he came to a high hover. Some trees near the stream, a stand of 20 foot bamboo, and troops already on the ground limited his touchdown choices. He started losing RPM in the hover and set down to the left of Reap. Both CH-46s were on uneven ground. YT-18 was only on the ground about four seconds before it meshed aft rotors with YT-15, which had already lowered its ramp and troops were leaving. Both aircraft began to shake and vibrate violently; then broke at the splice just forward of the aft pylon. The pylon dropped, injuring some men inside. YT-15's blades killed two Marines who had just left the aircraft. At 1815, while inserting a reaction company to guard the three CH-46s in LZ Crow, MARBLE MOUNTAIN-265's EP-171, flown by CPT T.C. McAllister with SGT R.R. Telfer as crew chief, was hit at 1,500 feet by 12.7 mm fire. Photos taken from the ground show smoke coming from the cockpit windows, and flames coming from the rear of the aircraft. When they tried landing on Crow, smoke filled the cockpit so no one could see. They overshot the LZ and crashed on the edge of the battalion's CP and 81 mortars. Thirteen Marines died, and three were injured in this incident. Thereafter, the Marines referred to the Ngan River Valley as "*Helicopter Valley.*"

July 15, 1966: Michael A. Cunnion, quarterback on the Holy Cross [Worcester, Mass] varsity football team, was Killed in Action along with 12 other Marines when his helicopter is hit by enemy fire and crashed in Quang Tri province. Submitted by Wally Beddoe, POPASMOKE Webmaster

VMO-2 escorted those CH-46's into LZ Crow and could only watch in horror as these mishaps mounted. Our squadron flew sorties around the clock providing gunship support and medevac relief for 48 consecutive hours.

I returned to Marble Mountain just in time to fly the General's chase plane. I managed one hour of flight time squeezed between 10 hours of waiting beside the plane. But it was a break from the up-tempo days I'd been having at Dong Ha. In my entire lifetime, I will never be able to forget the day we named Helicopter Valley.

While trying to catch a late movie at our open air,

walk-up theater last night, I became nostalgic watching beautiful actors portraying Americans wearing civilian clothes, engaging in ordinary activities, and enjoying a normal life. I arrived late and didn't catch the title of the movie. I found myself unable to focus on the dialogue and ended up daydreaming for an hour. I finally went home and fell into a deep sleep in my flight suit.

Things are going to change around here when the rainy season cranks up in September. We had a taste of it a couple of days ago with another torrential downpour. If the visibility deteriorates, the VC will take advantage of it. Weather adds an extra layer of excitement to our medevacs. The observation outposts that we resupply are high in the mountains and will be in the soup. We're the only lifeline those guys have and will fly into almost anything to support them. In September we'll lose 12 pilots to rotation. It's going to be difficult to train rookies in a monsoon. With all our resources being spent at the DMZ, there's no telling what kind of trouble is lurking for us at Marble Mountain.

26 July 1966 Tuesday (?) afternoon MMAF

Hastings is going better now that everybody understands the problem. All of our attention has been focused on that operation since Helicopter Valley. Rumor has it that the captured prisoner we brought in on the 5th of July told us there were three regiments of NVA already detached and more on the way. The prisoner spoke these words with great pride. There could be as many as 5000 troops in each of those three regiments, but even one regiment could be too much to handle in a game of attrition.

Meanwhile back at the Marble Mountain home front on the evening of the 23rd (three days ago), we had a rude awakening. As a light evening rain was cooling off the small stakes poker game in our hooch, we were interrupted by the KRUMPH, KRUMPH of incoming mortar fire. You don't have to ask if it's incoming. When it happens, there's no doubt. And as we like to tell the rookies, *"Incoming fire has the right of way."*

A mortar attack on our base was not a new one for me. I was a quick study and the first one in the sandbag bunker outside the hooch. Actually, we didn't go to the bunker that our hoochmates had built. We all headed for the one the guys next door had built, which was much better. Theirs was dug *under* their hooch, was deeper, and had a layer of sandbags over the top. We had been more like the grasshopper in that story about the ant, and we hadn't done a very good job on our bunker.

As we sat in our underwear in that dark bunker, we tried to guess where the mortars were landing. We knew that each one of these incoming rounds represented a three month journey, mostly on foot, all the way from Haiphong Harbor, and the VC had to make every one of them count. They weren't aimed at our poker game, but at the aircraft on the flight line, and most of the choppers were at Dong Ha. Waltrip suggested that we put on flight suits and run down there to evacuate those airplanes. It only took a few seconds to visualize not doing that in a million years.

The poker gang was wearing nothing but our dyed green jockey underwear with our holster belts and .38's around our hips like half-naked cowboys, wondering if it might come down to hand to hand combat. From the wisecracks that came out of that incident over the next 10 to 15 minutes, it was plain that we had all been seasoned by combat.

We also discussed why in the hell we couldn't secure our own little area. It seemed as if we were fighting a war with one hand tied behind our backs and always one step behind the enemy. We saw a couple of Hueys making gun runs a mile or so southwest of us, their red tracers glowing in the dark. After a brief encounter and exchange of fire, our sleepy little beach village returned to normal. We resumed our poker game. The players who had bad hands demanded a re-deal, and those with good hands were screwed.

The next morning we heard the details. No Hueys were hit, but a couple of 34's and 46's had some slight damage. At the time of the attack, we just happened to have three Hueys returning from Dong Ha. Kirby and Spink were in the first plane and had already landed and shut down, but the other two, led by Major Plamondon, responded immediately and were able to pick up the muzzle flashes from the mortars. They made a couple of gun runs and ended the fracas.

Spink told us his version of the incident. *"Kirby and I had shut down just as the first mortar rounds fell. Our engine was too hot to re-start without a cooling-off delay, so we pulled the rotor brake and ran with our crew to the nearest flight line bunker. (The bunkers on the flight line are nothing but a few layers of sandbags placed in a square formation on the perforated steel planking.) We hunkered down and listened to the incoming mortars while we hyperventilated. When the all-clear was spread from the ready room, we all started breathing again. Suddenly there was a loud boom just a few feet away, causing some of us to stain the laundry. One of our crew had accidentally discharged his .45 as he was returning it to its holster. Fortunately, only a sandbag was wounded."*

Today has been another respectable day without rain. The cloud cover is blocking the direct rays of the sun, making the tropical heat tolerable. Our hooches are undergoing a facelift at the hands of the engineers in preparation for the monsoon season. One hooch at a time is having the canvas covering removed and replaced with galvanized, corrugated metal panels. The canvas takes a beating during windy days, and it probably wouldn't hold up for another rainy season. The metal roof would have been a much cooler arrangement during the summer, but it hasn't been available until now. Sometimes, I wonder if we were ready for this war.

From what the veterans have told me, we have had a mild summer compared to *"what it used to be like."* The weatherman here, if we had one, would only need two words, *hot* and *rain*. They can be used alone or in combination. Flying in bad weather has always scared the hell out of me. This is mountainous terrain a few miles inland, and we obviously can't fly these missions on instruments.

We still don't have a hot water shower, only a crude, black solar convection 55 gallon drum that doesn't do the job on overcast days. One of the captains who went home gave me his water repellant, fire retardant flight suit. I also have inherited three or four sets of jungle utilities. We have to change clothes often, so a dry wardrobe is valuable. If you don't find a way to stay dry, your body will become a Petri dish for fungus. I have a blotch on my neck and around my waist. Once you control it in one spot, it creeps over to another. I try to stay out of the rain when I can and make full use of my vinyl plastic poncho. A hot plate is good for heating a can of beans or beef stew in the hooch for those dismal evenings when a rainy walk to the chow hall is too penalizing.

3 August 1966 Wednesday Night at Dong Ha

It's been medium-action day so far for the medevac plane. I'm flying gunship escort. The 34's are doing more medevac pickups now, simply because we don't have enough Hueys to do both the pickup and the gunship escort. We've been out about six times. It's 2200, starting to rain, and the weather is deteriorating. Hopefully, we can rest tonight.

Oops! Gotta go!

Well, I was interrupted there for about an hour while we transported some patients from the field hospital to the hospital ship Repose, a first class medical ship that is in the area supporting Operation Hastings. It's a much better facility than our field hospitals, especially where sterilization is critical, and some of the boys need every advantage they can find. The Repose will be like R&R for those fellows.

The concept of *triage* is a huge factor in combat. Prioritizing which patients receive what medical resources and when, wears heavy on the shoulders of the corpsmen, doctors, and medical staffs. The Repose has a triage nurse who makes those decisions. When a corpsman finds himself down to three or four bags of plasma, for example, and has more than one critically wounded soldier, he has a tough decision to make. I try not to look back there or become involved. My job is to keep my mind on flying the airplane. It's simply not possible to process the weight of everything that a war can throw at you. However, there is no doubt that these doctors will be some of the best in the world when they return to the states.

Landing on a rolling hospital ship in the middle of a black ocean at night with wounded Marines will definitely hone your shipboard procedures. Anyone who makes a run to the Repose has to remember the second most important part of the mission: *ice.* Those Navy ships have more ice than the Titanic, and we have zero at Dong Ha. Without it, our canned soft drinks and beer stay at a constant temperature of about 100 degrees. There are no generators or electricity at Dong Ha.

OPERATION PRAIRIE

Groucho Marx

6 Aug 1966 Dong Ha

On the sixth of August, two armed VMO-2 Hueys left Dong Ha to take on a target east of Cam Lo and south of the DMZ. Al Barbour was the flight leader in the lead aircraft and the first gunship to attack the target. Pianoman Dick Drury, an experienced and competent pilot as well as our only talented officer's club entertainment, was the pilot of the second Huey. Drury's copilot was a new major from the Marine Air Wing who had requested to fly on a live combat mission. Barbour had successfully pulled out of his run when Drury rolled in behind him. Drury's Huey was immediately hit with heavy caliber automatic weapons fire. The anti-aircraft fire came through the nose bubble and hit the flight controls where Drury's right hand was resting on the cyclic, destroying the pilot's fight control and taking part of his hand and arm. The copilot, whose name we don't know, reported the situation to Barbour who aborted the firing mission to lead them to the Phu Bai medical pad, where they did what they could for Drury's wounds including the removal of shrapnel from his feet to the hair on his

head. Due to the limitations of a field hospital, he was evacuated to Portsmouth Naval Hospital via Danang.

[Drury's dysfunctional military trip to Portsmouth took nearly ten days, during which, no medical attention was given to his arm. By the time his wounds could be evaluated, the doctors had decided to amputate because of gangrene. His wife Nancy, then living in Virginia, had come to Portsmouth to be at his side. She intervened vehemently at the suggestion of amputation. It took 14 months of multiple, complicated reconstructive surgeries to save his arm. He and his Distinguished Flying Cross and Purple Heart were medically released from the Marine Corps in 1967. He immediately started his own general contracting firm in Norfolk and began pursuing his MBA at Old Dominion University. In 1990 he joined the faculty of George Mason University to teach MBA students courses in strategic management and entrepreneurship, simultaneously earning his doctorate in education leadership. Nancy took a job with the Air Force as a congressional liaison at the Pentagon. She was knocked from her chair on September 11, 2001 when the hijacked American Airlines Flight 77 crashed into the Pentagon taking the lives of several of her good friends. She and Dr. Drury are now happily retired on the Eastern Shore of Virginia where he plays his piano on the banks of Chesapeake Bay.]

Operation Prairie is being fed primarily from intelligence gathered by small Marine reconnaissance teams operating out of Dong Ha. Insertions and extractions of these four to five man "Stingray" teams along known infiltration routes are a daily occurrence for VMO-2.

Their purpose is to determine the extent of NVA forces operating in the DMZ.

On the same day that Drury was shot, the 6th of August, we inserted a five-man team on the northern edge of the Punch Bowl, near the base of Mutter's Ridge about five clicks north of the Cam Lo River Valley. The recon mission was dubbed, Groucho Marx. The team immediately observed a small group of NVA but could not determine the size of their unit. Two days later, on the morning 8th of August, they spotted 15 uniformed NVA moving in a skirmish line, presumably looking for them.

The patrol leader radioed their commander at Dong Ha, who asked for two Hueys to cover them. The ground unit commander at Dong Ha decided to send a 40 man reaction (Sparrow Hawk) force to trap the 15 enemy soldiers and to capture one or two for intelligence purposes. After a futile search for the enemy troops, the reactionary force called for extraction. Several UH-34's were sent to retrieve them. The 34's came under heavy fire while picking up the troops. They were able to evacute only 20 of the 45 Marines. The platoon leader, Lieutenant Sherman, waived off the remainder of the 34's.

By now the NVA were in company force, ready to assault the Marine position. The Marines were able to hold off the assault but Lieutenant Sherman was killed. Back at Dong Ha, Captain Howard V. Lee asked to lead a group of seven volunteers to reinforce the heavily outnumbered Marines. Two Hueys from VMO-2 were sent to escort two UH-34's for the drop. Major Vincil Hazelbaker flew the first Huey, and I was his wingman in the second plane with no copilot. Enemy fire forced the 34's to land outside the Marine perimeter, and Captain Lee's men became separated. Lee and two other men were the only ones to reach the shrinking Marine perimeter. The four lost Marines popped a smoke grenade. Major Hazelbaker flew down to pick them up while I covered him without incident. We returned them to Dong Ha, refueled, and rearmed to return to the fray. A copilot volunteered to fly with me, and Tony Costa returned with Hazelbaker.

On the ground, Captain Lee took charge of the ground unit, which had now dug-in on top of a small hill. They repelled numerous assaults, sustaining heavy casualties while the Huey gunships raked the area with machine gun fire. Lee radioed his commander that he had only 16 men able to fight. He reported that they were running low on ammo. They were facing a force of 400 enemy troops, outnumbered 25 to one. Lee was reporting incoming fire from RPG-2's. (Shoulder-held, rocket propelled grenade launchers.) The incoming fire was constant and intense.

Overhead, Hazelbaker and I eventually determined that everything north and west of the hill was a free kill zone. We marked the hillside target north of their tiny hill and directed fixed wing to hit it with napalm to intimidate any enemy reinforcements. The 16 Marines on the ground were maintaining constant vigil in a 360 degree direction, running out of ammo and screaming for resupply. Without ammo they would be instantly overrun. This was by far the most horrific situation I had ever witnessed. Short of shooting among them, we felt powerless to help these beleaguered Marines. Any approach to that hill by a resupply helicopter would have been tantamount to a suicide mission.

Nevertheless, Hazelbaker and Costa agreed to do just that. With his fuel supply running low, Hazelbaker made a treetop approach to the top of the hill. Hovering over the ground, his crew kicked out all their remaining ammo, roughly 3000 rounds. They also evacuated some of the wounded. We covered their landing by shooting the remainder of our ammo around the small hill. As I looked down at Hazelbakers rotating beacon, and the tracers flying back and forth, I remember thanking God that there was room for only one chopper on that hill. My gun run was probably made from the highest altitude in the history of VMO-2. I also remember feeling incompetent that I could not keep a steady reference on the ground in the dark and fly the plane at the same time. I needed to be two people to do that. I couldn't understand how Hazelbaker, a relatively new pilot to the squadron and to the Huey, was able to manage it so skillfully. The rotating beacon in the LZ and the red tracers zipping across the top of it, provided the only light in the Cam Lo valley.

By the time we returned to Dong Ha, other planes and other pilots were gearing up to relieve us. Hazelbaker and Costa insisted that since they were the only ones who had seen the landing zone that they should go back and reinforce the recon team with a second resupply of ammo. Both men were insistant. A copilot volunteered to go back out with me to escort them. Major Jack Nolan and Lieutenant Al Barbour volunteered to take a second load of ammo for a kickout. Spink took a fourth gunship to provide additional fire support. When we returned to the sight, illumination flares were fired into the area by a nearby artillery battery to keep the area well lit. The ground troops reported seeing sillouettes of the NVA in the light of the flares. Bodies were all around them. The enemy would attack between flares.

Our only reference for the Marine position was flash-lights deep in the foxholes on the hill. They could only be seen from directly overhead. During Major Nolan's attempt to approach the hill, he became disoriented and "locked in" on the wrong hill. Despite repeated shouts from Barbour and the crew, he had tuned out the world and apparently heard no one. They landed on the wrong hill.

Hazelbaker decided to attempt a second resupply. Spink made a diving run with his running lights and landing lights on to provide a distraction for his ap-proach. Hazelbaker came in low from the opposite di-rection and was able to execute a second succesful ammo kick-out. But this time his luck ran out. While in a two-foot hover, their rotor head was struck by an explosive projectile of considerable force, probably an RPG. The crew chief, Corporal Ortiz was severely wounded when shrapnel entered from above and penetrated his flight helmet. The door gunner, Lance Corporal Jim McKay, was also injured by shrapnel. Costa was only slightly injured. The crew abandoned the crippled plane and joined the men on the ground in their dug-in positions. The beleaguered troops now had additional ammo and the Huey machine guns to boost their firepower.

Throughout the long night, Hazelbaker reported that they could hear the enemy talking as they tested their perimeter between parachute flares. Each time the

Marines fired at a silouette, it would be answered by a grenade. Hazelbaker had to order the Marines to stop shooting. By this time a "Spooky" had been dispatched and was orbiting the scene with a Gatling gun. Spooky is an Air Force C-47 or a C-130 cargo plane equipped with a side-firing .25 mm single barrel rapid-fire gun that can stay on target for long periods and provide 1800 rounds of surgical firepower per minute. Its high zoom and low splash damage make it very useful in close-quarter contact with the enemy. The night was crystal clear, and the red tracers spewing out of that gun resembled a flaming snake.

Captain Lee had multiple wounds but was still fighting. As he lost blood and grew weaker, he turned over command of the unit to Hazelbaker. All the men on the hill were wounded except for Hazelbaker. He took charge of the unit, redistributed the ammo and made sure the wounded were attended. He directed the overhead Hueys on our gun runs and radioed the Spooky to lay down a base of fire around their perimeter as close as possible. The Marines in the foxholes were so awed by Spooky's firepower that they asked the major not to do that again. As daylight approached, a reaction team was inserted to provide relief. The intensity of the situation had subsided. An A-4 fighter plane dropped a smoke screen to cover the landing while Huey gunships provided cover for all the Marines to be extracted. Fireballs from the smoke screen fell across the top of the zone burning holes in their clothing. Every helicopter at Dong Ha was in the air waiting to extract the beleagered Marines.

Captain Lee survived the ordeal and received the

Medal of Honor. The Huey crew would be highly decorated for their heroism, but not highly enough. These men deserved the Medal of Honor. Hazelbaker received the second highest honor, the Navy Cross, along with the highest respect of every pilot in the Wing. Costa was awarded a Silver Star.

VMO-2 pilots provided round-the-clock diligence to that recon team from their insertion until their extraction. My flight log indicates a total of 16 hours of flight time as we stayed on station throughout the evening. Al Barbour was one of the pilots who landed on the hill the next morning and reported having to work his skids around the bodies on the hill to find a flat place to rest the chopper. The ground troops reported bodies lying in piles around the base of the hill. When we checked the hill a day later, all the bodies were gone.

[Captain Howard V. Lee was promoted to major before his Medal of Honor citation could be processed. His story can be easily found on the Internet.]

The Groucho Marx incident was a Rubicon event for our squadron, the I Corps, the Marine Corps, and the Vietnam War. We all knew that operations around Marble Mountain and our little beach community would never be the same after that. MAG-16 immediately began shifting most of its focus to the Dong Ha area, where half our pilots were already located. For those of us available to come to it, Colonel Barden held an all-pilots meeting in the Marble Mountain ready room to emphasize the paradigm shift. Barden's talk turned into two completely different speeches. The beginning of his off-the-cuff remarks had a King Arthur ring to it, except that we sat at two long picnic tables. Barden told us that we were shining examples of everything the Marine Corps stood for, and our actions during the past few weeks had placed us far above any other men he had ever worked with. He said that we had proven to everyone exactly who the heroes were and, by contrast, we had properly identified the *goats*. His words flowed easily and not for a short time. When he began to ramble, we tried to help him close his talk by standing up to leave. While we were on our feet, he delivered the back half of his impromptu speech.

He apparently felt there was one more important thing his knights needed to know above all other considerations. This part of his speech was not as much fun nor as articulate as the first half, and I personally thought he should have quit when he was ahead. The gist of it was he wanted us to be absolutely certain we understood that no matter how stupid some of the orders might seem that we were being asked to perform, each of us was here for one purpose -- *to die,* if necessary, in the execution of those orders. Then, he went straight to his office without hanging around for chit-chat. We all looked at each other with puzzled expressions that all said the same thing: *"We love you Arne, but we ain't doing that!"*

[Arne Barden, our beloved skipper, retired as a colonel after 28 years of service. He then worked for General Dynamics as a systems engineer. He retired 15 years later. A victim of Alzheimer's disease, Arne died on 11 May, 2010. His son, Arnold W. Barden, Jr., was killed while piloting a Huey with the famed Seahawk unit in Vietnam on 20 September 1971. He was 25 years old.]

Much the delight of the fun loving flight line crew, Colonel Barden goes along with a mock ceremony to award a "Huey Gunship" award to Master Sargeant Lightfoot, who found himself in a fierce firefight while manning the door gun on a routine night mission.

According to official US Government and Marine archives, *Prairie* originated from Dong Ha, a series of battles to seek and destroy NVA forces in the foothills south of the DMZ. It lasted from early August through October of 1966. It was followed immediately by Prairie II, which was essentially the same, with more, but different, Marine ground troops gradually being brought into the action for another five months until March. The body count from Prairie II was 700 killed and 20 captured. Marine casualties were 93 killed and 500 wounded, primarily from mortar fire. Most of VMO-2's resources at Marble Mountain were shifted to Dong Ha to support these daily seek and destroy missions.

CHAPTER SEVEN

DEADLOCK OVER DONG HA

28 August 1966 Hue Phu Bai Sunday 2200

VMO-2 has two bases of operation now, and most of our flying is being done out of Dong Ha. We have a commitment of six gunships up there all the time. We also have a gunship assigned to Phu Bai, and it's my turn in the Phu Bai barrel this week.

I landed here this morning at daybreak and have flown six hours as a medevac gunship for a 34 and as a tactical air coordinator for troop lifts and recon insertions. Now, we are in an operation called Pawnee, which is taking place in the flatlands between Danang and Phu Bai.

One of the new pilots in the squadron found out that I was the embarkation officer. He approached me in a friendly way and said that he had been to embarkation school, too. That was a huge mistake. As soon as I could arrange an audience with the Skipper, we agreed that he should be promoted to that position. Unfortunately, that turned out to be a mistake on my part. The following day, I also received a promotion. One of the guys rotating home was the squadron adjutant. Normally, this is a legal position that usually implies a law background, but in this case, it meant that I would be in the admin office routing and reading, proofreading, and editing all squadron correspondence, both incoming and outgoing. I will be able to sign "by direction" for the Skipper and will need to be available for these dozens of pesky admin jobs in his absence -- all this in addition to my regular flying duties. Way to go, Boo! The only possible redeeming consolation is that my presence might be needed at base camp more than Dong Ha. They have hardback hooches with wooden floors at Dong Ha now, but it still makes the Amish look state-of-the-art.

We're losing 12 pilots in a couple of weeks, and that's not good for our already overstretched situation. It's difficult to keep a pattern going when we are bounced around for three or four days or a week at a time, but it makes the time go faster. I've been in country for six months, and September will be my "hump" month as well as my birthday. We don't celebrate things like birthdays over here. We should be like the Vietnamese who all become one year older on the first of each new year, like horses. They have a convenient way of celebrating everything at the same time in a two week celebration called TET.

We miss half our meals from flying so much, and I noticed that I had lost about 25 pounds since I've been here, from 180 to 155. Be careful what you wish for. I wanted to lose weight. The food is much better at Phu Bai than Marble Mountain for some reason. They have fresh eggs for breakfast and occasionally fresh donuts. I don't understand why there is such a disparity. Marble

Mountain is much closer to Danang's airport where food is delivered.

29 August 1966
Monday, 1400 Hue Phu Bai

I'm one of two Huey pilots up here for three days. We can never be more than five minutes from lift-off 24 hours a day. Being the wily veteran that I am, I devised a clever solution to ease the burden. I found a qualified Huey pilot from the 34 squadron who jumped at the chance to fly copilot with us and borrowed him to rotate in a three man standby. My copilot is Gus Plum, an experienced captain. Gus and I can rotate the pilot's seat and have a half day of slack time each day. Phu Bai doesn't have a beach, but it does have a great officer's club. I'm sitting at the club enjoying a cold Seven-Up while Gus takes the watch. If I knew we could keep this arrangement, I would ask to stay up here another week, but I've never had any luck volunteering for anything. The schedule officers at Marble Mountain probably think Gus and I are knocking ourselves out up here.

The O Club tape recorder is belting out another Beatles reel. John Lennon and the Beatles are in trouble from Lennon's commentary on the war. I guess it's tempting for entertainers to speak out when they stand so close to a microphone. As good as those kids are, they should stick to entertaining and leave politics alone. But, Great Britain is a free country, and you can't blame a person for saying what he thinks. That's what we're over here fighting for in the first place. If you're going to stand for freedom, you can't be a hypocrite. I hear that some Americans are sending money and medical supplies to the VC. Congress wants to make that a crime. This is quite a situation we have going here -- a real test of what we Americans really believe in. If you were to ask me, I'd say that every one of these people should have to spend a couple of years in the military.

3 Sep 1966 Saturday afternoon

On the 30th and 31st of August, I joined my buddies in Dong Ha again. Each time we go back, the Seebees have added a few more amenities and improved the living conditions. I returned to Marble on the evening of the 1st of September -- payday, but too late to collect my funny money.

My birthday, 2 September, usually falls on Labor Day weekend in the states. There's no such holiday here. There's also no such thing as Memorial Day, New Year's Day, Valentine's Day, Thanksgiving Day, or any holiday. They're all just days. Most of the time, nobody even knows what day of the week it is, except for Monday when we take a malaria pill. Three or four paydays can pile up before you get a chance to think about money. For the married men most of that is sent home to pay the rent and for the return postage to stay in touch.

One thing for sure, every day is flight schedule day,

and on my birthday, I was scheduled for a 0700 flight. It was to be a local TAOR recon, but it was cancelled for lack of aircraft and other priorities. So, by sheer *co-inky-dinky*, I had a leisure day on my birthday and decided to spend it on the beach. They have a supply of surfboards if you can believe it, and I had my first go at surfing. After an hour or so, I could see how surfing is done, but I don't know why anyone would want to do it more than once. I was exhausted from manipulating that board through those rough waves, getting up and falling down and swallowing sea water. A couple of our West Coast boys make it *look* easy, but they are not worth a damn at teaching someone from Tennessee. All I managed to do was return the board in one piece.

When the R&R situation came into better focus, I was given the Hong Kong quota on the 29th of this month. So, all in all, I had a pretty good 25th birthday yesterday.

I flew to Phu Bai this morning in complete darkness to repeat the same five days that I had just completed. My copilot, Major Ron Robson, is a brand new guy, just checked in. I will try to do a better job of showing the major the ropes, which is more than anybody did for me. They just set me on the bull. New pilots are checking in every week. Each one will receive his own unique initiation. I won't initiate them the way Goldfinger terrorized me on my first week in country. Robson is a pro who has five times the flight time that I do. It won't take long for him to climb the ladder. You can tell when a pilot has the right stuff.

Some squadrons are envious that senior officers fly as our copilots because their CO's don't operate the way Barden does. Then again, they don't wear blue bandanas. Barden considers experience and reputation over rank. The few times he has flown with me, he sat in the copilot's seat. This was a shock to me the first time we saddled up. His name was on the flight schedule as the pilot. This kind of behavior makes him enormously popular with the younger pilots, who like his rebel attitude. Barden feels that nobody knows the war better than the people fighting it. When Group Operations sends us a mission that doesn't make sense and takes up valuable resources, the bandana man will challenge them. The Group CO, Barden's boss, will meet with Barden to ask his advice on things. He may land that job at Group now that he is a full bird colonel, but I don't think he wants to leave his VMO-2 family.

For the third time in seven months, I may be leading the squadron in flight time with 115 hours, although we don't really keep up with that. We hear from some of the other squadron pilots who complain that they don't get to fly very much. A CH-46 squadron volunteered 10 of their pilots to ease our load. The high man in their squadron last month had 30 hours. They can only be our co-pilots, but that's better than flying alone. Hat's off to the man who came up with that idea. If they can land that complicated 46, they can sure land this pilot-friendly Huey. Having a backup in the left seat that can land the plane in an emergency is a handy insurance policy for the crew.

Deadlock (VMO-2) has earned itself a solid reputation over the last few months. Unique to Huey squadrons is the wide latitude for junior officers to exercise independent judgment. I am approaching the middle months of a 13-month tour. These are the months in which a pilot should reach his peak performance. By now we've had enough experience to know how to do the job and too much time left in country to be flying protectively like a short-timer. When Major Robson and I were talking this morning, I gave him my version of a perfect mission. The secret is to not waste a single bit of time, effort, energy, fuel, words, ammo, or emotion. There is a difference between being effective and being efficient. Effective means doing it the right way, but efficiency means doing it the right way as quickly as possible. After a complicated medevac, we are often surprised when we enter the flight time on the mission report that we were in the air only 30 minutes or so. VMO pilots average 600 missions per tour which is more than twice as many as the highest man in any other squadron. VMO-6 (Klondike) at Chu Lai has earned a similar distinction. With so much of our attention being focused in the north, they are being asked to help out at Marble Mountain. Most of the pilots know each other because we trained together as pups.

Because we're their lifeline, the grunts love the Hueys for their gunships, medevacs, and resupply. They know we'll come for them under any circumstances and do the job and then some. Captured VC documents confirm the enemy's opinion, *"The helicopters keep coming. There is no rest."* The two rotors make a popping noise that has a psychological effect. We could control the VC, over time, but it's those pesky regular NVA troops that are streaming through the DMZ that are taking over now. This is a new war, and those guys are well trained soldiers. We would be foolish not to respect both their cunning and their craft. I feel badly for them that so many of them will never experience a day of freedom. As Americans, we are each allowed to become the product of our own choices. Their choices are all made for them. The coming monsoons will provide some clues as to how well we can contain them.

On the 9th of September, the Marines will begin another operation further west of Dong Ha in the mountains near Khe Sahn. I have been over there a couple of times. It's very remote, almost in Laos. I don't envy those boys sitting out there in the middle of nowhere surrounded by thousands of invading enemy troops. Whose idea was that? Green Berets operating up there are trying to map and contain the supply highway that meanders through parts of Laos all the way to the Mekong Delta.

4 Sep 1966 Sunday

On our first day at Phu Bai, Robson and I were called out six times on day and night medevacs. An ARVN strike force northwest of Hue ran into trouble. An un-injured Arvin managed to stow himself onboard the medevac chopper to try to escape hell.

When they're caught doing this, they plead ignorance, which isn't difficult for them. Most of these guys were illiterate farmers when they were rushed into service, unlike the Ho Chi Minh faithful who've been honed in the art of guerilla warfare for generations. The choices are two for South Vietnamese boys -- the rice field or the Army. If they stay in the rice paddies, the VC will come get them anyway. The Army gives them a chance to get their hands on a little cash for the first time in their lives. (That pretty much describes what I'm doing over here.) None of them know the difference between communism and capitalism, and neither outcome would revolutionize their simple world.

In the mountains around the DMZ, in addition to our ARVN allies, we have two other groups that will rally to the American cause if the money is right. The first and most interesting are the Montangards (mount-n-yards). These men live deep in the jungles and are the direct descendents of the original inhabitants of Vietnam. There are places out there that have never come in contact with civilization. The Green Berets are good at recruiting some of these mountain people.

Montangards are similar to the Negritos that showed us the ropes in the Philippines. The Special Forces advisors go into their villages with an interpreter and some bartering capital. Then, they try to put together 30 or 40 of these hard core jungle rats and make a hatchet force out of them. They're honed in the art of survival and tribal warfare. Lopping off a man's head is an art form to them. After a few lessons with a firearm, the Green Berets have a ready and willing mercenary mini-army. They pay these fellows about three times what a South Vietnamese Army soldier is paid. They don't have to know that most of those missions are one-way trips.

A similar source of cannon fodder is the Nung. Nungs are Chinese mercenaries who escaped China for various personal reasons and fell in with other soldiers of fortune. Most of them live in the hills of Vietnam and are fierce fighters. Others are found in the cities hanging out in the pool halls and whorehouses looking for beer and their next meal, which in their pigeon English is "chop-chop." They also need money for their other secret pleasure which they refer to as "boom-boom." These fellows could be recruited fairly easily for 50 dollars up front and the promise of regular rations of beer, chop-chop, and boom-boom. A few items of clothing and a personal weapon and the Special Forces guys have an eager group of killers who just happen to hate the Vietnamese. However, they don't seem to have a problem with the Vietnamese women.

There are a few Cambodian men thrown among them who meander over the border to play the kill-for-money game. At Khe Sahn we see all these players among their interpreters and Special Forces advisors. They rarely make eye contact or speak to anyone other than their own kind. There is not an ounce of fat on any of them, and they love to strip down to the waste and sit on the ground, tribal fashion, with a loaded .45 between their legs. We see them playing cards on blankets spread out on the ground, just killing time, smoking C ration cigarettes, and chewing betel nut.

I escorted a CH-46 with a planeload of these assorted mercenaries on an insertion near Khe Sahn one afternoon. I felt as if I were working for the CIA. During the briefing in the Special Forces command bunker, I could sense that there were only two people (American advisors) who stood a decent chance of coming back. They already had their secret, *master disaster* pickup coordinates selected and gave them to the pilots at the briefing. I escorted the drop, but I wasn't included in the pickup a few days later, so I don't know the outcome of that mission.

Whenever I think of remote outposts like Khe Sanh, it reaffirms my decision to have become a pilot instead of an infantry officer. This hard-to-defend and difficult-to-resupply hilltop, situated in the "coffin corner" of the DMZ and Laos, right in the path of the NVA traffic pattern, is an easy target for mortars, enemy shellings, and sapper attacks. These isolated "listening posts" all remind me of Ashau Valley, which was constantly being harassed by the NVA and eventually overrun in a night assault. Who comes up with these satanic assignments for the grunts? *"Hail, horrors, I greet thee!"*

The music is blaring in the officer's club that Robson and I are using as a substitute ready room. Those floppy

haired Brits are by far the most popular. Anti-war or not, the men over here like John Lennon's music.

[Brigadier General Lowell English, my favorite general, was assigned the command of the Khe Sanh outpost and was in command during the eventual siege in 1968. The 77-day onslaught of the remote outpost lasted from Jan 21 until April. The eventual result was predictable and inevitable. The Marine generals had never been in favor of Westmoreland's idea to put it there in the first place. Lang Vei, the Special Forces camp near Khe Sanh, where I had supported the Green Berets on the drop into Laos, was overrun in less than 15 minutes by the NVA in 12 Russian tanks. General English resented Westmoreland's order to defend the area, which allowed Marines to be placed under U.S. Army command. Both English and Krulak regarded Khe Sanh as a trap which, according to General English, forced the Marines to *"expend unreasonable amounts of men and material to defend a piece of terrain that wasn't worth a damn."* General English died on September 25, 2005 at the age of 90.]

9 Sep 1966 Marble Mountain

Most of our flying yesterday was done at Dong Ha. We left after dark in weather so bad that we had to stop at Phu Bai to spend the night. A sea gull flew into the Plexiglas bubble on the way back to Marble Mountain, or maybe we flew into the sea gull. The reflection of

the blinking red port (left) running light off the white bird turned him into a "flaming missile" that absolutely scared the hell out of me. I'd have to say that the bird was a huge factor in our decision to land the plane at Phu Bai. My nerves were shot after that. Tomorrow, I have medevac and will probably go back to Dong Ha on September 12. Just trying to wrap my head around where I am -- thinking out loud.

12 Sep 1966 Monday 15:00

Yesterday, 11 September, they held the highly anticipated election in Danang, and I suppose, throughout the Republic of Vietnam. We saw the locals going to the polls as we were coming off medevac duty. We are not sure what they were voting on and not sure they knew either. The VC were supposed to terrorize the elections, and for three days and nights before the election, VMO-2 flew 24 hour border patrol looking for trouble. Dong Ha has taken a heavy toll on our available pilot pool. A day off after medevac is a thing of the past. You have to sleep whenever you can. Fortunately, I can sleep on a concrete slab, dumbing down with the best of them.

Recon team insertions are still the order of the day out of Dong Ha. When we aren't putting teams in or taking them out, we are scouting for new places to drop them. Many of the zones are booby trapped, so we have to strafe them with machine gun fire for precaution. One story involves a Huey pilot who landed in the elephant grass after strafing the zone and looked down between his legs to see a dead NVA "staring" up at him through the Plexiglas bubble.

We send two slicks and two gunships now on these insertions and are growing weary of flying into booby trapped landing zones. The few available clearings in the wooded mountains make landing a chopper a game of Russian roulette. The good news is that the flight leader is ultimately in charge of his mission, and a Huey pilot has the discretion to make the final call once he assesses the situation. This is where experience comes into play. We've learned to shoot up the zone *before* we attempt the landing. The element of surprise isn't working out there. So far, we have been the ones being surprised. The enemy is everywhere, and he's easier to manage on our terms -- while we're still in the air. We are cautioned to use discretion and have the guts to say *no* if the mission is too hazardous, but in truth, they all are. Life or death missions take on a code of their own and are not a quibbling matter. So it's rare for anyone to say no to anything. In the end, none of us wants to see Marines banged up or killed for no good reason. This isn't a John Wayne movie.

Yesterday, Puff Sweeney managed to clip a tree with his main rotor, and Captain Bob Brown caught his tail rotor. Nobody hurt, but two more planes out of commission.

14 Sep 1966 Dong Ha

Dong Ha is our new home away from home. I wonder who is perusing all of the skipper's correspondence while both of us are up here looking for places to put observation posts around the DMZ? A couple of months ago, this area was the Wild West. Most of the landmarks didn't have any names. Back in July when Puff and I wrecked that Huey, we were the only ones flying around out here in the badlands. We named most of the landmarks, and now, everybody calls them by the names we gave them: the Rockpile, Razorback Ridge, and the Punch Bowl. These are all prominent terrain features that we use to orient newcomers to the Quang Tri area, especially the fighter jocks (jet pilots).

"Just put those 500 pounders right along that razorback ridge just northwest of that rockpile. I'll go down first and mark it with some Willy Peter (white phosphorous rockets)." After a couple of weeks, those descriptions became proper nouns.

There is also a "Little Rockpile." Everybody needs to be properly oriented on the Dong Ha landmark vocabulary.

I keep a few Slim Jims (beef jerky-type bar snacks) in the map pocket of my flight suit and share them with the crew. They're salty, and they make you thirsty, which makes it easier to drink the warm water. Captain Brown's family sends him those round, red wax parcels of Gouda cheese that he shares with us during bridge games. Once you open cheese, you have to finish it because there's no place to keep it cool. The next day it will be nothing but a greasy spot. We have that same greasy-cheesy feeling when we pull our sticky selves off those rubber mattresses every morning.

Hygiene is a challenge. A toothbrush doesn't sound like much until you forget to bring one for a four-day trip. There's no drug store on the corner. Deodorant is a deal killer, too. I forgot that once, and in two days my flight suit was strong enough to fly by itself. These are just a few of the little things that occupy our thoughts when we're bored, which is whenever we aren't flying.

A few days ago at Danang, I flew a Mr. Hunt, who was a Code IV civilian and special advisor to President Johnson. He is involved in some sort of war crimes investigation. He sat in the left seat (copilot's seat), and his stomach was so big it actually touched the stick. This oversized, unpleasant man didn't appear to be thrilled with his assignment and seemed to want to take it out on me. He grunted his instructions for me to take him to Hill 55. I had to ask him to suck it in a couple of times in order to pull the stick back enough to control the plane.

"Okay Sir, I'm getting ready to lift off. I need just a little more back stick."

When I'm stuck with VIP's like this, I sometimes give them a special "tactical ride." I took Mr. Hunt over to Hill 55 with a few sharp banks to the left that forced him to lean on the door and contemplate his future in case that door accidentally swung open. I punctuated the landing with an unnecessarily big flare that caused the stick to press hard against his belt buckle. He didn't know any better, and it was fun for me. I may have been bored. Anyway, I thought he was a much nicer man after that.

When a congressman or a senator shows up for their re-election media opportunity, and they all do, they always requests a Huey tour of the Danang area for their entourage. The tour doesn't seem nearly as important as the photos of themselves and the media coverage. The aides, reporters, and photographers take a couple of valuable planes out of our fleet. It's part of our job to give that tour. One spectacle that I try to make sure they witness happens twice every day, early in the morning and again about dusk, coinciding with low tide.

The outskirts of Danang are somewhat primitive. Many of the residents near the beach come down first thing in the morning and line up along the tide line on China beach for their morning constitutional. There is a line of cheek-to-cheek squatters nearly three miles long. In a few hours the rising tide will flush all this activity out to sea. If the timing is right, I like to make a long low run down that coastline with my "Code 5 VIP," to kickoff his morning tour. They can't resist staring out the window in awe. At the end of the exhibit, I pull up sharply just so the congressman and his cameramen have the opportunity to check out their own plumbing.

"Is there any particular thing you would like to see today, Sir?"

His aides in the back are probably thinking, *"Take us back to Indiana."*

Hong Kong, however, has plenty of indoor plumbing

as well as spas. You can tell from my cynicism that I'm probably ready for a break. I will leave in a few days for five days of R&R on a luxury liner with an in-flight, Lew-Walt-style steak dinner served by gratuitous, round-eyed Pan Am hostesses. *Look out!* Lead me to the Hong Kong steam bath and massage parlor. I need to wash four months of this Dong Ha red clay out of my pores with a hot bath, a cold adult beverage, and some peace and quiet.

On 20 September, First Lieutenant John Kiser was providing gunship support for the VMO-2 medevac slick over a hot zone seven miles southeast of Danang. At exactly 1439, while engaging a target to secure the LZ for the pickup, small arms fire entered the honeycombed flooring of the Huey and exited through the overhead. Along the way, one of the rounds struck the crew chief's left wrist. Staff Sergeant Don Hankins never felt a thing when the round passed through the bone in his wrist and ripped off his brand new $25 Seiko. Kiser aborted the flight and called for a backup gunship in order to take Hankins to Charlie Med. Clearly in shock and still experiencing no pain, Hankins joked with the crew while his shattered tendons lay exposed outside his limp left arm. When he exited the plane at the hospital pad, Hank took 10 steps and passed out in the arms of the two men who came to assist him.

The next day, Colonel Barden and Doc Baker visited Hankins in the hospital and asked how he was doing. Hankins joked that he was okay, but he was plenty pissed off that he had lost his prized Sieko watch. Barden took the watch off his own wrist and handed it to Hank, and said, *"Here, take mine."* Barden was serious, but Hank was embarrassed to take the Skipper's watch and gave it back to him. A few minutes later, while Barden was visiting other wounded men, Doc Baker slipped back over to Hank's bed and laid his own watch on Hank's bed. On the way back to Marble Mountain, Doc told Barden not to worry that he had made sure that Hank received a new watch. Barden told Doc Baker in no uncertain terms to get his ass back over there and take that watch back. He gave the doctor his own watch and told him to make certain that Hank received the watch that Barden had offered him. Pieces of Hank's broken watch were eventually found inside the chopper and sent to him. The time and date were permanently frozen on its face, 20 SEP, 2:39.

23 Sep 1966 Friday morning Dong Ha

Our total pilot strength is now 27. The senior officers are Colonel Barden and five majors: Plamondon, Hazelbaker, Robson, Govani, and Cook. Of these, Cook and Govani are not yet qualified in the Huey model. When the other majors want time for their desk duties, all they have to do is request it. We have six captains: Brown, Davis, Thrash, Martin, Plum and Burkman. Burkman is out of the operational picture because he is now permanently assigned as General Walt's personal pilot. That leaves 15 lieutenants, three of which are not yet qualified, and six have been in country less than three months, which restricts them to copilot. We usually send three pilots on R&R each month, and one of our guys chases General Walt's plane. Our pilot commitment to Dong Ha is 10, and we usually have less than 20 airplanes effective at any given time. The bottom line from all of this is the lieutenants have no choice but to do most of the flying and not much flying is done at Marble Mountain.

Several key jobs, like aircraft maintenance and test pilots, are held by the captains, and they need ground time to handle those critical assignments. As adjutant, I have one of the heavier jobs but haven't seen my desk in six days because I have to pull my hitch up north along with someone else's. Two days ago I flew chase for Gen Walt from 0600 until 2130. We went from Khe Sahn to Chu Lai and all points in between. There wasn't enough time to drop by the VC barbershop for a 25 cent trim. (We call all the locals that work on base *VC*.)

Having bitched about all that, Dong Ha isn't that bad now. First of all, it's where my buddies are most of the time. We have activities. When it rains so hard that it's impossible to fly, we play mud football. We scrounge booze from the Seabees (who have everything) and run helicopter errands for them in return. One day we scheduled a mock recon flight in order to go out in the boonies and cut some wiener sticks for a wiener roast. It took two weeks for the mess chief to run down some hot dogs for us to have our weenie roast, only to discover that we didn't have any sticks. The marshmallows didn't make it off the supply plane.

To relieve the boredom between flights, we read our paperbacks and play chess, checkers, Tonk, Oh Hell, Acey-Duecy, poker, darts, and anything else we can make up. We play battery operated radios and listen to Peking Polly talk about how screwed up the Marines are. She said that all the "liberating forces" needed to do was to leave the Marines alone, and they would eventually destroy themselves. Whoa – that hurt! We work on our sandbag bunker, and make fun of anything that moves or makes a noise. When an O1-C spotter plane landed with half its port wing shot off, that entertained us for a whole day. Nobody was hurt. We had no idea any plane could fly with one wing.

We see elephants in the jungle. They look pink from the red dirt they throw on their backs to keep cool. We drop Special Forces into remote villages among aborigines who still live the way they did thousands of years ago. They know how to capture elephants and train them. We take pictures of these things that look just like the pictures in *National Geographic*. Still, it's nice to go back home to our beach front property and crash on my own bed, a real Vietnamese mattress that I inherited from Doc Zimpher. After lights-out, I find myself groping for my flashlight to find that little window on my Japanese Seiko watch that tells what day it is. It won't be long 'til my Hong Kong R&R on the 28th.

25 Sep 1966 Sunday

Today' *Stars and Stripes* newspaper featured a non-aviator friend of mine on the front page above the headline. Frank H. Adams, of Nashville, an aerial reconnaissance officer, was flying in the back of an Army O1 Birddog when his pilot was struck and killed by automatic weapons fire. The pilot had descended to have a better look at a man in a camouflage uniform.

"Suddenly, they started coming out of the woodwork," according to Frank. *"Three different groups were firing automatic weapons at us. There must have been 50 of them."* A split second later, the pilot slumped forward and called out, *"My God, I'm hit."*

Before Frank could unstrap his control stick, the plane was down to 100 feet. The dead pilot was slumped over the instrument panel, obscuring the airspeed and altitude indicators from Frank's vision. His foot was also pressed against the right rudder, which Frank tried to offset by pushing hard against the left rudder. Frank managed to fly the Birddog in a hard crab for about 18 miles until another Army pilot came alongside and guided him to an airstrip. Twenty five minutes later, Frank skidded off the runway and crashed into a pile of empty ammo boxes, flipping the plane over. He was unhurt. We had become good friends during our training at New River in North Carolina, but I have not seen him since.

In the same newspaper, the headline featured a picture of Soviet Foreign Minister Andrei A. Gromyko addressing the United Nations General Assembly rejecting a three point Vietnam peace plan presented to him by US Ambassador Arthur Goldberg. He told the assembly that the immediate withdrawal of all US troops in Vietnam was the only path to peace, pure and simple. *"Unconditional cessation of all bombing ... and the granting of the Vietnamese people of a chance to settle their internal problems themselves,"* he demanded.

Johnson signed a bill into law that would increase the minimum wage from $1.25 an hour to $1.40. The Dow Jones Industrial average closed Friday at 790. Typhoon Ida threatened to dump ten inches of rain on Okinawa with winds up to 94 miles per hour, and Tropical Storm Helen was pounding Japan. The Monsoon season is upon us.

27 Sep 1966, Marble Mountain

There is a large collection of paperback books in our ready room that people send. Some of us enjoy reading and discussing the same books. It's nice to have more to talk about than telling lies about how magnificent we are and what jerks other people are that don't agree with us. During my all-night operations duty in the ready room last night, I read Bel Kaufman's *Up the Down Staircase*.

Kaufman's book centers on a young, idealistic English teacher who takes a job in a big city public high school and sets out to teach formative youngsters about the passions of reading and writing. From day one, she is confronted with the realities of her unmotivated students, the incompetency of some of her fellow teachers, and the petty bureaucracy of the system imposed by an out-of-touch public school administration. On about page 20, I started thinking, *"Hey, this sounds like a metaphor for Vietnam."*

The book is written in epistolary form which means the story is crafted through letters, memos, and notes that allow the reader to piece the fragments together for themselves and draw their own conclusions. The out-of touch principal fires out regular edicts from his corner office in whatever untimely way he can make their lives as ludicrous as possible. The book is totally hilarious, and not unlike the real world. Especially ours!

The teacher reaches her breaking point when one of her favorite, and most promising students, is suspended for breaking an asinine rule by going up a staircase that the principal had declared to be a "down" staircase. Just as she is about to chuck the whole public school thing for a more sane, elite, private school setting, something happens to make her "get it," and she realizes that she not only can make a difference in peoples' lives, she already *has* made a difference in practically everyone she has touched at the school. The realization that she was being appreciated was an epiphany for her. And it changed her life.

It also tore my insides out.

I like a book that can bring you back from the edge of tears, send a message, and suddenly have you laughing out loud. This is such a book. Someday, I would love to be able to write that way.

This morning I received a trunk from Okinawa that I shipped from North Carolina on 14 January. Slower than a government refund check! I had given up on this footlocker. I can use the civilian suit in Hong Kong and my summer Marine uniform when, *and if*, I ever go back to the states. The rest of the stuff in the trunk is useless now. I plan to buy a tailor-made suit in Hong Kong and have it shipped home, but not by the military.

Today is like a beautiful fall day in the states, the kind that makes you smell pigskin in the air and makes you want to watch a college football game. Baseball is the only live sport on Armed Forces radio. Who has the attention span for that? I would love to listen to an SEC football game between UT and Ole Miss or maybe even a Vanderbilt game, although the result of that one would be predictable.

28 Sep 1966 Morning

First thing this morning, I shined my brass while the maid put my clothes in order for Hong Kong. She ironed my trousers, but I had to iron my own shirts after I witnessed her makeshift "steam iron" technique. She filled her mouth from a glass of water and sprayed it all over my trousers. *Whoa, back! Let's swap jobs.* You shine the brass.

I'm on standby today for VIP, and they have a Jeep ready to come for me if needed. The only thing left for me to do now is to show up tomorrow morning at 1130 for the manifest. I already stopped by sick bay to make sure my shot records were up to date. Good thing I did that, especially after I saw what she did to my trousers. Doc Baker said I needed only one shot for cholera.

For the first few weeks I tried to keep up with my flight time and count the missions for air medals, but after a while, it became meaningless. I think I have already earned 20 air medals. What the hell am I supposed to do with 20 air medals? After the first one, we don't even receive a medal. Instead, they give us a *"gold star in lieu of a medal."* *A gold star!* Sounds like grade school.

HONG KONG

30 Sep 1966 Hong Kong

I left Danang yesterday in a deluge that drenched my uniform completely in the first three minutes, then waited four hours in the open air terminal amid the swarm of swarthy Marines and the acrid smell of Vietnam. Eau de Danang, that ever-present fragrance of spent fireworks and human excrement that lingers in the nostrils.

My clothes dried in place on the three hour flight. The only emotion I remember was total exhaustion. I couldn't even muster enough energy to eat the little beef filet they prepared for us aboard the Pan Am DC-6. It was a burden to lift my hand with the fork in it.

This morning started with a 0730 breakfast at The President Hotel. The bill was under six dollars Hong Kong which is about a buck and a quarter. I think I'm going to like this place.

I've been referred to Rene'l Clothiers for my custom suits. They were on our US preferred vender list, and several guys on our flight have appointments with a hustler named Arvie, the owner. Arvie is an Indian whose family does the selling and fitting while the clothing is probably put together on a Cantonese assembly line somewhere in Hong Kong; one of those sweatshop factories, most likely, from looking at the prices. I can buy a custom Harris Tweed overcoat for 55 dollars and a suit for 60. Hong Kong is a shopping mecca and a trading center. The China Fleet Club has samples of the most popular items for military shoppers to see how much popular items *should* cost. If you can't buy the item from them, they will recommend where to buy it.

Arvie's chartered shuttle bus picked us up at the hotel. Tour cars were lined up for us, and we were invited to a gourmet Indian dinner at his family's restaurant. All ten of us are going including a colonel who has done this before and told us not to miss the dinner. Arvie instructed the driver to take us anywhere we wanted to go and to take good care of us.

The city tour had its ups and downs. Beautiful places one minute and heart wrenching poverty the next. Hoards of Chinese refugees in the Aberdeen district were snuggled up to luxury high rise apartments and a popular floating restaurant. I studied it all as though one day I may be called on to tell the world about this mess. But at the moment, no words would come. The only thing that I knew for certain was that my home and my family were far away. There was a sense of hopelessness in myself and in the poorest of these people. I couldn't blame them for begging for anything the tourists might have to give them. I didn't appreciate the tourists taking pictures of these people. I didn't want to be there, watching any of it. I could see why China wanted all that rice in South Vietnam, and I wished I had a couple of those big bags of it for the Aberdeen people. It was easy to see why many Asians would fight and die for it.

Shopping day was tiring and frustrating. Junk sitting next to junk! I stared helplessly in a daze, unwilling and not capable of making decisions. Funny thing, I know exactly what to do when that medevac phone rings, but suddenly I was immobilized and unmotivated. I wanted to do some Christmas shopping but didn't want to catch that Oriental shopping virus that haunts military men. Here, I can buy 12 tailored dress shirts from Arvie for 30 bucks, with monogram. I could start my own shirt business. But what kind of man really wants a monogrammed shirt? My mind was trashed. Why was I so worthless? Part of my ennui was psychological. I still had those beggars on my mind. I remembered a haunting quote from one of my college literature classes.

*"Providence sends a few people into this world ready booted and spurred to ride, and millions of others ready saddled and bridled, to be ridden."**

I was probably just homesick.

*(Quote attributed to a 17th century English politician on his gallows, just before he was hanged. It was later rephrased by Thomas Jefferson and many others.)

1 Oct 1966

My first fitting was first class, and Arvie had people swarming all over us with hundreds of fabric selections to choose from. Standing in front of that mirror, a full 25 pounds lighter than my normal weight, it never occurred to me that I would ever have a spare tire again for the rest of my life. I looked like Paul Newman, and as far as I was concerned, I would always be this size.

"A little tighter in the waist please!"

There's a big red star on the Bank of China building, the tallest structure in Hong Kong. The symbol of Communism! The very thing we are fighting against in Vietnam. Half the people here are Nationalists, and half are Communists. This is a British Crown Colony under a 99 year lease from China. Plenty of Brits, Japanese, Portuguese, Filipinos, and Americans operate freely, and they all seem to speak English. About 40 miles up the coast is the island of Macao, black market to the world. It sits along the same South China Sea that we swim in at Marble Mountain, and it's one of the richest places in the world. And then there's Arvie, our Indian clothing merchant who doesn't give a damn about any of that. He's just taking care of business and is probably smarter than any of them.

Hong Kong is in three parts. Mountainous Victoria Island is where the more wealthy residents live, the mansion-on-the-hill type thing. The industrialized Kowloon

Peninsula is separated from Hong Kong by the harbor. The only link between the two is the hold-on-to-your-wallet Star Ferry. The colony's agrarian district is called the New Territories, also leased from Red China in 1898 for a period of 99 years.

We drove all over the island, and I took plenty of pictures with my Canon QL 19. The Tiger Balm Gardens and the Floating Seafood Restaurant, where Steve McQueen was supposedly having lunch, completed our tour. I took pictures of all this, but exposed none of my film. I had a little pilot error loading the film. Again, no accident report was filed. After the tour I came back to the hotel for a nap, still exhausted. Later, the hotel bar was almost deserted, except for two couples at the tables and an old gentleman at the bar by himself. I opted for the bar. After some quiet time, I opened a conversation with him by asking if he thought it was a little chilly in the bar. He said he was from Finland and preferred this temperature to the current street temperature.

Well, okay! I guess I wasn't used to air conditioning.

We talked for three hours. He spoke five languages, and we were conversing in his fourth. He knew Swedish, French, German, English, and a "smattering" of Russian. He was a Finnish physician who'd once cured a patient from South Carolina by mail. He'd been just about everywhere but America and had spent the previous two nights in Tokyo and Stockholm, traveling alone on business. His English was quite good but more formal, and it took all my concentration to pull the meaning out of some of his sentences. He went off on a tirade about the French Impressionists and the deterioration of the arts in Finland. He mentioned frequent trips to Russia, and I was wondering if he was a Communist (not that I cared). He cleared that up by commenting on how peculiar it was that in Hong Kong the free world seems to have no problem trading freely with the Communists. He asked me if I knew what their formula was. When I suggested that the common denominator might be the almighty US dollar, he seemed puzzled by my answer. So we just went on in a sort of quasi-intellectual conversation in his fourth language with me in my first and only, trying to keep up with him. He talked about the commercialization of Japan in the last five years and even drew a picture of his dream home on a napkin. It was a curious blend of Russian and Colonial architecture. His picture brought my big Saturday night in Hong Kong to a yawning conclusion.

He was probably lonely, too.

6 Oct 1966 Dong Ha

I asked everybody in the room what day it was and received four different answers: Thursday, Friday, Saturday, and Monday. The names of days may not be that important. I'll just say it's Thursday.

The day after I returned from Hong Kong, I was back in the Dong Ha grinder flying night medevac. At 0200 I was hoisting a wounded Marine out of a 200 foot canopy while sandwiched between a 1000 foot cloud ceiling and a 600 foot hill in a situation that we like to refer to as a "bucket of worms." The tempo has intensified around the DMZ, and the Army has sent a detachment of four Hueys to add to our seven. We work pretty well together. Turns out, those guys are just like us, only better equipped.

While I was on R&R and Colonel Barden was in Hawaii, we had a squadron shakeup. While our beloved skipper was away on R&R, the group commander, Colonel Hunt, quietly slipped through the paperwork to have Barden transferred out of our squadron and into a desk job at Group. Now, they have the bandana man inside their tent pissing out, instead of outside pissing in. Most likely, it was just part of his promotion. After all, a full bird colonel shouldn't have to fly copilot to a first lieutenant for Pete's sake. All we know is that we lost the best skipper and best friend that VMO had. Spink raised holy hell and threatened to turn in his wings. Surprised us all! The next thing we knew, Spink was transferred to Group along with Barden. Now, he'll be flying a desk, too, so we lost another good pilot. Major Plamondon, a tall affable, dark haired man with a gentle disposition, who likes me, has been promoted to CO.

One of the first things our new commanding officer did was to call me into his office. He handed me two pieces of paper and shook my hand. I walked out of his office a captain. This was a totally unexpected surprise, and I didn't even have any captain's bars. Spink was also promoted and must have been better prepared because he had already purchased a couple of sets of his new insignia. He gave me a pair of his captain's bars and pinned them on me in the ready room. With this simple gesture, he and I had come full circle since February. He had a sharp wit, but he also had a more analytical, serious personality. I felt badly for not allowing myself the chance to know this warm and fuzzy side of him.

I took quite a ribbing from my buddies in the lieutenant fraternity. *"Hey, is it Captain Boo, sir?" "Here comes Captain Radley." "Look at that lieutenant with those captain's bars on." "Squadron, Atten-Hut!" "Can I have your old lieutenant's bars."* I put up with all this because I would be making some real money now, almost a hundred dollars more per month.

All my hoochmates have rotated back to the states, some of them 20 or 30 days past their rotation dates. There is a backlog of people waiting to go home, and there isn't a pipeline to replace them. I'm undergoing the veteran metamorphosis, becoming a teacher instead of a student. I find myself being more impatient with careless rookie mistakes. One of my copilots experienced vertigo in a cloud bank while I was looking for a landmark on a map. When I looked up, the Huey was in a 20 degree left bank. Fortunately, we were in a patchy cloud layer and in a valley. A helicopter isn't like a regular airplane that flies straight and level. It has to be constantly monitored.

Gus Plum had to go home for a month because his wife had a serious personal problem. We weren't told what. She had been having issues with his being over here in the first place.

As soon as the pilots reach the 13 month mark, they're usually cut some slack on the flight schedule and don't have to fly the hairy stuff. They call it *"closing out the flight book."* Some of the older guys have three or four kids at home, so you can bet your last dong (piaster) that they'll be taking advantage of that tradition, and I plan to do the same.

I took quite a ribbing from my buddies in the lieutenant fraternity.

8 Oct 1966 Dong Ha, inside the "Plamondon Bunker"

I'm in the new VMO-2 bunker at Dong Ha. It took us two weeks to build the five foot deep, 10 foot square sandbag fortress with three feet of sandbags piled on top of it. Heavily fortified on all four sides, our fortress has a sculpted dirt bench around three sides and four dirt steps leading down into the belly of this masterpiece. If the camp was overrun, we could probably hold out about 10 minutes with our 38 pea shooters until a sapper tossed a Russian grenade in here. It should be safe enough for the standard mortar attack, however.

It's not cave temperature, but it is cooler than anything else we have. Our new CO did the engineering and supervision on the construction project. One of his hobbies is working with wood, but all we had to work with is bags of sand. We don't know if he was thinking of our welfare or his five kids, but to his credit, he was the only senior man that lifted a finger to work on it. When it was finished, Bob (Beetle) Bailey took a pen and scratched an inscription over the entrance:

THIS BUNKER IS DEDICATED TO

MAJOR R.A. PLAMONDON

ANTI-HUMOUSLY

THAT HE MAY REMAIN SO!

I come down here on hot, muggy days because it's 15% cooler, and we keep the ice from the USS Repose down here. A good place to write and think! We have two commandeered Styrofoam boxes from the Repose filled with ice and cold drinks. The boxes were used by the medical corps to store whole blood. They have two-inch red letters on all four sides -- HUMAN BLOOD. We wondered if just the word *BLOOD* wouldn't have sufficed, or if perhaps they had a variety of animals to choose from.

The cold drinks are almost as valuable as human blood. Hydration is a major issue in this kind of heat, but for some odd reason, Marines don't care for the taste of warm water. We come down here to stretch out and nap on the cool dirt bench. It's better than sitting on an empty barbed wire spool. Our new barebones wood-framed hooch sleeps about eight guys and has no chairs or furniture. We sit on boxes, cots, or stools. We play nickel-dime poker at night on boxes until our sore butts and back pains send us to our canvas cots. My new rank hasn't earned me any special privileges.

CHAPTER EIGHT

THE SECRETARY OF DEFENSE

12 Oct 1966 Marble Mountain

While I was cat-napping in the general's lounge at the III MAF headquarters this morning, something monumental broke. Except for Air Force One, this is as hot as the VIP business gets. McNamara's coming. SECDEF, himself! I guarantee that nobody at VMO-2 knew about this when the flight schedule was filled out, or they would not have sent Boo Radley over here. I will be flying the second plane behind Bob Burkman, Walt's personal pilot. *"The sky is falling,"* and the Chicken-Littles are in a ten foot hover.

The first thing you learn in the military is not to believe the first thing you hear, so I would hope this is all a false alarm, at least on my watch. Nothing good could possibly come from a meeting between me and Secretary of Defense Robert S. McNamara especially for me. However, it would be fun to see the three-stars pee their pants when their boss pops in on them. The pecking order will definitely change, as well as who sits where in the Huey. I'll be the absolute lowest person on this food chain, of course.

The Alpha Dog doesn't exactly telegraph his passes for security reasons, so you never know what his plans really are. If he does come, there is no chance he will ride in my chase plane. I won't be able to give him the China Beach bathroom tour. But he will have a grand entourage, so I should have important people in my plane. I don't envy Burkman's job. Tagging along behind like a little brother is a piece of cake.

```
                    MARINE OBSERVATION SQUADRON 2
                       Marine Aircraft Group 16
                  1st Marine Aircraft Wing, FMF Pacific
                   C/O FPO, San Francisco, California 96602

FLIGHT SCHEDULE                           WEDNESDAY 12 OCTOBER 1966

ODO: CAPT DAVIS (0730-1830)          SDO: LT KNOWLES (1800-0800)
MTP: MAJ PLAMONDON

SUNRISE: 0639                              SUNSET: 1828
A/C NO FLT NO BRIEF ETD ETR  A/C COMDER    CO PILOT  MISSION  CODE  NOTE

       1-0   TBA  0700 W/D  BURKMAN         c/c       777     1R7   (1)
       1-2    "   0715  "   WILLIS           "        778      "     "

       2-0   TBA  0730 0730 MAJ ROBSON      HEALY     788     1T4   (2)

       3-0   W/D  W/D  W/D  BROWN           SMITH     783     1T4   (3)
       3-2    "    "    "   BARBOUR         BACCITICH  "       "     "
       3-3    "    "    "   LARSON          THRASH     "       "     "
       3-4    "    "    "   PLUM            GOVONI     "       "     "
       3-5    "    "    "   KIRBY           KISER      "       "     "

       4-0   TBA  0900 STBY COL HUNT        c/c       783     1R4   (4)

       5-0   1400 1430 W/D  CORLEY          BRADLY    783     1T4   (5)
       5-2    "    "    "   SWEENEY         MASSARI    "       "     "
       5-3    "    "    "   OSBORNE         c/c        "       "     "

       6-0   1830 STBY 0730 MELENDEZ        A/O       786     3V3   (6)
       6-2    "    "    "   BARBOUR         c/c        "       3T4   (7)

       7-0   0730 0800 W/D  MAJ COOKE       HENRY     783     1T4   (8)

NOTES: (1) GEN WALT
       (2) MED EVAC ESCORT  (TIL KLONDIKE APPEARS)
       (3) DONG HA
       (4) COL HUNT  (STBY)
       (5) DONG HA RELIEF
       (6) NIGHT TAOR
       (7) ESCORT  (NIGHT TAOR)
       (8) SLICK OR DIRTY SLICK TO DONG HA

       STBY PILOTS: BURKMAN, WILLIS, MAJ ROBSON, MAJ PLAMONDON, DAVIS, SWEENEY


DRAFTED BY:                     LT KEEFE
LT CORLEY                       SQUADRON DUTY OFFICER
```

344

The following morning . . .

Well, McNamara came to Danang. He showed up four hours earlier than expected, and then with only a 30 minute notice. The III MAF staff was in a panic. General Walt and his chief of staff, Brigadier General Jonas M. Platt, personally briefed Burkman and me for the pick-up of his party and for the possibility of a tour of the Danang TAOR.

After a tension-charged morning, McNamara suddenly emerged from out of nowhere. He looked like a disheveled aviator: greasy headed and needing a haircut. With him were generals Westmoreland, Katzenbach, two Navy admirals, and a bunch of other people I didn't recognize. McNamara rejected the standard offer of local tour and opted for a fixed-wing ride with the two admirals out to a carrier to spend the night. *Smart choice chief, they have ice cream out there.* What drove his decision to come all the way to Vietnam and then spend the night on a ship was not clear. But people at that level don't shoot from the hip, and this was not a casual call. There is another war going on in North Vietnam that's being conducted from platforms like the carrier Kitty Hawk. I'm sure those two admirals had more serious issues to discuss than ice cream.

We took Westmoreland and his party back to Walt's beach house to get reorganized. They had a major pow-wow that excluded the pilots, followed by dinner at Walt's beach house. The cook earned his money that night. This was the first time I'd ever been included for dinner. We had prime rib, shrimp cocktail, stuffed baked potatoes, green beans, a good red wine, and pecan pie with -- you guessed it, ice cream. Burkman and I dined in a small conference room with the generals' aides. Then, they had a private after-dinner party with coffee, drinks, and cigars. We could only catch glimpses of the party that spilled over into the kitchen area while we played Gin Rummy and went over all the plans for tomorrow. I was back at Marble Mountain by midnight after taking a planeload of loaded generals to their respective quarters.

Bright and early the next morning, McNamara was scheduled for a tour of the DMZ and the Dong Ha area. Since I was familiar with the plans, all four of them -- A, B, C, and D, Burkman asked me to escort him on the tour. Plan A called for two planeloads of VIP's, and I would take one of them since they didn't want to put all these important people in the same aircraft. I was to start with the US Attorney General Nicholas Katzenbach and everyone junior to him, while Bob would take Mac, Westy, Walt, and a couple of Navy admirals.

We assembled at 0700. After sorting out the pecking order, we made it to Dong Ha at 0800, right on schedule with Plan A. I could have taken some fantastic pictures of all that, but it doesn't look professional to be juggling a camera while flying the plane with your knees, especially with "codes" on board. We were received at Dong Ha by a small militia of high-ranking party crashers and every officer and enlisted man who owned a camera -- which was everybody at Dong Ha except the Huey gunship that was flying security overhead. The cadre of gawkers from VMO-2 poked their heads through the crowd, and they were easy to spot with their blue bandanas and slept-in flight suits.

Some higher-ups, who had all night to think about this, had other ideas about how the rest of McNamara's tour would be conducted. After much handshaking and discussion of the new *Plan "E,"* the entire senior command of the United States Army, Navy, and Marine Corps were ushered to their respective helicopters by as many full colonels and unit commanders as could finagle a ticket to the big show. Everybody wanted to see and be seen by Westmoreland and McNamara.

My fifteen minutes of fame fizzled fast. I was totally bumped. But some of the guys had seen me standing next to five-star Westy, and my stock shot up a couple of points, briefly anyway. There must have been 20 helicopters in their gaggle when they took off toward the Rockpile. I watched with both relief and rejection as my big brother, Burkman, flew off without me. A couple of CH-46's had about 40 reporters and cameramen stuffed inside. We never heard anything about what they learned out there. They could have saved a lot of trouble by asking the lieutenants.

The October 7, 1966 cover of *TIME* featured a picture of the Rockpile and a long article on the tough terrain around the DMZ likening the Marine assignment around Dong Ha to places like Guadalcanal. The 9th of July edition featured the bespectacled McNamara on the cover, looking somewhat pensive, if not perplexed. He was an accounting teacher at Harvard before being pressed into this service, and no doubt, the chief scorekeeper of the war of attrition. Maybe, those two *TIME* articles precipitated this trip to Dong Ha. McNamara didn't want some magazine reporter to know more about his war than he did. The issue that featured the Rockpile was a little dramatic but a good account, I thought. The best part was the way the writers used the names of the landmarks that VMO-2 nicknamed. The Rockpile, the Razor Back Ridge, the Witch's Tit, and the Little Rockpile were all given their names back in late June and early July. The Rockpile is becoming a symbol for the Vietnam War. They will fly close enough to have a good view of Helicopter Valley. Some of the 46 hulls are still there. I wonder if Walt will show McNamara that. Those were all the places that the Secretary of Defense wanted to see with his own eyes and take back to the Pentagon with him. We were told that they also landed at Khe Sanh, almost on the Laotian border, and close to The Trail. Very interesting!

Only one thing is certain about this visit by the head honcho: *they are cooking up something sinister for us in those hills.* It never fails.

Robert Strange NcNamara, an accounting teacher at Harvard before serving for two Presidents as Secretary of Defense, and the most likely architect of the war of attrition conducted by Westmoreland, became disenchanted with the war effort in 1967. A former Price Waterhouse consultant, he tried to lead the military with a business mentality. In his memoir on Vietnam, he admitted that he knew all along that the war was a mistake.

General William Childs Westmoreland was relieved of his command in 1968 shortly after the Tet Offensive. While his strategy of attrition may have been effective by statistical standards, his legacy suffered a humiliating blow when he was publically accused of underestimating the strength of the enemy and exaggerating enemy casualty reports in an interview by Mike Wallace on *Sixty Minutes.* He lived to be 91.

SAINT CRISPEN'S DAY

Oct 25, 1966

I'm probably the only Marine over here that knows that tomorrow is Saint Crispen's Day, the anniversary of the Battle of Agincourt, Shakespeare's Henry V story that helped lure me into the Marine Corps. This was a weather-related tale about a heavy downpour that determined King Henry's fate and saved his small band of beleaguered Brits. The spirited new horses that were carrying the French noblemen, who were leading the charge against Henry, lost their footing in the muddy terrain and fell into a useless pile at the bottom of the bowled battlefield while Henry's archers rained arrows down on them.

Who would the rainy weather favor in this war: the swarming regiments of North Vietnamese regulars slogging unchecked down Ho Chi Minh's new interstate highway or the sleek thoroughbred Hueys stuck in the Dong Ha mud unable to negotiate the weather to stop them? Only the mind of an English major could entertain itself with such a bizarre analogy.

26 Oct 1966 Tuesday, Saint Crispen's Day

Yesterday was a Monday that VMO won't forget for a long time. I'm sure it was one of the most colorful in our short history.

The day began early, as all of them do, with Major Cooke (a new pilot from the VMO training unit in California) launching at 0200 in bad weather to escort a UH-34 on a medevac pickup in the mountains around Dong Ha. The 34 completed its mission, taking his evacuee to the Repose and returning safely. After a little while, we became concerned about Major Cooke, who had not returned or reported in. The tops of the mountains were in the soup on a dark and ugly night. Major Hazelbaker, who is not exactly a brand new pilot but new to the Huey, was the operations duty officer, and most of the other pilots were asleep in the hooch. Hazelbaker decided to launch a search plane and took it upon himself to volunteer for it. That was a mistake. He was inexperienced in that terrain, and he managed to compound the situation by driving his Huey into a river.

By daybreak we were all in the air searching for all of them. Hazelbaker and his crew were pulled from the river with cuts, bruises, and broken bones. The plane was completely destroyed. We found Cooke, who had driven his gunbird into a tree at an apparently low airspeed. He and his crew were banged up, but none were seriously hurt. Cooke will be back in action in about

six weeks, and Hazelbaker broke his nose and rammed something through the palm of his hand.

The following is Major Hazelbaker's incident report of his flight into the water:

"I was the operations officer. The new Executive Officer hit a tree while escorting a medevac to Con Tein in typical bad weather in the dark of night. I launched, routinely, from Dong Ha, to find and pick up his crew. Anyway, my plan was to turn on the search light and fly the tree top radial to Con Tien; routine, except for the search light. I was on instruments and partial VFR. My copilot was looking for the tree line. I was holding 50 ft off the water and comfortable. The crew chief was working on the radios between the front seats. We were in a slick. I turned on the radial to Con Tein and felt for the switch to turn the search light on. I must have leaned forward a bit, wasn't used to feeling for the switch. Obviously broke my scan. When the search light came on, the skids were water skiing. My reaction was a quick back pressure on the stick and must have sunk the tail. The water, in cascading lights, flowed back over the windshield. We stopped. All four of us got out. 100% pilot error. The slick had settled on the bottom of the swollen, but shallow, Dong Ha River. Blades and transmission were somewhere forward. We four waited on top of the slick until daylight. I talked to my wingman, Major Robson, "Could you believe that I just landed in the river?" Or similar words and was assured that someone would come pick us up shortly. The one thing that I can't get out of my dreams, you all must have them, is when the slick came out of Dong Ha and hovered over our position, I helped the other three climb up, and when I grabbed the

skid and tried to climb up, I couldn't make it. A couple of Marines reached down and pulled me up. One said, 'that vest is sure heavy.' Lesson learned was to get rid of the vest when in the water.

The night before those mishaps, Bill Kirby and Ron Corley were flying home to Marble Mountain from Phu Bai and stopped to refuel at the Phu Bai fuel dump. In the dark, the crew chief mistakenly grabbed a pressurized nozzle used by the C-130's. When he activated the nozzle, it knocked him backwards and sprayed raw fuel all over the chopper. The plane was still turned up, and the turbine engine burner basket was an open fire pit. The whole plane lit up like a Christmas tree. The way I heard the story, his wingman sitting behind him saw the whole thing and pulled his plane into a hover to escape the anticipated explosion. The blast from his rotor wash blew the flame out. There were some tense moments as everybody scrambled to regain their composure. It was all over in a *flash,* and the crew inside the flaming Huey didn't even see any of it happen. After that, they decided they didn't need any fuel after all. They spent the night in Phu Bai to examine any damage in the light of day.

Another new pilot, Lou Larsen, had his engine flame out Monday. Fortunately, he was on the ground when it happened and not out in the jungle. He ran out of gas with the fuel indicator showing 200 pounds in the tank. Add faulty fuel gauges to our long list of concerns.

To cap off a spectacular Monday, Captain Bob Burkman, respected friend, confidant, all around good guy, and General Lew Walt's personal taxi-cab pilot, was summarily discharged of his VIP duty, on-the-spot, by our fearless three star commander. Bob said the general told him that that he was *"flippant, irresponsible, immature, and way too casual and cocky."* Don't you hate it when somebody knows you that well?

I'm not sure if Burkman's dismissal had anything to do with his performance during McNamara's visit, but I doubt it. Walt would not have taken that long to make a decision. Some of us are nervous about who will be tagged to replace Burkman. Every single one of us fits Walt's description of Burkman. Trying to eliminate myself from consideration, I told Plamondon that I was everything that Walt said Bob was, plus I didn't like being treated rudely. Plamondon said he wouldn't make anyone do it who didn't want to, but it would need to be someone who knew the ropes over there. He wasn't ruling me out.

All in all, St. Crispen's Day was almost as dramatic as Shakespeare's play without a single shot being fired. Peking Polly may have been on to something when she said that if the "freedom fighters" would leave the Marines alone they would eventually destroy themselves.

Four days ago, during a troop insertion south of the DMZ. One of the guys in my plane became overly excited and jumped out of the plane before we reached the landing zone. He misjudged the distance and jumped about 15 feet with heavy equipment on. I think he may have broken his back. Gus Plum landed on a stump and broke out the Plexiglas bubble. Jim Sweeney has two sets of rotor blades to his credit since our (or his) July tail rotor incident. We have had three planes grounded because of enemy fire this week, no injuries, but more downtime for the planes.

MONSOONS

Water, water everywhere! The monsoon season is upon us, contributing several inches of heavy rain each week to an already saturated South Vietnam. The weather is responsible for many of our flight issues. The roads now look like small rivers covered with mud. The rivers have spread out into lakes. Our TAOR around Danang looks like the Florida Everglades, and there are new waterfalls spilling out of the mountains. The rice paddies are one to three feet underwater.

We joke about the endless rain and are dumbfounded by it. We stare at it as if it were a train wreck and repeat the same thing over and over, *"I have never seen anything like this."* Then, it rains harder, so it's okay to say it again. You can't see through it. The tents leak. Everything is wet, and nothing can dry. It rains sideways in one direction, then suddenly switches directions. We try to cover things with plastic. Anything that resembles metal has rust on it. Paper wilts in your hand. Food spoils. Our clothes are soggy. Our books are mildewed. Our boots and socks are soaking wet. Our new hooch has mold already, and our skin has blotches of fungus that won't go away. The fence washed away on the beach at Marble Mountain. An entire bridge washed away at Dong Ha.

But, the jokes keep coming, almost as relentless as the rain. The beach is closed for swimming, and the outdoor showers are colder without the solar effect. When the generator floods, the electricity drowns. Once a week we might catch a glimpse of the sun but forget about the stars.

Our only entertainment is each other and the club at Marble Mountain. The newest craze at the club is a drink called a Flaming Hooker. Any kind of booze that can be set on fire in a shot glass, which is just about anything with enough alcohol, is lit with a flame. The challenge is to carefully sip the flaming time bomb from underneath the flame without setting yourself and the club on fire. Then, you are an official member of the flaming hooker club. It requires getting your head back far enough so that the flame doesn't touch the tip of your nose. Becoming tickled and snorting must be avoided at all cost. There are mustaches that have to be avoided, as most of the guys who like this kind of challenge are also fans of big mustaches. The many slips between the cup and the lips make these fire-breathing magic shows popular diversions, and they usually draw a standing audience. I say standing, because if you sit, you might be talked into trying it, or worse, sprayed with liquid fire. It's not a good idea to be directly in the line of fire without a flame retardant flight suit.

In the ready room, Chris Bradley and I provide most of the entertainment. We have already anticipated our Christmas program, and a choral group is being actively recruited.

31 Oct 1966 III MAF Headquarters

In 14 hours October will be history, stored in the few remaining brain cells I have left, along with the other seven dwarfs, March through September. I don't know if I'm being tricked or treated today, as ordinarily this would be Halloween, but once again I'm escorting Lew Walt's plane.

No, I'm not the general's new pilot. That dubious honor fell upon our good friend Mr. Bill Kirby, who, according to Plamondon's selection promise, apparently did not protest too much. *Thank you, Lord!* Burkman is back on the farm with the rest of us lowlies and now has to learn to be a fighter pilot all over again. Bob took his "demotion" in stride and chalked everything up to experience. Kirby will have access to more prime rib dinners but will have to trade in some of his sarcastic irreverence. Kirby is a good choice. He's as big a smart-ass as any of us, but he has another gear to go to when he needs it. He can be serious and professional when he has to play the game. No more days off. No more R&R. No more squadron life. No more nothing -- just round the clock VIP duty at III MAF Headquarters.

Lieutenant General Krulak, commanding general of the Fleet Marine Forces, Pacific (that's three stars) whom we nicknamed "The Little Giant" (because he's little), and probably the next commandant of the Marine Corps, was here this morning. When he's in Vietnam, he stays in the Chu Lai area and has a Huey pilot from

VMO-6 assigned as his personal pilot. We share our VIP war stories with his pilot, Brooke Shadburn, who tells us Krulak has a collection of swagger sticks. He carries a different stick with him each day. Swagger sticks were discouraged by Commandant Shoup in 1959, and they are considered by most Marine officers to be the epitome of military affectation. One of Krulak's sticks is a riding crop, commonly used to whip race-horses down the stretch. When he talks to Brooke, he sometimes unconsciously taps him on the shoulder with this riding crop. Unbelievable!

[Krulak named Chu Lai after himself, having been the General who first flew over the area and selected the site. There were no towns nearby, just a wide open area, so he called it Chu Lai, which means Krulak in Mandarin Chinese. (From the book *Brute,* by Robert Coram, 2010.)]

Kirby and I took all these generals to Air Force Ops to catch a fixed-wing plane to Phu Bai and Dong Ha. They wouldn't be going up there if they weren't cooking up something special for us which I will probably write about later. That seems to be the pattern. Wherever the brass visits, somebody is going to have to saddle up for drama.

Speaking of drama, President Johnson came to Vietnam on 26 October, a couple of weeks after McNamara was here. Mac may have suggested it. Presidents like to pay their war a visit at least once during their term in office, especially if polls are sagging. It wouldn't look good to ignore this tradition. But the President did not make the Marines and the I Corps part of his visit. I guess he heard about all of our mishaps on the 25th and wanted no part of VMO-2. On the way back to Washington from his SEATO Summit meeting in Manila, LBJ met with Army troops at Cam Ranh Bay, a relatively secure area in a deep water bay a couple of hundred miles north of Saigon and way south of Danang.

People coming back from R&R in the Philippines tell us that Manila was steeped with excitement about the Summit meeting. Johnson and his bosom buddy, Premier Ky met with Ferdinand Marcos and the heads of state of Australia, Korea, Thailand, and New Zealand. These are the Domino countries that we don't want to fall to Communism, remember?

The three day summit meeting was to drum up support for Vietnam and encourage these allies to send more warm bodies for the war of attrition to help bring *"peace to the Asian and Pacific Areas."* One benefit to coming to the III MAF headquarters is that you can read these things in newspapers that we don't see at Marble Mountain.

The President's visit may have loosened up some supply planes. We had charcoaled steaks at MMAF last night and carved roast beef the night before. We have a new mess officer and the menu has been punched up. Apparently, the right person in charge of the mess hall makes all the difference.

[Lieutenant General Victor H. (Brute) Krulak, the stick-wielding commander of the Fleet Marine Forces and arguably the best strategist of the Vietnam era, coveted the title of commandant. His meeting with President Johnson, in which he proposed the mining on Haiphong Harbor, may have deprived him that promotion. His son Charles, born in Quantico in 1942, eventually became commandant in 1995, 13 years before his father died. Brooke Shadburn, Krulac's personal Huey pilot from VMO-6, was killed on 5 April 1967, after having asked to be relieved from duty as Krulak's pilot. Shadburn had protested repeated incidents in which Krulak tapped him with a riding crop, and he asked to be returned to regular squadron duty. A short time after he returned to VMO-6, the medevac plane he was piloting triggered a booby-trapped 500 pound bomb in a landing zone. The bomb completely obliterated his medevac slick and killed 17 other Marines.]

3 November 1966

We have television at Marble Mountain. They've been talking about this for months, but nobody believed it. The recorded programs are allegedly beamed from a plane in Saigon, but who really knows how television works? Snippets of World Series reruns and part of a *Ted Mack Amateur Hour* are all I've seen so far. There's a TV in the line shack for the troops, and all the clubs have one.

Last night we had another wiener roast at Dong Ha. Despite Chris Bradley breaking a quart jar of French's mustard on the floor of our hooch, we turned it into an "event." A special task force took a Huey out in the boonies to cut some wiener sticks, since there was not a stick of wood or a coat hanger inside Dong Ha's barbed-wire perimeter. I was the pilot, and Lou Larsen was copilot of the Code IV wiener-stick-snatch-and-grab-mission.

Major Dave Andrews took his K-Bar survival knife to cut the sticks, while Bradley provided security with a broom from the hooch that was supposed to be an AR-15 automatic rifle. We landed a few hundred yards outside the perimeter in the nearest place where there appeared to be enough scrubby bushes to cut some sticks. Larsen and I sat in the turned-up plane and watched with tears running down our cheeks as Bradley, the exhibitionist, cut a bush to camouflage himself and shadowed Major Andrews providing "armed-escort" with his broom. This set the tone for an outrageous evening of foolishness that went late into the night.

With new people coming into the squadron we are starting to rebuild the camaraderie that was decimated by a wave of departing pilots and the loss of Barden. For a while we had the charisma sucked out of us.

Immediately following an invigorating outdoor November shower, there's a small window where you have to towel off with a stiff wind blowing between your legs. It keeps you on your tippy-toes. The water we use for showers at Dong Ha has been collected from standing water and is not much different from bathing in a clear rice paddy puddle. (Keep those shot records up to date.) They're trying to put heating elements in the shower barrels, under the assumption that the generator would work long enough to heat it. Like the TV, we'll believe it when we see it.

One of the pilots received a letter from his wife admonishing him for not writing his thank you notes to friends and family on appropriate thank you cards rather than using our standard lined notebook paper. He read it to us and asked us what we thought of it. We were astonished. It made us realize how difficult it was going to be to fit in back home with people who would dispense that kind of advice to a combat soldier.

8 Nov 1966

Every pilot develops his own style with experience, and we each have our own way of doing things. I've tried to apply my own brand of common sense to some of these dangerous missions. There are several things that I do differently from most of the other pilots. For example, when I am flying the medevac slick, I think it's very important to get into the LZ as *quickly as possible*. Not just because there is a wounded soldier down there, but because the more you buzz around, the more the enemy has time to set up a surprise for you. A treetop approach is less likely to draw fire than a high altitude approach.

I let my gunship escort reach the landing area *first,* so he can check out anything suspicious near the landing zone. If Charlie is out there, *let him see the guns first* and not the slick. The pickup plane doesn't have any guns, and the VC aren't stupid. They know a medevac slick by now, and they know that they land near green smoke. In fact, they have been known to pop a green smoke just for bait. Let bad guys see the gunship first. It might make them head for their spider holes.

When I am about five miles out, I ask the ground troops to toss a red smoke outside their perimeter in the direction of the bad guys. This, too, might make them think we have come to kill them, not pick up a medevac. This not only tells me where the good guys are, but it also gives me the wind direction. I know they can't toss a smoke grenade far from their own position. As soon as I decide on the direction of the approach, I ask for another smoke for the LZ, and I set my wingman up to make a gun run while I come in from a completely different direction about treetop high. They might think there are two gunships coming for them. The idea is to use the gunship as a diversion, and sneak into the LZ before they know what's happening. While I'm making the pickup in the zone, my wingman has time to set up for another gun run. I try to time my departure out of the zone just as he starts his second run. Hopefully, this keeps Charlie focused on digging a hole instead of using me as target practice.

I try to block out the combat part and stay completely focused on flying the chopper. The combination of efficiency and surprise finishes the task quickly, before the enemy has a chance to make a plan. These ideas are not entirely original, but a combination of the rebel tactics that the lieutenants decided would improve our chances of success, part of which is our own survival. We have seen our share of body bags and don't want to go home in one.

During the pickup, I try to look straight ahead and gather an awareness of the scene outside the chopper. Some of the sights and smells of the wounded can be overwhelming. I look back there as little as possible.

Most of the pilots don't have any medical experience, and the last thing we need is to become emotionally devastated during a medevac. On the way to the hospital, after the pickup, I ask the ground troops if they need any more firepower on the enemy positions. If so, I contact some fighter jocks and hook them up with the ground troops. Let them have some fun with that. All in all, this simple system sends a message to Charlie (VC). *If you see a Huey and you decide to mess with it, we will not only come for you, but we have friends that will come for you, too.*

In my early days over here, I flew copilot with some people who would spend 10 or 15 minutes circling the landing zone like a buzzard. Then, they made a conventional, into-the-wind approach, like they were landing at Chicago O'Hare or a training hop at New River. I don't think it matters which way you approach, as long as you turn into the wind and have everything under control at the last second. The slick doesn't weigh that much going in, so unless the wind is howling, it's not a big concern until *after the plane is loaded.* Once you know where the landing zone is, come in so nobody knows where you are until you are on top of the zone; then, you can do a side flare to lose airspeed or a complete 180 if you have to, and just sort of flop into the zone. All Charlie hears is the popping of those rotor blades -- which sounds like gunfire anyway.

The point is, don't telegraph your plan. It's like the old joke about never calling your wife from a bar. You'll be yelled at on the phone and ambushed again when you come home. Sneak in late with your shoes off.

COMPLETE LUNACY!

The real character in our squadron is Chris Bradley, a one-of-a-kind comedian who attracts all the attention. He looks the part of an entertainer with his tall, gangly looks and oversized schnozz, and he is always up for fun. Bradley invites insults in order to sting his assailant with one of his corny African proverbs.

"When the elephant leaves the jungle, the buffalo is a great beast." Or this one: *"Only a fool would test the depth of a river with both feet."*

Do not, I repeat, do not enter into a battle of wits with Bradley unless you are heavily armed. We called him Ichabod for a long time, until one day we saw a gaunt figure walking across the tarmac in the pouring rain with his poncho hood pulled down across his face. I was in the ready room and told everybody that it looked as if we were being visited by the Grim Reaper. All he needed was the scythe. *"Grim"* is all we ever called him after that.

It's been quiet around Danang. We joke that the VC are using the city for R&R, implying that it's in their best interest to keep their playground peaceful. The truth is that it's quiet because our airplanes are elsewhere. Pilots from VMO-6 (Chu Lai) have to come up here to help us out when we need it, a common occurrence lately. Our commitment to Dong Ha is for 10 planes now, and with the two we provide for General Walt, sometimes we don't even have ten planes to send. The generals at Dong Ha have been cued in on the Huey taxi service, so we provide that service to the field commanders as well. The 34's are taking on more of the role of the medevac slicks, and the Hueys provide gunship support. Barden and Spink, in their new roles at group headquarters, may have something to do with this new trend.

Dean Martin starred in tonight's outdoor movie, *The Silencers*, a spy spoof with Martin as Matt Helm. Some of the guys are into the James Bond phenomenon and talk about every detail as though it's nonfiction. This movie threw some cold water on the Bond mystique by poking fun at it. Somebody needed to punch some holes in the Bond persona. Sean Connery couldn't lift the gear that a bush Marine carries every day.

I'm reading a book called *Live with Lightening* by Mitchell Wilson. It's over my head, but I'm determined to finish it. Who knows why we become attached to some of the things we read? Escapism, I guess. Jose Melendez likes flying saucer books, and you have to be prepared to discuss aliens if you spend time with him.

11 Nov 1966

Someone wrote a letter asking why we wear green underwear. Tidy white makes a great target, for one reason, especially in the jungle at night if we ever found ourselves in that unfortunate situation.

Occasionally, pilots are assigned temporarily as forward air controllers (FAC's) to embed with the troops to call in tactical air support. Our experience as helicopter pilots assumes we have some special knowledge of fixed wing capabilities. That's a tall assumption since we are helicopter pilots. This isn't a job any pilot would want and another good reason to stay on the skipper's good side in case he received a random allotment to fill one of those FAC billets.

The 10th of November is the birthday of the Marine Corps -- a busy day for the band. Yesterday, we were 191 years old. If we were back in the states we would all be hung over from last night's big party. Here, the celebration was more austere. The Seabees constructed a big sign for us. We mustered in formation and listened to a recorded message from the commandant. Then, we had a steak cookout and a sparsely attended party with an oversized sheet cake -- chocolate, underneath all the red, white, and blue icing. The Marine band from Danang played for us for about an hour while we kept time with sticks and empty soft drink cans. We had a short poker game and hit the sack. Yee haw!

After lunch today I headed back to Dong Ha for the new seven-day rotation. We've added Khe Sanh to our rotation. This was originally a small group of Special Forces crazies on a small mountaintop outpost about 20 miles west of Dong Ha near the Laotian border. Under Westmoreland's instructions, the Marines have assumed control of this outpost. The word is that they aren't thrilled over the idea of being stuck out in the middle of nowhere guarding a piece of remote jungle in the middle of no man's land. They've added a runway for C-130's to land and expanded it over the last several months. Some of the ultra-crazy Army Special Ops guys have set up an even smaller camp a couple of miles west of Khe Sanh called Lang Vei.

Martha Raye has been over here for a couple of weeks. She will entertain tonight at Dong Ha. Kirby and Walt will have to perform that celebrity dance. Her stage will be, of all places, on top of the Plamondon Bunker that we worked so hard on for the last couple of months. There is also a group of professional baseball players making the rounds, and Kirby has been flying them around for the last couple of days. Ron Corley asked Kirby to try to get some autographs. I'm scheduled to fly my favorite VIP, General English, tomorrow. He's an exceptional man with no swagger stick and a pleasant demeanor. He actually calls me by name and asks me personal questions about my wife and my son, Kirk. I'd like to think the general requested me as his pilot, but I know better. Once while I was running an errand at Danang Airport, he spotted me walking to the plane and asked his Jeep driver to give me a lift.

I managed to make contact with Kirby while writing this book. In order to validate the story of the baseball players, I asked if he remembered their names, and he flashed me this email:

Bud,

The players were Hank Aaron (Braves), Stan Musial (Cardinals), Brooks Robinson (Orioles), and Joe Torre (Cardinals, Braves, Mets). Also Mel Allen (Yankee lead broadcaster, late 40's to early 60's). I had lunch with them at Gen. Walt's residence. That's how he entertained non-

military guests. I don't remember anything about auto-graphs, however. No opportunity for that and nothing the general tolerated. For celebrities, it was usually a quick, courtesy in and out, all business.

Here's how I got to go to occasional celebrity lunches and dinners: the general didn't like empty chairs at his table, so a sometime collateral duty of his Huey pilot was "seat filler" when there were fewer than 10 places oc-cupied. Like King Arthur's, the table was round. These were short-notice invitations, and casual conversation with guests was not encouraged. No lingering over coffee. He regularly served broccoli with parmesan cheese. I still like it that way.

FYI: Walt had special affection for Martha Raye, from when she started touring Pacific islands during WW II. She showed up several times. She was the real deal, I thought. By Vietnam her career was about finished, so publicity didn't matter. Still liked hanging out with the troops, I guess, and still had the time. Maybe you knew she was authorized to wear an Army Nurse Corps colonel's uniform. Don't know why. She had the right connections. If she needed a ride anywhere in I Corps, the general took care of it. Once sent a plane to Saigon for her. Grumbled about it, but couldn't say no. Bill

Bill Kirby left the Marine Corps immediately after his return from Vietnam to continue his education. He worked as a part-time flight instructor and charter pilot while he completed graduate studies in English Literature at the University of Connecticut. He completed a long career as a fundraiser in 2002 and continues to work in public education. An accomplished fly fisherman, Bill and his wife Toni have two daughters and five grandchildren. In February 1967, General Walt sent a brigadier general to meet with Kirby to inform him that Walt wanted to present him with an award to recognize his outstanding performance as his personal pilot. He offered Kirby a choice of a second DFC or a Navy Commendation Medal. Walt presented the medal, along with a letter of recommendation in his own handwriting, on Kirby's last week in Vietnam. During my tour of duty, Kirby was the only one of Walt's pilots to receive such an honor.

General William Lewis Walt was featured in the May 26, 1967 issue of *Life Magazine* in its cover story, praising the success of his combined action company initiative to win the hearts and minds of the Vietnamese people. Lew Walt served as the commander of the Third Marine Amphibious Force and the Third Marine Division until June of 1967. He was eventually promoted to assistant commandant of the Marine Corps and was awarded a fourth star by President Nixon, the only assistant commandant to receive such an honor. He lived to be 74. The following email from Bill Kirby adds depth to the character of this extraordinary Marine and the impression he made on the people who served close to him.

"From late October 66 to February 67, I spent every day with General Walt with no days off and no R&R. He was totally committed to advancing the complex mission of his Marines in I Corps, to maximizing their performance in battle and civic action both, and to keeping them healthy and whole in dangerous situations. To inform himself, Walt preferred first-hand briefings in the field, and used his Huey to visit even remote units. He held his subordinate

commanders to a tough standard, perhaps a near impossible one. Pity the battalion or regimental commander who wasn't ready for the general's questions. He had little patience, and it was a lot easier to be a rifleman around Walt than an officer. Walt reserved his rare moments of tenderness for the wounded Marines he visited frequently at the Danang Naval Hospital, and to whom he personally awarded the Purple Heart."

17 Nov 1966 Phu Bai

I just got back from a five hour flight without shutting the plane down. Longest flight I've had in a long time. We inserted four recon teams and extracted two others. One team was in a fire fight surrounded by NVA, and we successfully managed that without hurting any good guys. We had to abort one insertion due to bad weather; too risky, especially in light of the previous mission. It was a full morning with plenty of excitement.

CHAPTER NINE

LANG VEI

21 November 1966

There's a typhoon hanging in the South China Sea about 500 miles away that's expected to make a direct hit on Dong Ha. Ironically, we have mixed feelings about it. A typhoon could do more damage to the enemy than we could. If it went north of us, it might hurt their supply lines north of the DMZ or do a number on Haiphong Harbor. We'll see which side God is on, if or when it actually arrives. Right now, the typhoon is stalled out, killing time and not bothering anyone -- just like we are.

Tomorrow morning I have been asked to take two Hueys to Khe Sanh for what was described as a *"deep-recon insertion."* So deep, in fact, they are doctoring up the airplanes and painting over the Marine logo on the sides of the aircraft. We have been asked to also remove our names from our flight suits, so this should be interesting. I suppose we could refuse to do these clandestine assignments, but these are high priority tasks that they don't hand out to just anybody. The intrigue and mystery add excitement, "re-tell" value, and high drama that can be more interesting than our paperback novels. In other words, it makes for good story-telling around the ready room picnic table.

23 November 1966 Khe Sahn

I'm not sure I should even be writing about the events of the last two days. They have convinced me that we have entered into a new and expanded phase of this war; at least it's new to me. I feel as if I have just returned from McNamara's secret bunker.

I was the flight leader of a two plane detachment sent to Khe Sanh to support a clandestine Army Special Forces unit operating in a remote mountainous outpost within spitting distance of Laos and the DMZ. We were asked to remove all forms of personal identification, empty our pockets, and remove our dog tags. The planes had been stripped of identification. The maintenance logs and serial numbers were removed. Our landing coordinates took us to the Special Forces camp at Lang Vei, about seven clicks further west of Khe Sanh. This place was literally in the exact center of no-man's land. If you wanted to give the world an enema, this would be the spot to plug in.

As soon as we landed, we were met at the choppers and directed to an underground command center the size of a small town high school basketball court. On the way to the bunker we walked past a group of about 20 or so bandito mercenaries who were sitting cross-legged on ponchos near the entrance to the bunker. They were playing cards for paper money and smoking cigarettes with their .45 pistols shoved between their legs, supporting and underscoring their manhood. An Army Green Beret lieutenant was standing nearby with a hand-held radio keeping a close eye on them.

The command bunker was alive with communications equipment, stacked three or four components high in a great semi-circle with several operators listening to the incomprehensible zapping and buzzing coming out of them. The scene resembled a page out of Jose Melendez's space ship novels. The bunker was dimly lit, but the radios were crackling with energy and their multi-colored lights provided most of the light in the bunker. A short, burly, no nonsense, Green Beret major was in charge. He seemed like one of those officers who had been passed over for promotion a few times and stayed perpetually pissed-off. How else could he have drawn this godforsaken assignment?

The copilots behind me were wide-eyed, as I was, and we all had the feeling that this bunker was connected directly to the CIA or the Pentagon. Was this McNamara's bunker? While the major was briefing us on the mission, he was interrupted half a dozen times by a voice in his headphones. Several times he put one side of the headset up to his right ear and barked out a mouthful of acronyms I'd never heard before. Whatever business we were involved in was certainly going to be serious business with this man in charge. The major was taking his orders from someone with super-charged huevos.

Our mission was to provide gunship escort to two CH-46's that would be taking three Special Forces officers and a hatchet force of 35 of those jungle rats to drop them onto a small hill within three or four clicks of the Ho Chi Minh Trail. They showed us an aerial photo of the site, and the trail was clearly visible in the blown-up picture. In fact, it was no trail at all. The dirt road was wider than most of the streets in my hometown. The hatchet force would then perform a delicate snatch and grab mission to capture a couple of stragglers and bring them back for interrogation. The mercenaries were to be the kidnappers and would do the delicate job of snatching the prisoners and dragging them back to the Americans. They would then high-tail-it to a pre-determined secondary zone for extraction, a safe distance away. The pilots were instructed to return to the command bunker after the insertion and standby to extract them after they had the "package." This might be hours, or it might take days.

The weather would determine the time of insertion, and the highly constipated major would make that call at a time of his choosing. We were not invited to wait in the clandestine bunker, which appeared to be built to withstand a small atomic bomb. Instead, we were told to sit by the planes, within earshot until further notice. Whatever they were smoking in that bunker, they didn't give us any.

The CH-46's were standing-by to make the troop insertion and had already been briefed. My little section of two Huey gunships would provide fire support in case the testosterone loaded Green Beret cowboys found the hilltops of Laos a little less than receptive. The major wanted one of the Hueys to make a dummy run, sort of a diversionary landing, to make sure the zone was secure enough before the cowboys went in. In other words, we were to make a mock landing and hover in the zone for a few seconds to see if we drew fire. (At this point, I'm thinking maybe I should have lobbied harder for the job of General Walt's personal pilot.) If I drew fire, then a secondary plan and different course of action would be necessary. *No kidding!*

All this brilliant strategy had been devised in that underground spaceship by America's best and brightest soldiers. After the briefing, we retreated to our planes and were told to be ready to go at a moment's notice. The weather would be the determining factor. Every thirty minutes or so a Green Beret captain would come out of the bunker and look up at the sky and murmur something into a hand-held radio. After about two hours of this looking up and muttering, I decided to gather all the pilots together for a private discussion. I suggested that after we became airborne, the constipated major notwithstanding, that we would ultimately be in charge of the flight portion of this mission, so we might as well have our own plan. I could see relief in the faces of the 46 driver's. My wingman and I were going to go ahead of the 46's and not behind them. They would wait at a safe distance away while the two Hueys made low passes on either side of the LZ before I circled back around and into the wind for a fast taxi across the zone to appease the major. My wingman would be covering me during this maneuver. If all went well, the 46 leader would then make his approach and landing while both Hueys flanked the 46 with alternating low passes drawing attention away from the zone while he made the insertion. If there was any shooting involved, the mission would have to be aborted.

If the stuff hit the fan during or after the insertion, it had already been made clear to us that the only thing we were to concern ourselves with were the three Americans. That was fine with us. Hopefully, the "advisors" would be smart enough to exit the plane *last* and not first.

If there were only those three to pick up, the 46 would not make that pickup. The faster, more maneuverable Huey, i.e., me, would spend its ammo to lighten its load to accommodate the Americans. The scary part of all this was that we were given explicit instructions that under no circumstances would we leave any American, dead or alive, in that area. I wasn't thrilled with the idea that our crew chief and door gunner might have to leap out of the plane to go after some of these characters.

After lying around in the chopper until mid afternoon, one of the copilots suggested that we could fly out there to check the weather at the drop zone. I wasn't too keen on volunteering myself as the leading man in this little romance, but I had to admit that it made more sense than looking up at the clouds miles away from the drop zone. I suggested that the copilot who came up with the idea go over and tell the meteorologically impaired captain his idea and added that one of the Green Berets should go along with us, so he could communicate the information directly with his boss. It took another 30 minutes for that information to be processed inside the "intelligence" bunker. Finally, one of the Green Berets came out and said that the major had decided to launch a recon flight to see what the weather was like around the zone. It was also his idea that the recon leader should go with us. My copilot looked at me and winked.

We flew westerly for longer than I expected. Boundary lines were not obvious on the maps we were given. We were definitely going into a place where we wouldn't need our dog tags. There was less than a 1000' ceiling with a solid cloud cover, and I felt as if we were being squeezed between the rising mountains and the ominous clouds. Finally, we saw the landing zone, a smaller hill between two larger mountains on either side, about two miles from Ho's freeway. The tip of the high ground on the western side was already slightly obscured by ground scud. I could see why they had chosen to land in that saddle because the trees had been thinned by either a defoliant or a bomb blast. But was it safer with high ground on either side?

We had a small space in which to operate four aircraft with high ground on two sides and no bailout areas. We were also far away from our main support network. Personally, I would have made the insertion the next morning, but I was not in charge. It would be almost impossible to call in fixed wing support if we needed it, and there was not that much daylight left in this day in case of trouble. I wasn't sure that fixed wing support could even be an option since we were not in Vietnam anymore.

The major must have wanted that promotion badly because less than an hour after the airborne weatherman reported what he had seen in the landing area, he mustered the hatchet force for the drop. On the way back out to the landing site with the troops, we caught a glimpse of sunlight through the bubble. The big ball was about five fingers from the horizon, which I figured was less than an hour of daylight.

We did the insertion exactly as the pilots had discussed without incident. No additional adrenilin was needed. Afterwards, we were back before sunset and ate our first meal of the day and retired to our makeshift living quarters. The crew chiefs preferred to bed down in the planes.

Around nine o'clock we were ordered back to the command bunker immediately. The radios were cracking again. The hatchet force had come under fire and had taken heavy casualties. One of the Green Berets was dead, and another had been shot in the leg. The two Green Berets, along with about half of the mercenaries, were humping their way to the emergency pick-up zone in pitch black darkness about two and half clicks (30 football fields) to the northeast, through heavy jungle. It would take awhile to go that distance with a wounded man. We puckered pilots were told to be prepared to launch at any moment, according to the major, who was now belligerent because they did not have their dead comrade with them. The code of any elite force is to leave no man behind, but now they were also playing high stakes poker with the rules of the Geneva Convention. If this recon leader made it out of there alive, he was going to join the major on the short list of Green Berets to be passed over for promotion.

We waited. We waited -- with the worst possible scenarios playing in our heads. At 0200 we were told that we would not launch before dawn. For the remainder of the night, we heard massive explosions and saw flashes of light through the clouds, all coming from the direction of our LZ. When we arrived at the bunker just before dawn, the major was curiously calm. Overnight, he had called a "homerun" on the LZ and everything west of it, including Ho's highway. They dropped every available bomb from every available plane on top of that LZ and the larger mountain to the west of it. When we returned to the site, it was unrecognizable. The two landmarks were gone, flattened like a parking lot. No one near any of those three hills could have survived that barrage.

We escorted a single 46 out there to pick up the two Green Berets and what was left of the hatchet force, who had humped through the night to a safe distance at an incredible speed and had no doubt called in the air strike. The 46 took the wounded to a medical unit. We came back to Khe Sanh and were told by the major that we could go home. We took our time and had a leisurely lunch. They actually had a cook at this isolated outpost. After all, they were the *Army*. The Marines would have had canned lima beans and ham.

With all the pressure off, we joked that we could go anywhere we wanted now and do anything we pleased because we had no identity. We wondered how many infantry soldiers had actually done that very thing. We were temporarily incognito, just like all those college kids hiding out in Canada. We had helicopters and plenty of ammo and fuel. Where could *we* go for a few days and hide out? We were in the twilight zone with no one to report to.

No one to report to! So this is what real freedom felt like? Freedom was exactly what we were fighting for in Vietnam, but so far, I had felt very little of it. Reality set in quickly, and we wanted to go back to see what had happened to our wallets. My poker money was in there.

We listened to the VHF radio on the way back and heard Johnny Rivers' hit song *Secret Agent Man*. *"They've given you a number and taken away your name."*

The 1962 Geneva Accords had declared the countries that bordered all of Vietnam neutral, and, therefore, off-limits to any type of military involvement. This did not stop Ho Chi Minh from enlisting Laotian revolutionaries to join with his forces to create a system of passageways that connected North and South Vietnam and bypassed the demilitarized zone. As the conflict escalated so did his network of roads which became known as the Ho Chi Minh Trail. Aerial reconnaissance and covert Special Forces units were monitoring these activities, but their efforts were being hampered by the dense foliage of the tropical jungle. An operation called Tiger Hound which dated back to November of 1965, involved massive bombing and defoliation tactics determined to halt the progress of Ho's Trail. While more bombs were being dropped in 1966 than in all other wars combined, millions of gallons of herbicides were also sprayed on tactical operations areas and "enemy rice crops." One mission described a highly successful attack in northern Laos on an "enemy rice crop" that destroyed 4000 acres just before harvest time. *"Enemy rice"* is rice that is up to something, I suppose.

The herbicide called *Orange* did not achieve its more sinister brand, "Agent Orange," until after the war. While we were winning the hearts and minds of the farmers in South Vietnam, we also destroyed over 20,000 acres of *"VC rice,"* which infuriated organizations supporting the International Rice Research Institute. No information on these deadly toxic defoliation tactics was made available to the pilots or to the troops that had to slog around in it, nor was any consideration given to the health hazards for our troops, the populous, the environment, or our adversaries who were exposed to it.

I do remember this; there was not a more beautiful place on God's green Earth than those tropical jungles in the mountains of Laos, Cambodia, and Vietnam. Sometimes, when we were flying between two mountains, we might see a spectacular waterfall shooting out of the side of one of the hills and dropping 200 feet or so into a crystal pond below. Pure, unadulterated wilderness! Well -- almost unadulterated, anyway!

OLD SALTS

While VMO-2 and its pilots were preoccupied with the Ho Chi Minh Trail and the NVA problems of the northern portion of the I Corps area, VMO-6 out of Chu Lai, already shorthanded, was being asked regularly to supply planes and pilots to Marble Mountain for priority missions in our neglected Danang tactical area. While I was at Dong Ha on the 14th of November and Major Plamondon was our commanding officer at Marble Mountain, Tony Pecoraro was one of two pilots assigned to assist with our squadron workload. The story that unfolded on that day would make VMO history, and it involved one of the most decorated pilots in all of Marine Corps aviation. I was able to hear pieces of that story from others but had never heard it directly from Tony until 2009. Here is the story in Tony's words:

"By November 1966 some of us were becoming Old Salts in our squadron. All the original VMO-6 guys were gone, and there were about six of us who had been in the squadron for almost 10 months, and we were the work horses of the squadron. There were only 10 pilots left and we were supposed to have 22. We flew every day and some nights without a break. Most flights did not have a copilot. I remember flying with the disbursing officer, and once with the chaplain in the left seat. They wanted to get a taste of combat, and they liked to take pictures to bring home.

On the morning of November 14, Gordon Chadwick and I were asked to go to Marble Mountain to help VMO-2. We were told to take two gunships to VMO-2, and we would pick up co-pilots there.

Off we went. I don't remember who the lead pilot was, not that it mattered, but we arrived and landed at the tarmac at VMO-2 as we had done several times. We walked in to the ready room, and the operations officer said they were glad to see us as they were running ragged and needed our help. He said he had a mission for each of us, and he handed us each an envelope with a mission description and contact information. I asked him if he had a co-pilot for me, and he said he did not.

My mission was a truck convoy escort, something I have done many times and had never had an incident. For this reason, I thought flying with an empty left seat would not be a big deal. I was in a hurry to get going, so without talking to Chadwick or asking him what he was doing, I fired up my Huey and went to work. I made radio contact with the convoy, and everything went according to script. The convoy had a smooth ride with no enemy contact. I stayed with them until the last vehicle pulled in to its destination and then said my "adios" and headed back to Marble Mountain. After landing, I air-taxied to the VMO-2 parking area to refuel. On the way to the fuel truck, I noticed that the atmosphere was eerily different. Everything was quiet and completely still. Something was making the hair stand up on the back of my neck and arms. I can't describe, it but I knew something was terribly wrong. As I was shutting down the engine, I saw a group of three or four officers, two of them wearing khakis, walking toward me. When I got out and approached them, they told me that Chadwick had been killed.

I was dumbstruck and shaken. What happened? We

each got a mission envelope, and mine went as smooth as silk. Chadwick was a quiet guy and an experienced pilot. We were not that close, maybe because I am anything but quiet, but on this day we could have been brothers. They told me he was flying as a gun support in a troop insertion. The CO of MAG-16 had asked to fly as his copilot. They thought they had been shot down while making a gun run.

The CO was still alive, but Chadwick was burned beyond recognition. Doc Brown, the VMO-2 squadron doctor, asked me if I could fly back to VMO-6 and get Gordon's dental records, so they could make a positive identification.

Chadwick was kind of a loner, and now I felt like I knew him for the first time. Flying back to Chu Lai alone, I started sorting through the many questions flashing in my mind. What if I had gotten his envelope? If he had a real copilot instead of a non-qualified passenger could things have been different? Was he trying to impress the bird colonel? Or worse, did he let the CO make that gun run? How would we ever know?

I flew back to my squadron and gave everyone the news. No one cried. No one was emotional. Everyone seemed to assimilate the facts of the incident and processed them the same way we processed the other hundreds of events that had bombarded us for the last 10 months. They asked me if I would take our own squadron doctor back to Marble Mountain, so he could be the one to identify the body with dental records. I flew Doc Moffert back that night and returned after the Doc did his thing. Suddenly, I was the reclusive one, and all I could think about was how fragile and insignificant we all are.

The next day Chadwick's belongings were packed and shipped back home to his family. In less than a week, a new pilot was in his cubical, living in his space, sleeping in his bed, as though Gordon Chadwick had never existed.

Chadwick was the third pilot to be killed in our squadron in those last few months."

As told to me by Tony Pecoraro in 2009.

I did some further research after talking to Tony to find out what happened to Chadwick's copilot. His name was Colonel Kenneth L. Ruesser, our MAG 16 Group Commander and one of the most decorated pilots in the history of the Marine Corps. He had been shot down in three different wars and stories of his unprecedented flying feats can be found easily on the Internet.

Colonel Reusser apparently wanted to be on the scene to direct and coordinate the recovery of a downed CH-46 on what would turn out to be his last combat flight. The 46 had been shot down the day before. Chadwick's Huey had stumbled into a perfectly executed ambush prepared by the North Vietnamese. I found Harley L. Wedel of Fairview, Oregon, who has written a short biography of Ruesser which includes details of this incident. With his permission, I include what he wrote:

"Heavy fire hit them instantly and killed the pilot (Chadwick). Ruesser was hit in the leg with a large caliber round, and the chopper's controls were shattered. The only place for the chopper to go was down. Slamming into a rice paddy, the chopper was immediately engulfed in flames. The fuel-fed fire swirled into the cockpit from behind, and Ruesser found his shoulder harness quick release

mechanism refused to let go. The Huey was broken and partially crushed, and the men in the back were trapped in the flames. Knowing if he was to see another sunset, he would have to rescue himself. Ruesser leaned back into the flames hoping to burn through his unyielding harness. As the fire became more aggressive, it melted the Styrofoam lining in his helmet, badly burning his scalp and ear, and eaten its way down his neck and shoulder. Yet he still was not free.

Over and over he lunged against the burning harness until, with one final heave, it parted, allowing him to escape the cockpit and flop into the cooling waters of the rice field. Though his flight suit was still smoldering, Ruesser began pulling and tugging to free the men in the back, all the time being fired upon, and being hit again by small arms fire from the North Vietnamese from their hidden positions. Across the paddy, a corpsman with the ground Marines, ran through a hail of fire and knocked Ruesser to the ground. After rolling him around in the rice paddy, he picked him up and carried him to another CH-46 and evacuated the colonel to the nearest medical unit. He was in critical condition with burns over 35% of his body and two bullet wounds.

That night Ruesser overheard the doctors saying that there was no way he would live through the night, but this die-hard Marine recovered with skin grafts and reconstructive surgery to live until 2009."

26 Nov 1966 Phu Bai

Steady rain for two days. We go outside as little as possible. Anyone with active kidneys is going to be wet one way or another. Our weather minimums are regarded more carefully since the Cooke/Hazelbaker fiasco when they flew their planes into the ground. Pilots who are too aggressive in bad weather usually end up on the hospital ship Repose. Some of the clouds have trees and rocks in them. There is a saying about being lonely in a crowd, but it can be very lonely in a cloud. And when you find yourself in one, you can only hope that you are the only lonely one.

We play cards on days like this. Bridge is popular for the serious moments, and a card game called *Smoke* when we're really bored. Smoke involves cheating as much as possible without being caught. Each time you're caught, there is a five point penalty, and as soon as someone shows some promise of winning, the others gang up on him. Friends betraying friends can only end up in loud, funny arguments which seem to be the sole point of the game. Nobody has ever won a game of Smoke, which means nobody ever loses, but it's a guaranteed shouting match.

We had our Thanksgiving dinner at Dong Ha on the 24th. Not exactly like home cooking - more like the first Thanksgiving without the Indians, primitive, but festive. It was another typical out-of-place holiday in Vietnam. I flew 5.6 hours and about seven missions at Khe Sanh that day, and later that night I went to Phu Bai for an all night medevac standby.

On the 18th of November, at Marble, MAG-16 requested that one of our pilots with ten months experience come over to take a desk job with Barden and Spink in group operations. This is a 12-hour-a-day and sometimes all-night job with no flying. There are three people that fit that description, me, Gus Plum and our CO, Major Plamondon. Naturally, the CO isn't going, so that left me and Gus Elihu Plum. I wasn't around at the time so Plamondon sent Gus. Not a bad choice since Gus's wife has had some problems since he's been over here. That can't be helping Gus's frame of mind. So at least Gus was taken out of the shooting war.

Plamondon has five kids, and he has pretty much taken himself out of the high risk adventures. Of the three people who came to the squadron together in February, I'm the only one still flying strikes. I wouldn't be cut out for that group job. There isn't enough humor over there for my oddball personality. My smart mouth would get me in trouble. I like the idea of being both in and out of the mainstream as a squadron pilot. Fly my missions -- leave me alone!

I knew that Tony had been disgruntled at Chu Lai for a long time. The episode with Chadwick hadn't helped matters. A few days ago, when he was sitting around the ready room at Chu Lai complaining, a call came in to fly a chaplain to the scene of a helicopter crash.

The chaplain was to deliver last rites to a pilot who was pinned inside a CH-46 that had overshot a landing zone on top of a steep mountain and crashed halfway down the mountain. The 46 came to rest on a thin ledge. The wreckage was precariously teetering on a sliver of land with a badly injured pilot trapped inside.

When Tony's Huey arrived at the scene, a small group of troops was assembled. He and his copilot had to sit down and slide on their hands and feet to get down to the site. They were surprised that nobody seemed to be making the slightest effort to rescue the pilot. The chaplain didn't even attempt the steep trip down to the ledge. The trapped pilot was in bad shape but still very much alive. There was a 1000 foot drop from the chopper to the trees below. The only thing holding the 46 to the ground was a large rock that was pressed against the instrument panel -- the same rock that was pushing the instrument panel against the pilot, pinning him inside. His legs were so badly broken that both his feet were pointing in the wrong direction.

After a careful analysis, the situation did seem hopeless, but Tony was not about to let this man die without a fight. They were waiting for an Army Crane (large helicopter) to fly out to perform an external lift with a cable hoist to pull the crashed chopper off the side of the cliff. Tony felt that the rotor wash of the hovering Crane could dislodge the plane. If the 46 started sliding down that mountain, there would be no way save the pilot.

Tony took charge of the rescue and called off the Crane. He ordered the men to find some tin snips and to bring the hacksaw blade from the Huey survival kit. Using crude tools, he hacked his way into the cockpit, only to find a thick piece of armor-plating in the way. He then devised a plan to dig a tunnel underneath the 46. Once inside the tunnel, he was able to cut through the skin of the plane and access the cockpit from underneath.

He now had a better view of the large rock that was holding the instrument panel of the plane against the pilot. He ordered the men to dig a second tunnel to the rock in order to maneuver it. Inside the second tunnel, the men would be able to adjust the rock and free the pilot. Tony positioned himself underneath the pilot and asked them to move the rock that was pinning him. Everybody on the scene knew that if the movement of that rock upset the precariously perched helicopter, our hero would be in serious trouble. But Tony was confident, and his adrenalin was pumping. He ordered them to remove the rock anyway.

Working as a team, they wiggled the rock far enough into the freshly dug tunnel to free the pilot. Then, Tony dragged the injured pilot out to safety through the first tunnel. Enough of the rock was still in place to prevent the chopper from slipping off the mountain. Still, the job was far from finished.

The ledge was too small to land a Huey, and the men could not drag the badly wounded pilot all the way back up the mountain to Tony's Huey. Tony selected a suitable spot where he thought he might be able to hover safely enough for the others to load the man into his Huey and crawled on his hands and knees back to the top of the hill. He and the copilot and wide-eyed chaplain then flew down to the site and hovered dangerously close to the side of the mountain while the others loaded the wounded pilot aboard the chopper. They then carried him to the hospital. Thanks to Tony, no last rites had to be administered that day.

I told Tony that I would submit his name to be entered into the smallest book in the world, *The Book of Italian War Heroes*. He was recommended for the Silver Star, the third highest award for heroism, and I hope he receives it because he earned every bit of it. Less than one week later, Tony was given the job as the R&R officer in the Philippines and will spend the rest of his tour in a plush office in Manila, behind a Philippine mahogany desk. He has already made arrangements for Helen and his son, Tyrone, to join him for the balance of his tour. Well done, Tony!

In 2009, I sent Tony an email at his home in New Jersey asking him to confirm the story from my 44 year old journal.

"The story is pretty much the way you wrote it. The pilot of the 46, whose name I never knew, but would love to see him again, was a very brave man. Both his legs were crushed and turned in the wrong direction. He never complained. I told him we would get him out of there and he said, "Yeah; right."

We finally used the saw blade from the survival kit to cut away the skin of the 46. When I went back to pick him up, I had the crew chief throw a smoke grenade down there, so I could see the wind direction. The crew chief chose red smoke which caused a tense moment. That was the color we normally used to mark enemy positions. Hovering at that altitude, and trying to get the skid close enough to the ground, and wondering if my rotor tips were going to clip the side of the mountain gave me a few long minutes of pucker-time. My legs completely turned to rubber when we finished the job. I remember the feeling of relief when I turned the stick over to my copilot. All the energy was instantly sucked out of my body."

Tony Pecoraro left the Marine Corps in 1968 and took a position with Union Camp as a manager trainee in Allentown, N.J. After two years, he founded a corrugated box company with his wife, Helen. They had no money, no customers, and no real plans. Through their hard work and ingenuity the company became very successful. Trenton Corrugated Products has thrived for 40 years and is now run by the second generation of Pecoraros. They have also been successful in racing and breeding horses on their 25 acre farm in Crème Ridge, NJ. He continued his passion for flying and flew his own private aircraft until his recent retirement. Tony and I have managed to reconnect through the writing of this book and have become close friends again.

CHRISTMAS CHOIR

7 Dec 1966 Dong Ha

On the 30th of November, Major Plamondon was replaced as interim CO by Lieutenant Colonel William F. Harrell. This was not a demotion, as the job calls for a lieutenant colonel. Major Bob held the job exactly two months and is now back to being, XO, second-in-command. Of the four pilots who rode in on the plane together to Danang, Tony and Gus are now sitting behind desks, and Plamondon is our squadron XO. Yours truly is flying weiner stick missions, but we're all very much alive and kicking.

Six pilots who were tired of moving back and forth decided to volunteer full time at Dong Ha. Al Barbour spearheaded this movement and cleaned out his Marble Mountain hooch to underscore the commitment. He brought in his stereo system, so we can have music when the generator is working.

About two months ago, we were told that there would be a third Huey squadron, VMO-3, that would take over our Dong Ha commitment in November, so we could focus on the business of securing the Danang area. They keep extending the promise. It may be January or February before that happens.

We have a scraggly little Christmas tree with decorations and some stockings hanging around, as if Santa would actually land on our rickety roof. We receive fruitcakes in the mail, which we eat instantly because it reminds us of home. Other popular holiday items are spiced cider, cookies, and hot cocoa with mini-marshmallows. We heat the cocoa on top of an old Kerosene heater. Except for our location and the reality of what we do, we manage to have fun with a great family of guys who love each other but would never actually say it, precisely like any ordinary, dysfunctional American family.

There are plenty of artillery guns close by that are constantly working targets. The veterans are accustomed to the sporadic booms but occasionally somebody yells, *"Incoming,"* just to watch the rookies scramble. They figure it out after a while.

Good news! Cease-fires are planned for Christmas, New Year, and Tet. This is what we are being told, but I'm being sarcastic, of course. It speaks well of our fine leaders that they would want to work something like that out for us. How about weekends off too, and maybe knock off work at five. Now, you understand why we have to laugh or go crazy. Nobody over here could possibly take a ceasefire seriously. We need to *go hard* or *go home.* Most everybody over here would take either one of those choices in lieu of a political "cease fire."

Last month we started a 'Mustache by Christmas' contest. Mine turned out red and thin on the right side. Comical! Some have already quit the contest out of humiliation.

10 Dec 1966 Saturday Dong Ha

The sun broke through and invigorated us. We flew several missions, and by noon our muddy field had dried out enough for a late afternoon game of rugged two-on-two football. I collided with a pass defender and skidded though a pile of sharp rocks and gravel, tearing up an old flight suit. Al Barbour stepped in a hole full of water up to his knee; lucky he wasn't hurt. Trying to be annoying, Corley stood on the sidelines casually chunking rocks at the players. Our only football rolled into a muddy culvert and mercifully ended the game. Al volunteered to retrieve the football (his) by being inserted 10 feet into the muddy culvert on a long wooden plank. We flipped the plank over on him claiming it slipped. He took it well and went straight to the shower.

23 Dec 1966 Friday Marble Mountain

I just returned from a week at Phu Bai. As soon as I landed and turned in my flight reports, I was tagged for what was described as a top secret mission. The weather is so bad I had trouble finding my way in from Phu Bai. Somebody needs to tell these people that it is not possible to complete a mission if you can't see what you are doing.

24 Dec Saturday Christmas Eve 1966

This morning, Christmas Eve, the sound of rain was still on the metal roof. I walked over to Bob Williams's tent. He's the Bell Helicopter rep, and he has a small television. Nothing was on TV, but we listened to a couple of Christmas songs before I had to go to an eight o'clock meeting in the ready room. I had to fly a short test hop to check out a plane with a faulty hydraulic system, as one of my collateral duties is "test pilot." I received this maintenance pilot designation a while back which I tried to avoid but couldn't. It's another job to do. After a plane is repaired or has a part replaced, it has to be tested by a maintenance pilot. Even though we have a maintenance officer, he can't do everything, so we need four or five of these maintenance pilots. The term *test pilot* is somewhat of a misnomer, and it might infer that we are systems experts. That may be true with some of the pilots, but not me. The crew chiefs are the experts, and I simply do what they tell me to do.

My clandestine flight in the middle of the night prompted questions around the ready room as to what I was doing since I was the only plane flying in that bad weather. I told them that it was codenamed Rudolph and was top secret. This prompted a long sarcastic discussion about flying reindeer, how Santa kept his pipe lit, and who could remember the words to *"Twelve Days of Christmas."* We played around with clever lyrics changes to Christmas carols, but we couldn't get anyone to volunteer to type the funny song sheets. Nobody wanted any extra work.

Writing home is more difficult than ever. There's nothing left to say. Most of the missions are similar, except for the one last night, and that's classified, so I can't write about it -- might get *fired*. Let's just say it involved the delivery of a "package."

My sister asked me to write a letter for her to read to her church group about what Christmas is like in Vietnam. I wrote that if Christmas was on a Monday we would take a malaria pill. It was a long sarcastic letter, and I didn't feel good about it after I mailed it.

Time goes by faster when I'm flying and staying busy. When I sit down to write, especially during holidays, I seem to babble, very much like I'm doing now, and talk about coming home. That's not good. I need to stay sharp. It reminds me of the summers I spent as a counselor at Culver Military Academy. We had to keep the kids active and occupied, so they wouldn't be homesick. These last few weeks in country will be a balancing act. I won't be avoiding flight time, but I don't care to do as much of the heavy lifting either.

The ceasefire began at 0700 this morning, and at 0730 the medevac plane got shot up. The VC didn't receive the memo. Same thing happened last year. We never learn. When I left Phu Bai, there was a good fight going on up there between a Marine battalion and the NVA between Hue and Quang Tri. The Marines were trying to mop up during the day, and the guerillas would counter with mortars at night. As I said, same old stuff.

That Rudolph run last night, flown in the worst weather I've ever been in, kept me out past midnight. I was never more than 100 feet above the ground. I mostly navigated on the river. I walked back to the hooch in a violent rainstorm without dinner. No big deal. I've gained five pounds since all these holiday goodies have been coming in -- never could resist a cookie. There are several Christmas packages waiting for me in the ready room that I didn't want to carry in a monsoon.

As soon as I changed into dry clothes and settled in, I had another emergency mission. A nature call! Got soaked again, dried off again, and changed clothes again. When I sat down to write, the lights went out. The rain on the metal roof was about to put me to sleep when I heard the familiar sound of our old friend "Krumph," followed closely by his two best friends, Krumph II and Krumph III. I watched eight of these things land south of the runway -- one for each reindeer. Thankfully, none of the mortars landed on my roof. At 2200 the power was restored, and it was time for lights out. I had enough strength remaining for a quick "whore bath" and crawled into my rice bed. It's been a cold, wet, miserable day.

Merry Christmas! Welcome to my world.

I had almost stopped writing altogether and was mostly making those little tape recordings with long, pregnant pauses between rambling sentences that went round and round in circles with very little content. Everything had already been said, and I had run out of creative ways to say

I wanted to go home. Saying that more than once seemed childish.

One of the fellows in our hooch received a tape from his wife who was sobbing uncontrollably. Toward the end of the tape he finally understood what she was crying about. Her younger sister was pregnant by her college boyfriend. He had flown a particularly long day and night of medevac sorties the day before and had been looking forward to listening to his wife's voice on the tape. He said he ripped the tape out of the recorder, walked down to the beach, and threw it far out into the Tonkin Gulf. He didn't need to explain to any of us why he did that. But he did anyway.

"They're at home having sex and crying about it. We're hauling these kids out of the jungle, none of us knowing if we'll be alive tomorrow."

In re-reading my letters home and my journal, I can see that I had grown more cynical as my tour progressed. By Christmas, I was no longer objective about our circumstances. Like the cockfights in Alongapo, I had too much sympathy for the roosters and too little for the people benefiting from the fight, whoever they were. I also had spent too many nights lying on those rubber mattresses wondering where the bullet might rip through my flesh. Would it be in my right ankle, where my foot sat on the floor of the plane on the rudder pedal? That wouldn't be so bad. Nobody ever died from a busted ankle. But suppose the lucky round took out my right knee or my whole right leg? I imagined my life with no right leg, and then with no legs, eventually working my way up the right side and down the left until I fell asleep. This was similar to counting sheep, only I was counting body parts, and fanaticizing life scenarios with wounds I had witnessed on those medevacs. I pictured beautiful movie stars visiting my hospital bed and asking me dumb questions about my injuries.

Sometime during the period between Thanksgiving and Christmas, something happened to cause a complete and permanent change in me. As the pilot of the medevac slick, I was summoned to evacuate one wounded Marine about 12 miles south of Danang. The young man was missing his left leg, his left arm, an eye and an ear. His arm and leg were wrapped in his vinyl poncho, and the poncho was placed in the plane beside his stretcher. As the corpsman and crew chief attempted to comfort the Marine with morphine and plasma, he never whimpered. When we landed at the hospital pad, the doctors ran out to assist with his stretcher and the poncho. I was preparing to lift off and leave the area when an extraordinary thing happened.

When the stretcher reached the front door of the hospital, one of the doctors ran back to the Huey and summoned the crew chief back to the stretcher. I could see the wounded man motion for the crew chief to lean forward, so he could tell him something over the noise of the rotor blades. When he returned to the chopper, tears were streaming from his eyes. I gave him a few minutes to collect himself before asking him what happened back there.

"Captain Willis, do you know what he said to me? He said to tell the pilot *thanks for the ride.*"

On the way back to Marble Mountain to refuel, we were all bawling like babies. I still cry when I think about it. When we landed and shut the plane down, we all just sat in the plane for a long time without saying anything. After we shut the plane down, I told the crew that I hoped that young man would survive to change as many lives as he had that day with his amazing gesture of gratitude. Any soldier who could see through those incredible circumstances and still have the presence of mind to say *"thank you,"* sent a powerful message through me. I took it personally, since he said, *"tell the pilot,"* and tried to make a commitment to remember to thank people every day. No individual before or since has had more influence on my life than that young Marine.

25 Dec 1966 Christmas Day Marble Mountain

We opened our packages from home, and the choir held its Christmas program in the ready room. Marines don't swap gifts, so audience participation was sparse. If you showed up, you sang in the choir. Bradley and I cajoled a few others into singing with us. Corley was supposed to sing and decided at the last minute to serve as choir director since he didn't know the words and can't sing a lick. That was fine because it gave us all something to focus on instead of looking at each other. We had not rehearsed, so it did not go well. We slogged our way through *The Twelve Days of Christmas,* an ambitious song with no cheat sheets. We'd planned to do caroling for the other squadrons, but after we heard ourselves, there wasn't much enthusiasm for it. We murdered three songs and ate some cookies.

Colonel Barden and Shep Spink came down to spend

some time with us. Spink joined the choir. Barden kept his distance, so he wouldn't be hit by choir shrapnel. Singing is not his bag. We suspected that he snuck off for a nip of vodka. They both look happy and rested in their new jobs. My big gift came in the form of an R&R that materialized out of nowhere. My plan worked. Three people passed up a billet to Hong Kong again to wait for Hawaii, which moved me to the top of the Hong Kong list. Colonel Barden and "Puff" Sweeney are also going. We all leave together tomorrow for five beautiful days.

Alleluia!

Corley, Bradley, Spink, Kirby, Barbour, and Willis stumble through the *Twelve Days of Christmas.*

Shep Spink left Vietnam in Feburary, 1967 and took a job with the New Yorker Magazine. His cushy corner office in New York, left him unfulfilled. He and another VMO-

2 veteran, Dick Lewer, became drawn to the plight of the Biafra refugees in Nigeria. They organized a helicopter-borne relief group to airlift supplies to the refugees. In 1969, he began a career in international banking with Citicorp, developing emerging markets in Asia and Africa. He and Isobel are now retired in Ponte Vedra Beach, FL. My first contact with him after 44 years occurred on 19 October, 2010, which just happened to be his 70th birthday.

CHAPTER TEN

THE COMMANDANT AND THE DOG PLATOON

2 Jan 1967 Marble Mountain

Medevac standby at Marble Mountain. Twenty four hours of waiting for statistics. Now, the rain is shrieking sideways against the chilled metal tents that haven't seen the sun in more than a week. I came back from Hong Kong to this.

I stayed at the Hong Kong Hilton this time and had two very good friends with me, Arne and Puff. I did none of the sightseeing things from the first trip, spending my time mostly in nicer restaurants and places that looked civilized. The highlight of the trip was phoning home. You have to give your phone information to the operator, and she places the call for you while you wait in the room. Sometimes, this process can take hours.

It was good to be a part of a peaceful society again. The only war going on in Hong Kong is the daily battle for the almighty dollar. I finally shaved off my red moustache as soon as I came close to hot water. It had filled out respectably, but it was still *red*. I had been using black mascara and an old toothbrush to give the illusion of fullness, but I was fooling no one. Some of those guys already had handlebars.

It's good to see 1967 on the calendar and know that time (and my tour) marches on. Rainy season should end this month, and we can begin the process of drying out.

7 Jan 1967 III MAF Headquarters

It isn't every day that you are asked to fly the Commandant of the Marine Corps, but we are quite busy shuttling the brass from pillar to post while they plan their strategies in the ongoing Prairie II operation around Dong Ha. This is my second time to be honored to be in the entourage with four-star General Wallace M. Greene. He doesn't make much eye contact or small talk with his pilot, but I would have to say that he is a very impressive man and a true gentleman. He has plenty of swagger, but no stick.

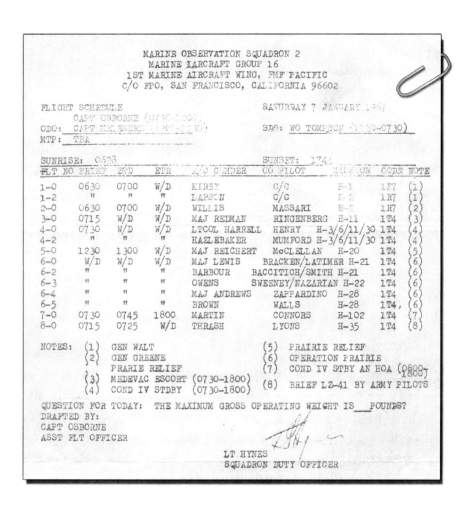

MARINE OBSERVATION SQUADRON 2
MARINE AIRCRAFT GROUP 16
1ST MARINE AIRCRAFT WING, FMF PACIFIC
c/o FPO, SAN FRANCISCO, CALIFORNIA 96602

FLIGHT SCHEDULE   SATURDAY 7 JANUARY 1961
    CAPT OSBORNE (0730-1200)
ODO: CAPT HELENBECK (1200-2030)   SDO: WO TOMPSON (2130-0730)
MTP: TBA

SUNRISE: 0628   SUNSET: 1744

FLT NO	PRIEF	ETD	ETR	A/C CMDER	CO PILOT		MISSION	CODE	NOTE
1-0	0630	0700	W/D	KIRBY	C/C	H-1		1F7	(1)
1-2	"	"	"	LARSON	C/C	H-2		1R7	(1)
2-0	0630	0700	W/D	WILLIS	MASSARI	H-3		1R7	(2)
3-0	0715	W/D	W/D	MAJ REDMAN	RINGENBERG	H-11		1T4	(3)
4-0	0730	W/D	W/D	LTCOL HARRELL	HENRY	H-3/6/11/30	1T4	(4)
4-2	"	"	"	HAZLEBAKER	MUMFORD	H-3/6/11/30	1T4	(4)
5-0	1230	1300	W/D	MAJ REICHERT	McCLELLAN	H-20		1T4	(5)
6-0	W/D	W/D	W/D	MAJ LEWIS	BRACKEN/LATIMER	H-21		1T4	(6)
6-2	"	"	"	BARBOUR	BACCITICH/SMITH	H-21		1T4	(6)
6-3	"	"	"	OWENS	SWEENEY/NAZARIAN	H-22		1T4	(6)
6-4	"	"	"	MAJ ANDREWS	ZAPPARDINO	H-28		1T4	(6)
6-5	"	"	"	BROWN	WALLS	H-28		1T4,	(6)
7-0	0730	0745	1800	MARTIN	CONNORS	H-102		1T4	(7)
8-0	0715	0725	W/D	THRASH	LYONS	H-35		1T4	(8)

NOTES: (1) GEN WALT   (5) PRAIRIE RELIEF
        (2) GEN GREENE   (6) OPERATION PRAIRIE
             PRARIE RELIEF   (7) COND IV STBY AN HOA (0800-
        (3) MEDEVAC ESCORT (0730-1800)   1800)
        (4) COND IV STBY (0730-1800)   (8) BRIEF LZ-41 BY ARMY PILOTS

QUESTION FOR TODAY: THE MAXIMUM GROSS OPERATING WEIGHT IS___POUNDS?
DRAFTED BY:
CAPT OSBORNE
ASST FLT OFFICER

                                    LT HYNES
                                    SQUADRON DUTY OFFICER

It isn't every day that you are asked to fly the Commandant
of the Marine Corps.

9 Jan 1967 Dong Ha

I finally figured out what an ear block is. I'm back at Dong Ha with a slight head cold that is a little uncomfortable in this weather. The northern portion of South Vietnam is still rainy and cold with a sharp wind from the north. We have stoves in the tents made from 55 gallon drums. We burn scrap wood and aviation gas or JP fuel, which is the same low grade, stinky kerosene that we burn in the Huey. It takes the chill off and helps keep our boots and socks somewhat dry. Wet feet can cause problems.

Flying is sparse in this weather, but not for lack of enemy activity. They take full advantage of our 1500' ceiling minimums and are constantly on the move like ants. This is a scrappy bunch we're up against. We also need two miles visibility. If the mission is an emergency we try to go no matter what. The group is trying to protect the airplanes as much as anything. Without the Hueys we're out of business. Sometimes, they don't come back in bad weather. We haven't been able to complete a entire mission in two days. We brief, we wait, we launch, we abort, and we wait. To pass the time, we play bridge and chess. I'm not much good at either because they both require patience and concentration which I don't seem to have.

The six pilots who asked to be permanently assigned to Dong Ha have worked to make this place livable for the rest of us. Those guys know the area like the inside of their footlockers -- very useful information in this poor visibility. They brought up a refrigerator, chairs, and a few creature comforts for the pilots' quarters. The new mess hall is in full swing, serving fresh food now. They show movies at night in the mess hall, but both the picture and sound quality are pathetic. There are no TV's at all up here.

The ceasefire was a predictable bust as I'm sure you saw on the evening news. Nothing really changed.

*

The asterisk represents an elapsed time of 30 minutes while we briefed a recon insertion that is on hold until the weather breaks. We also had three reports of fuel contamination from all this rain. Fuel samples are being pulled on all the birds as I write this. If water finds its way into the fuel tank, it can cause an engine flameout. One more thing to manage!

I was at Phu Bai for five days the week before Christmas supporting Operation Chinook. There was plenty of enemy contact and some positive battle damage assessments. I left the night before the "ceasefire" and the battle was in high gear.

About three weeks ago on 15 December, four of our pilots went on a temporary shipboard assignment for 30 days -- another landing force exercise into the Mekong Delta. I was at Dong Ha and was late hearing about it, or I would probably have been sent. We were told that 15 of the 30 days would be spent at Cubi Point in the Philippines. Once again I was in the wrong place because the last we heard, Chris Bradley and Ron Corley were in the Cubi "O" Club throwing champagne glasses in the fireplace on New Year's Eve. Plamondon and John Kiser also went. Our new CO said my name had come up, but he didn't think I would want to go. Thanks Coach.

In exchange for those four experienced pilots, the squadron received four brand new pilots from that phantom squadron we keep hearing about that has pilots but no airplanes, VMO-3. We will have to check each one of them out. So we trade four experienced pilots for four rookie copilots. Thanks again.

11 Jan 1967

A few days ago when Commandant Wallace M. Greene came for his semi-annual visit to III MAF with General Walt, I didn't have time to write about it, but I have been thinking about it ever since. He visited places I have never heard of, including a POW camp and the Dog Platoon. The meetings lasted long enough for me to get out of the plane and talk to some of the Marines who work at those places.

The dog camp is a specialized training center for scout dogs, usually German Shepherds, trained to go out on patrols with the troops. These stealthy sentry dogs can locate the enemy before the troops see them and help capture prisoners. The dogs are "lifers," and some have had many handlers, so the camp is as much for the handlers as the animals. They performed a demonstration with one of the dogs that scared the hell out of me. When an attack dog locks his black eyes on you, it is a defining moment. The dog isn't concerned about his own welfare at that moment, only his mission. It's all about training, and it was impressive to see the kind of discipline that can be instilled into an animal. Once the exercise was over, the dog was as gentle as a house pet. If it had opposing thumbs, we could have put him in a uniform and taught him to salute.

The POW's hardly looked like prisoners. In fact, they looked happy to be there. They're probably treated better than they were in their own units. Some of them were NVA and certainly better off than those machine gunners who were found chained to their weapons. They were as friendly and tame as house pets. Being at both these places on the same day formed a curious analogy for me. Ho Chi Minh is training his young pups to perform their mission without thinking, just like those dogs. The kids in the POW camp are probably his fourth generation of trained animals, each of them capable of raw terror or devoted friendship.

It's almost impossible to receive any current news about anything unless you can spend some time at the general's quarters. The *Stars and Stripes,* a weekly military newspaper, is a simple piece of journalism that isn't much better than these notes, offering encouraging reports on how badly we're defeating the enemy. But I don't see us gaining any ground. It's as if we are trying to hold back water. We read old copies of *TIME* and *Newsweek,* sent to us in bundles when others are finished reading them, but nothing on US current events.

We know the mini skirt is popular. Nancy Sinatra wore a tight, white leather one when she came over with her leather boots (that were made for walking) and strutted around for the troops for a few days. Her singing is only a couple notches up from our Christmas choir, but she's one of Kirby's favorites.

I'm reading the *Ugly American* for the second time. Even though the book is fiction, I would have to agree that there is an American swagger in this part of the world that is not attractive. I read part of Johnson's comments at the SEATO Summit in Manila and thought of him while reading the book. The fine line between power and arrogance is an easy line to cross. People seem to understand when you make a mistake because everybody in the world does. But while they may forgive ignorance easily, most people simply will not tolerate arrogance.

We are making Dong Ha hot apple cider toddies on a hotplate. Perfect weather for a few drops of rum in a hot cup of cider! If we only had some snow, some ski partners, and a ski resort, and could ski. We have a roaring fire in our oil drum heater, and I have a chess challenge waiting for me. Hey, it's not *all* bad.

That white space represents a two hour time lapse for an emergency extraction of a recon team just south of the DMZ. They weren't under attack, but they had been out there for a week. They were sore, sick, hungry, and exhausted. While we were out there, we decided to recover two teams in one trip since another unit had also completed its mission. Those were some happy guys. The Marine lieutenant in charge of the team that I picked up shouted his thanks close to the ear of my flight helmet. His breath was as strong as burnt napalm. This told me that his stomach hadn't had anything in it for at least two days. Not all missions have to be life-or-death to be rewarding. Even though we had to *'bust our minimums'* for those guys, it was worth sticking our necks out. I like taking them out better than putting them in, but I have a hunch they are a just like us and become addicted to the action. They'll probably have a big meal now and sleep for a couple of days.

BRADLEY AND RINGENBERG

26 January 1967 Marble

Last night at Marble Mountain, around midnight, we got a call from Spink at Group to frag a gunship to Khe Sanh, an outpost northwest of Dong Ha near Laos and the DMZ. Chris Bradley and a relatively new copilot named Jerry Ringenberg were called from the hooches to take the assignment. The weather was horrible, and those mountains up there are no picnic in broad daylight. I was on the top bunk in the ready room standing the medevac watch. Bradley had flown medevac the night before and had enjoyed a day of rest. In checking the mail, he noticed that he had a reel of tape from his wife, Judy. He wouldn't be able to play the tape until he came back from the mission, so he stopped at the door and flamboyantly flipped the tape across the room to me. I was lying with my hands behind my head when the tape landed on my midsection. In typical smartass fashion, as was our mantra, he said if he didn't make it back that I could enjoy his wife's tape.

I put my cap over my eyes and went to sleep. Four hours later, I awoke to a commotion in the ready room. When I sat up and swung my legs off the bunk, Judy Bradley's tape tumbled onto the floor. Three or four senior officers were already in the ready room, which is highly unusual. Two Hueys were missing somewhere in the area of Quang Tri. Rumors were flying, and details were sketchy. All pilots had been summoned in the event a search and rescue mission was needed. The sketchy rumor had Al Barbour leading a two-plane "section" on a Khe Sanh night strike with Bradley as his wingman. Critically low on fuel, they were coming back to Dong Ha to refuel when the weather went to zero-zero. It would take a miracle for them to land safely in a situation like that. That was all we knew at that point.

Later, more information trickled in. Barbour, who had volunteered himself permanently at Dong Ha and knew the area like the back of his hand, was able to dead-reckon the heading where the river and Route 16 led through the river valley to Dong Ha. With Bradley following close behind, Barbour caught a glimpse of the road through the ground scud and made a break for it. On what fumes they had remaining, they were going to try to make it to the nearby Quang Tri Army compound where he knew there was a flat soccer field where he could land and have some fuel delivered. Somewhere in that transition, Bradley lost sight of the lead aircraft.

In the ready room at Marble, we waited nervously for more information, fearing the worst. I put the Bradley tape back in the mail slot for good luck and paced the floor with the others. I was rested and ready to go if needed, although I still had medevac till 0700. More than an hour passed until we heard that Barbour and his copilot, Pete Conners, had somehow managed to land in a soccer field at the Army outpost. There was

no sign of Bradley and Ringenberg. Barbour had been on the radio with Bradley just before the radio went dead. After sunup, we were able to piece together the full story. Corporal James Shriver, the door gunner in the lead aircraft, wrote this report of the incident.

"We were returning from Khe Sanh area to Dong Ha. Dong Ha was 0/0, socked in. We could not land and elected to try to reach Quang Tri Army compound. Our aircraft (the lead one) affected a safe landing with barely more than fumes in the tank. The second aircraft was very close behind in the fog. When we touched down, visual contact was lost with the second aircraft. Outside the Army base perimeter we saw the rotating beacon of the second Huey blinking in the distance through the fog. Not sure how far. There was no radio contact, and we assumed they had crashed. The crew immediately deplaned and started running toward the rotating beacon to assist.

We only slowed down long enough to be warned by the tower sentry that we would be shot if we proceeded. We shouted for them to do whatever they needed to do, but we did not slow our efforts to recover the crew.

Bradley's armor plated pilot's seat had been ripped from its mounting at impact and thrown 25 yards clear of the wreckage. Bradley had managed to release his seat belt and shoulder harness and was stumbling toward the crew in shock as we ran toward the scene. The Huey was decimated. The two crewmen were injured but alive. Lt. Ringenberg was killed instantly. His seatbelt did not appear to be fastened, and his head impacted the cyclic (flight control stick) when the aircraft tail rotor clipped an unmarked Vietnamese grave. Ringenberg's body and the two injured crewmen were taken to the dispensary at Quang Tri. At daybreak an H-34 brought us some fuel in 55 gallon drums, so we could return to Khe Sahn and resume our mission.

Ironically, Corporal Dupee, the injured door gunner of the second Huey, had shoved me aside for some reason, so he could be the gunner on that aircraft. I think about that a lot."

Bradley took only a few days off before he was back in the saddle again. We discussed this incident from every possible angle, looking for as many details as possible in order to learn anything we could from it. Bradley told us he had visual contact with the ground and had the landing under control until he was about 10 feet off the ground. Then, a solid blanket of fog enveloped the plane. In the next few seconds of complete disorientation, he did not realize he was flying backwards when he clipped the mound of dirt.

The consensus among the pilots was that two out of three conditions that cause fog were in perfect harmony as Bradley approached the ground for his landing. When the temperature and the dew point are within one or two degrees of each other, you only need one other ingredient to create fog. His rotor wash provided that third component when it stirred up the inevitable cyclone that normally accompanies a chopper landing. Meteorologists call it condensation nuclei. We just know it as dust.

We also had to admire Al Barbour's judgment in asking to be permanently assigned up there, as well as his flying skills. He knew every single kilometer of those mountains, and he probably saved four lives that morning, including his own.

Al Barbour completed his tour in the Marine Corps at Camp Pendleton as a flight instructor in May of 68. He accepted a position with United Airlines for pilot training in Denver, CO, and was initially assigned to LaGuardia/JFK where he commuted from his hometown of Sagaponack, NY. After 33 years as an aircraft captain he retired from United at the mandatory age of 60 while flying out of Washington Dulles on the European routes. He and his wife, Susan, of 37 years have four children and nine grandchildren. More than anyone I know, Al has continued to honor the memory of the Marines who perished while serving their country out of Marble Mountain and Dong Ha; both as president of the USMC Combat Helicopter Association www.popasmoke. com, and his ongoing role as their research historian. He developed an additional website that covers the history of VMO-2 that emphasizes the contributions of over 1750 Marines during the Vietnam War, www.anglefire.com/ va/cherrydeuce. Al has a woodworking shop in Marshall, VA where he spends his leisure time building homes and furniture.

Chris Bradley left Vietnam in July, 1967 to be stationed at Quantico where both his children were born. He then left the Marine Corps and accepted employment as a Special Agent in the Drug Enforcement Administration. Because of his flying experience he became involved in establishing the DEA Air Wing, serving in Mexico, Jamaica, South America. His family moved to Air Wing Headquarters in Dallas in 1978 where he was promoted to Deputy Chief Pilot. He served in Turkey as Resident Agent in Charge and retired in 1994. He has spent the intervening years teaching the American Civil War, visiting battlefields, writing poetry and homesteading in the Mountains of WV. His wife Judith of 41 years died in 2005 from cancer. *"I often think of the death of my co-pilot Jerome Ringenberg. I had never flown with him before and thus hardly knew him, yet his last gasps have found places in my poetry. There have been times in my life when I've paused to say, 'this is for Jerry'."*

Bradleys armor plated seat (shown in foreground) was thrown 25 yards from the wreckage.

JACK OWENS

March 1967

On the 17th day of March 1967, I closed out my combat flight log ..."*twelve and twenty,*" as it is known throughout the ranks. With ten days remaining on a 13 month tour, it is understood that a soldier isn't as likely to make his best decisions, so they put him in the back of the room, so he won't hurt anybody. I was no exception to this rule. By then I was just going through the motions. I flew a few admin hops, a handful of test hops, and VIP sorties, but I wasn't asked to do any more heavy lifting. It was accepted that I had served my time. Now, it was time for me to take my place on the short timer's roster as one of the seasoned Old Salts, relegated to the role of wizened warrior. I had cheated death for 385 days and made it through the Ides of March twice. McNamara's promise of the "*maximum 12 month tour*" had been more than satisfied.

My orders were slow to come in. I had two weeks in this twilight zone. The lieutenants that were in my hooch when I moved in had long since been promoted to captain and had one by one rotated back home. Some of them promised, or threatened, to write, to taunt us with tales of extravagant luxury and incredible sex.

Charlie Plunkett, Steve Waltrip, and Poop Ashbury, who

had entertained me with their antics for months, all become quiet and reclusive during their end days. Theirs was an odd withdrawal, which I shared, as they entered into their own personal transitions. They all prepared themselves to go home in similar fashion. They spent more time alone, writing home, reflecting, and talking quietly with each other. There was no fanfare for their departure, nor did they want any. They just sort of dissolved. One day their duffel bag rested on the floor; the next day while you were flying medevac, they were gone. We may have received a post card with a witty comment but no sex stories. New officers appeared in their places and rearranged their spaces to suit themselves.

A senior captain named Jack Owens asked to be put into a hooch with a seasoned pilot, and they put him in next to me. He snored so loudly that we accused him of blistering the plywood on the ceiling. We offered to pay him to be the last person to go to bed, so we could fall asleep before he did. He knew his problem and told us to wake him whenever we needed to, and we frequently obliged. One night he came over and sat on the end of my bed and told me that I was one of the most respected pilots in the squadron. He said he had asked the CO to be in my tent. This compliment made me tolerate his snoring somewhat. We had several such conversations after that, and I told him everything that I knew about flying into hot zones and how to protect himself with common sense.

One night after lights out, he got out of bed and came over to ask me if I had a relationship with Jesus Christ and if I had ever accepted him as my personal savior. I told him that I had screamed his name a few times on some of those missions. He chuckled uncomfortably because he knew he was going deep on me. I could tell he had too much on his mind because he wasn't snoring. I told him that I was a Christian if that's what he meant. He said that was part of it, but if I ever wanted to talk about anything like that, he was there for me. I always respected him for that, for not being just another cowboy. But we never went there again. I think he just wanted to know where my calmness came from. I wish I could have given him the answer he was looking for.

I used to play sports against opponents who would do things like cross themselves before shooting a free throw. I remember thinking that I hoped God had better things to do than be watching a high school basketball game that night.

My new hoochmate, Jack Owens, was an All-American guy and a good pilot. There was something about his perfect look, his affable personality, and his name that reminded me of one of my best childhood friends in Tullahoma, Frank Owen. This went back to when I was 14 years old in 1955. It was during the Christmas holiday break from school, and I was leaving the house for my part-time job at the Dairy Queen when I received a phone call from a girlfriend who asked if I had any news about Frank. She told me that he had been hit by a car while he and another buddy, Billy Murphy, were riding their bikes to Carroll Cave about six miles from Tullahoma near Ovoca Lake. She heard he was rushed to the hospital, and it was not good. I knew Frank's phone number by heart and dialed it immediately to separate fact from fiction. His dad answered and was breathing hard. He said he knew something was wrong because his wife and the family car were gone. Families only had one car in those days. Frank's dad, who was also Frank, didn't know anything about this, and I was dumbstruck for a few seconds having to tell him what I had just heard. He dropped the phone without hanging it up and ran the three miles to the emergency room. By the time he arrived, his only son was dead. I ran to the hospital, too, and I wish I hadn't. Watching the family reaction overwhelmed me. I had never seen grief like that. I was dizzy and sick to my stomach and had to leave immediately. I had been invited to be on that bike ride with them that day but had to work at the Dairy Queen instead.

The little Baptist Church where Frank and I went to Sunday school was overflowing for his funeral. I was there at the appointed time but had to sit in a folding chair, even though I was one of the pallbearers. His dad could hardly stand. Frank was his pride and joy and the perfect kid. We all wanted to be like him and knew that he would be the one who would amount to something. He just did the right things naturally. A great looking guy with coal dark hair that was trimmed and perfect. He always had his book turned to the right page and even carried a spare pencil. The church wasted no time holding a big revival, and every kid in school was on high alert. It was a two-night affair and nearly 100 kids joined the church that week. The pastor mostly talked about hellfire and damnation. Two of my friends came down the aisle to personally escort me down front, even though I had already been baptized. Nobody wanted to burn in Hell that week.

Trying to sort through my feelings about Frank, his dad, and the poor fellow that accidentally hit him with the car, I couldn't decide which one of them I'd rather be. Considering what the two men must have had to go through, maybe Frank had the easiest part. I also thought about all the people who didn't know about any of this and were unaffected by any part of it. Maybe, they just saw a name in the obituaries. And then there was my phone call? Why was I chosen to break the news to Mr. Owen?

I knew way back then that I would have to come to terms with how I felt about my own death. I finally came to the conclusion that no matter how complicated life becomes, death should be the easy part. There are a million things out there that can kill us, and it can happen to anyone at any time. We just have to be decent people and stay mentally alert. When someone we know dies, we have to hitch up our trousers and go on. It's going to happen to all of us sooner or later, and when it happens to me, I'm not going to be stupid and pretend I didn't know it would happen. I knew that the fear of dying was high on everyone's stress chart, but I just could not tolerate the idea of being a chicken-shit about it.

Two years after Frank died, almost to the day, on the school Christmas break, 16 year old J.W. Keller was killed. He was a year ahead of me in school, but we both played on the varsity basketball team. J.W. and I dated twin sisters, and we were supposed to double date that night for a Christmas party at the Lakewood Country Club. On the way to her house, he was hit by a train right in the middle of town. He was alone in the car and was broadsided by a train. If there was a more perfect kid in the world, I never knew him. The very next week when basketball practice resumed, the coach asked me to take the guard position vacated by J.W.

Two of my buddies were plucked from the pack before their prime. If those two didn't have a chance to grow up and change the world, what will happen to a guy who can't even find his pencil? Had I been with them, perhaps I could have made a difference. My connection to each of them, plus the timing and the freakish way they were both killed made me feel singular, as though I was being sent a series of messages. The fragile nature of a man's life was being explained to me. I knew way back then that I would need to prepare myself with a special set of survival skills.

And then I remembered the young Marine who jumped off the stretcher with no legs. The bones in the stumps of his legs stuck into the dirt as he hung there by his elbows while his two stretcher bearers tried to help the panic stricken boy back on the stretcher. The last thing I saw out of the corner of my eye was the red cloud of dirt and dust that I stirred up around them. Jesus Christ!

Seeing these new people come into the squadron, seasoned pilots, but green to combat, robbed me of some of the excitement of going home. I didn't want to fly their missions for them, but I also didn't feel good about just leaving them there to figure it out for themselves. There was too much for them to learn without someone to mentor them. They had never even seen the Rockpile. We all have our vulnerabilities, and I had learned the hard way that the confidence that comes from experience was the single biggest key to pilot longevity in combat.

I knew that I would never experience a bond like I had with these men, the same way I knew that I would probably never see any of them again when this was over. I don't even know the names of any of those boys that I'd been pulling out of those jungles. The only thing I really knew for certain was that I loved these guys. Those grunts who fought and slept out there in those horrific situations were doing the kinds of things that I was not man enough to do.

I would have done anything for them. Anything except stay in that country one day longer than I had to!

After a while I hear loud snoring. I just lie there in the dark staring at the plywood ceiling, waiting for my mind to shut up. An occasional night flare flickers shadows into the hooch, and I look down at my legs to make sure they are still attached. I feel my arms at my side and wait for sleep to come as I watch the plywood blister.

FINAL CHAPTER

THE LONG RIDE HOME

Eventually, my orders to go home arrived. Being the adjutant, I was the first to see them. Gus Plum and Major Plamondon received their orders at the same time. Apparently, I had not prepared to go home any better that I had prepared to go to war. The first rule of a good scout is to be prepared, and I couldn't even find my garrison cover (hat), a fore and aft, flat "piss-cutter" as we called it, that went with the jungle utilities that we were to wear on the plane home. I gave my Vietnamese mattress that I had inherited from Doc Zimpher to the senior member of our hooch. It was a real bed with a mattress stuffed with chopped rice stalks and covered with rice cloth. The other stuff went to whoever asked me for it.

There was some concern that the Pan American, Boeing 707 that would be taking us back to the states via Okinawa would not be able to land at Danang because of all the political shenanigans. Of the four horsemen who flew in together 13 months ago, there were only three of us going back together. A Jeep driver picked us up at our respective hooches and drove us to the ready room to say our good-byes, but only a few pilots were there. I spent several minutes in the line shack where the crew chiefs and corpsmen hang out, thanking them and shaking hands. Plamondon took a couple of pictures, and the medevac pilot cranked up the slick and loaded us in for the two-minute flight to Danang.

We sat in the back of the Huey on a stretcher that served as a bench for the short ride over. The stretcher was installed on the lowest level of a three tiered system that mounted on the back bulkhead of the Huey. This was a fairly new Huey, but the stretcher had been used hundreds of times and was stained brown with dried blood. We didn't even bother to use a seat belt and just sat lightly on the edge of the stretcher, leaning forward. Plum sat on his duffel bag facing us with his back against the center console with his legs crossed like an American Indian. A crew chief went along and opened and closed the cargo doors for us. We could see the long white 707 sitting where it was supposed to be, but none of this seemed to be sinking in for me. My mind was like a dimmer switch that had been turned to its lowest setting.

It took an hour or so before anyone was allowed to board the plane while the flight crew tidied it up from the previous flight. It occurred to me that it may have been the same plane that brought me here and that it had just offloaded a new batch of rookies. I saw a handful of men who stood out in the crowd because their skin was chalky pale. I figured that they had just flown in from the States. God bless 'em!

Plamondon was practically giddy in anticipation of going home to his wife and kids, taking pictures of everything with his new Polaroid. He wanted to take a picture of me in front of the plane that would take us back to Okinawa. In less than a minute he handed the finished picture to me. Amazing! He never asked and I never told him why I didn't have my hat on when he took the picture. I figured if that hat was the only thing that I had lost over there, then that was the very least of my problems. Besides, who was going to call me to account on that? It was just so typical of me not to have all my Marine shit together as would be expected of a real soldier.

When it was time to go home, I couldn't even find my cover (hat), and I could only locate one collar insignia.

Doc Baker had given me a couple of sleeping pills for the long flight in case I was too wired to sleep on the plane. The obligatory stop through Okinawa for refueling and processing added an extra day to an already extraordinarily long 23- hour flight. I had never had any trouble sleeping through anything and barely paid attention to Doc's medical advice. Once we were inside the plane and the flight attendant closed the door, it finally hit me that I would not be coming back to Marble Mountain.

When the pilot began taxiing to runway 34 for takeoff my mind started cascading irrationally. I had survived my combat ordeal and was going home, but instead of elation, I was being bombarded with an overwhelming feeling of anxiety and guilt. I had almost expected not to make it out of there alive, and I wondered why I could be so lucky when all those other men didn't. I believe the number was over 30,000 by now and still counting. I wondered if the medevac slick had been called out since it dropped us off. My mind began playing tricks on me that I was part of a cruel joke, and everybody on the plane was going to die in a spectacular crash at sea. Everything started slowing down dramatically to the point where I thought my new Japanese self-winding R&R Seiko watch had completely stopped. I tapped on the crystal lens a couple of times to wake up the sweep hand. It had the same time as the Swiss Army watch on the left hand of a right handed Marine major sitting across the aisle from me. He had his garrison cap lying across his left thigh with his gold oak-leaf insignia pinned precisely in the proper place. He must have been a real Marine who kept up with his shit. I was still leaning forward in my seat, not willing to become too attached to it just yet, a position we refer to as *"at the ready."*

An Army officer sitting in the middle seat next to me was reading a new book written by a United States Senator, James William Fulbright. Fulbright published *The Arrogance of Power* in 1966. The Southern Democrat from Arkansas was strongly opposed to the war, and his book attacked the justification of it, as well as Congress's failure to set limits on it. He had his own interesting explanation for our reasons for being there. Stupid me didn't bring a book, so I read along with him for about 40 minutes as he turned the pages before I could finish reading them. Why does everybody read faster than I do?

Fulbright blamed our involvement on Cold War geopolitics, claiming that America is cursed with a Puritan spirit that leads us to look at the world through a distorted prism of angry moralism. Our puritanical nature is interpreted as a sign of God's favor, which confers on us a special responsibility to impose our will on lesser nations, trying to make them richer and better in our own shining image. In other words, according to the senator, our nation has a glorified image of itself in believing that it's our duty to do God's work. The United States had apparently risen to a level of world power that afforded us the special privilege of omniscience. This flew in the face of my half-baked theory that we had been there to capture the rice fields, and the senator was far more articulate. It made me wonder if the people who are responsible for creating wars actually know why we fight them. I promised myself that I would buy that book and read more than the few pages that I could steal from the one that he said his father had sent him -- but I never did that.

The three hour flight to *"Oki-Knock-Knock"* seemed as if it lasted three days. It was a quiet flight, not quite full, and not many were sleeping or talking. I couldn't (or wouldn't) allow myself to enjoy the satisfaction of going home. The nagging feeling of foreboding wouldn't leave me alone. I could feel the lumps of Doc Baker's two sleeping pills laying loose in the left front pocket of my shirt, but I had waited too long to take one now. I just sat there like a feral cat that had been forced into a strange domestic environment. My senses were hovering on the edge of anxiety, waiting for the inevitable emergency.

After landing in Okinawa, we spent the rest of the day standing in line being processed. I joked that they should quarantine us until we were vetted or put us into a decompression chamber. We underwent a cursory physical exam with the customary coughing for the doctor, taking temperatures, and so forth. No mental exam, which would have been more appropriate. It was a relief that I didn't have a hernia, but I did have a blotch of fungus on my neck about the size of a dollar bill, and the doctor gave me something to rub on it. Any shots we might need we would receive in San Francisco.

I had to check three different times before they found the duffel bag I left with them 13 months ago. I found an extra cover (hat) in there that I was able to put to immediate use. That night we went back to the Kadena Officer's club, where it all started. We had planned to have dinner at the club but they were having some sort of change of command party with cheap drinks and free hors d'oerves. We pretended the party was for us and made a meal of it. When we returned to our quarters, Major Plamondon brought Gus and me the bad news.

That morning, the 28 day of March, 1967, the day my plane left for Okinawa, my snoring roommate Jack Owens was killed while flying a routine recon mission out of Dong Ha. He was flying at less than 100 feet when his plane was riddled with both heavy caliber and small arms fire, killing him instantly. Doc Baker was in the left seat with him flying as an observer, presumably earning the necessary four hours of monthly flight time to receive his flight pay. The 22 year old door gunner, Corporal Paul Edward Albano, and 19 year old crew chief George Mark Stevenson, both of whom I spent time with in the line shack before I left, also perished in the crash. Doc Baker was not a pilot, and the plane inverted and crashed nose first when Jack was hit. This incident strangely coincided with my irrational anxiety attack on the long plane ride to Okinawa. Doctor Curtis Richard Baker perished before I could swallow the two sleeping pills he had given me to relax.

By the time we boarded our flight to San Francisco at 1000 the next morning, I was starting to feel as if my entire tour was nothing more than a dream, similar to being involved in a long novel that I couldn't put down until I had finished it. However, the novel wasn't finished, and it would be up to me to write the ending. Certainly, I didn't want it to end with a plane crash at sea with a planeload of more good people aboard. I allowed myself to start thinking about the landing in California, and if I might get down on my knees and kiss the ground when my feet hit American soil. That seemed a little dramatic even for a writer. As soon as the stewardess handed me a Coke, I swallowed one of those pills Doc Baker had given me.

The pill didn't work. I browsed through every magazine on the plane, and we hadn't even taken off yet. I asked for a pencil and some scratch paper, and they found some things for me to make some notes for the journal that I had been gradually losing interest in keeping. My brain refused to shut down and would not focus. The blank paper just stared back at me while time stood deathly still. All those nights of lying awake thinking about bullets ripping through various parts of my body came creeping back into my thoughts. I didn't have to worry about that now. I had subconsciously convinced myself that I wouldn't make it home, but if you don't count the fungus, I didn't have a scratch on me.

The second pill didn't work either. I wondered if Doc Baker had given me an amphetamine as a practical joke. I'm not sure how the plane stayed in the air for five years without refueling. When we finally landed in San Francisco, I was so subdued that I barely remember the 200 yard walk across the tarmac to the terminal. We were escorted to a processing facility where our shot records were examined. I had already taken care of most of this with Doc Baker because I didn't want three more days of fever and chills. I needed only one shot. I said my goodbyes to Gus, and we promised to stay in touch. All the men split up to go to their respective boarding gates where their family members would be waiting for them. I still had to cheat death for several more hours because I had another long flight to Tennessee waiting for me.

[Gus Plum was killed on the 13th of April 1967, less than two weeks after he came home from Vietnam. He was riding as an observer on an orientation flight in El Toro, California. Their helicopter crashed into a mountain in bad weather, killing everyone on board.

Bob Plamondon left the Marines Corps in 1971 and settled with his family in Central Falls, RI, where he pursued his passion for carpentry. He and his wife, Claire, of 54 years now live in Woonsocket, RI. They have seven children, and ten grandchildren.]

Waiting in California for my flight to Tennessee and reading an American newspaper helped put my mind at ease. The long shapely legs of those California ladies clicking their high heels through the terminal perked up my sagging spirits. A man came over to shake my hand and thanked me for my service to the country, something I wasn't expecting in San Francisco considering what I had been reading in the paper. I bought a beer in one of the bars at the airport and watched the frost melt on the cold glass while I sipped from the bottle. Two and a half dollars seemed expensive for a beer. The bartender wouldn't let me pay for it.

In the airspace between the Golden Gate Bridge and the Statue of Liberty, my brain fog lifted. I stared out the window at the snow-capped Rocky Mountains and anything else the pilot brought to our attention. Suddenly, I was a child on my very first ride in an airplane. The closer we came to my home state of Tennessee, the more I began to realize I might be out of the woods. The small bones in the bridge of my nose were vibrating like a tuning fork as we approached that twangy, nasal country music that I woke up to every day of my childhood. I could hear Johnny Cash down there singing, *"Understand Your Man."* It dawned on me that people wouldn't be shooting at me anymore, and whatever challenges might be thrown my way I wouldn't have to die if I made a wrong decision. I promised myself that I would never worry about anything else for the rest of my life because the worst was behind me.

There was plenty of time before the landing to reflect

on the positive things I'd gleaned from my combat experiences. I searched my pockets for pen and paper again. Did I ever learn the answer I was looking for about whether I would turn out to be like my sorry-ass father? Not really! I was no hero either -- no better or worse than any other man who ever served his country. We were all just soldiers doing a job. All that mattered now was that I survived. It didn't matter if I had 42 air medals or none. When it was all said and done, I was just Boo Radley, a complicated mixture of my kinfolks and everybody else I'd ever met. But I knew I wasn't the same person that left home 13 months ago. That guy was never coming home.

I also knew I'd picked up a few idiosyncrasies that I'd have to work through. I could no longer tolerate whining and selfish behavior. I seemed to have developed a hyper-sense of awareness of any movement around me. In my peripheral vision, I could see the flight attendant and her cherry red fingernail polish. *"Sir, I need you to put your seat forward for me,"* every word carefully crafted from her corporate training. The seatbacks only moved an inch or two, but that was the difference between life and death with Pan American Airlines, I suppose. Her beverage smile was gone now as she was giving the landing a more serious demeanor, collecting empty cups, and checking laps for loose seat belts. Laughing broke out near the front of the plane that caused everyone sitting on the aisles to stick their heads out to see what was funny.

The door to the cockpit was open. I could see movement by the pilot and co-pilot. They were going through their pre-landing procedures and talking to the air traffic controller. Reading material was being stowed. Five reading lights were on. A fellow in the back had to be asked to take a seat. A sergeant coming back from the lavatory pulled on the back of my seat as he went by. He had a window seat in row 16. The men at the windows were staring intently down to earth. Most of the men on the aisle looked straight forward, watching the pilots. The seat belt light came on and made three soft tones.

Just before the pilot keyed the intercom and gave us his standard seat belt and tray table speech, I dug the ballpoint pen out of the right front pocket of my utility trousers and used a Pan Am cocktail napkin to see if I could still remember the oath that I had made as a 12 year old.

On my honor, I will do my *best* ... to do my *duty* ... to *God* and my *country* ...

I had no idea what would be waiting for me in the mystery world that I left behind so many lives ago, but those simple words seemed to be as good a place as any to start my new life over again. I knew that this landing would not mean the end of Vietnam for me or for any soldier on that airplane. This war would never end. But my seatbelt and tray table were once again in the full upright and closed position, and I was ready for landing.

JARGON

Alphabet (military) Universal radio code for English speaking military: alpha, bravo, Charlie, delta, echo, foxtrot, golf, hotel, India, Juliet, kilo, Lima, mike, November, Oscar, papa, Quebec, Romeo, sierra, tango, uniform, victor, whiskey, x-ray, yankee, zulu. **Numbers:** wun, two, tree, fow-ar, fife, six, sev-en, ait, niner, zero.

ARVN The Army of the Republic of South Vietnam, our not-so-well-trained allies, usually reluctant ex-farmers.

Arvie Our nickname for an ARVN soldier.

bird Any airplane or chopper, also aircraft or plane.

bulkhead Any wall; not to be confused with **head**, which is what Navy-types call the bathroom.

Charlie VC, Victor Charlie, shortened to just plain Charlie. The term *VC* or *Charlie* can be singular or plural.

CO Commanding Officer, Skipper, the boss, the Six. The **XO**, or Executive Officer is second in command under the CO.

Chop-chop Vietnamese pigeon English for *eat*, also means *hurry up*, or **ASAP**, as soon as possible or right now.

CH-46 Tandem rotor multipurpose Marine chopper, usually used for inserting and extracting combat Marines.

CH-47 Beefed-up Army version of the Marine's CH-46

chart Same as a map. Many of our charts were old maps made by the French and not very accurate. This is very disconcerting for ground troops calling in close artillery support.

click 1000 meters on a map; a **grid square** is a 1000 meter square.

coordinates Grid identifiers on standard topographic maps, read right and down to pinpoint locations, usually to 10 meters.

corpsman Navy medic assigned to the Marine Corps to provide medical attention to casualties under the direction of a **flight surgeon** who is a civilian doctor with a temporary officer's rank.

crew chief A helicopter repair specialist who has responsibility for some part of the aircraft; could be a mechanic, avionics specialist or other. Huey crew chiefs were responsible for everything that went on behind the cockpit, including assisting the corpsmen and serving as an additional door gunner on gunships. They were highly competent, versatile, and indispensible. The pilots often showed them how to land the Huey in the event of an extreme emergency.

c-rations Individual canned food kits generally considered a single meal, containing an entrée such as spaghetti and meatballs accompanied by cheese and crackers or maybe cookies. Usually heated with Sterno or a heat tab. The kit sometimes included a small can opener called a John Wayne.

dee-dee Leave the scene, vanish, disappear; from the Vietnamese *didi mao* meaning go quickly. We might say something like, *"They shot at us, then dee-deed."*

DMZ Demilitarized Zone defined as a three-mile-wide buffer area at the 17th parallel; part of a post WWII treaty that separated French controlled South Vietnam from Communist North Vietnam.

Dog tags Identification tags worn around a soldier's neck, containing name, serial number, blood type, and religious preference.

frag Short for fragmentation order; an addendum to a larger set of directives. A "frag order" would be used to dispatch a Huey for a medevac pickup or a VIP pickup. All **sorties** had to be official military business, and every single mission was recorded as such.

Home Run A casual term for an all-out aerial bombing assault on a known concentration of enemy troops using B52s and any available fixed wing aircraft that carried large bombs. **Arc Lights** were heavier B-52 bombing missions originating from Guam.

hooch Any shelter or sleeping quarters.

Huey UH1-E; the primary helicopter flown by VMO-2 discussed in detail in this book. Also known by many other names such as gunbird, slick, helo, chopper, aircraft, airplane, a/c, bird, plane; forerunner to the Cobra.

hump, humping Infantry Marines on the move, on foot. From the stooped-over position required to carry heavy equipment across their backs.

IFR Instrument flight rules; using cockpit instruments for navigation in bad weather when there is no visual reference to the ground or horizon. **VFR** Visual flight rules: visual reference with the ground during good weather.

infantry Ground troops, Marine rifleman, real soldiers. Note: *all Marines are trained as riflemen.*

I CORPS The Northern-most area of four "CORPS" designated by the US military during the Vietnam War. The I CORPS was controlled by the Marines and commanded by Lieutenant General Lew Walt.

K-bar knife Survival knife with a seven-inch blade carried in a leather scabbard by every Marine on his utility belt.

KIA Killed in action. **WIA** Wounded in action.

Lyndon B. Johnson Our 36th president, a former Naval reservist who never saw combat but never-the–less was awarded a silver star by General Douglas McArthur. He escalated the Vietnam War dramatically after Kennedy's assassination. As the war dragged on, his popularity suffered, and he grew weary of criticism and mounting American casualties. In March of 1968, he made a surprise announcement on television that he would not seek the nomination nor run for re-election. After the Tet Offensive in 1968, popular newscaster Walter Cronkite reported that the war was unwinnable. LBJ said that he knew then that he had lost the support of the American people when he lost Cronkite. A heavy smoker, LBJ died in Jan of 1973 of a heart attack on his Texas ranch. The following day, a ceasefire agreement was signed in Vietnam. He was 64. There are those who would argue that he rendered the mission of the Marine Corps obsolete when he changed their mission in 1965, re-creating the Marines in the image of the Army.

LZ Any area designated as a place for a helicopter to land. Landing zone.

MAF Marine Air Facility.

MAG Marine Air Group. In our case, MAG 16, commanded by General Louis Robertson in the I CORPS area.

MMAF Marble Mountain Air Facility.

M16 Standard military weapon issued to Marine infantry soldiers. It could be fired in semi-automatic or fully-automatic configuration. Enemy soldiers used an **AR15** Russian made rifle.

M79 A fragmentation grenade shaped like a large bullet fired from a M79 hand-held grenade launcher.

mike-mike Millimeter.

napalm Congealed gasoline delivered in a bomb canister by a fixed wing attack aircraft such as an F-4.

NAS Naval Air Station; in our case, Pensacola NAS.

NVA North Vietnamese Army.

Officer's pecking order The lowest ranking commissioned Marine infantry officer is a 2nd Lieutenant (one gold bar). He aspires to command a *platoon* of about 44 men. He is usually promoted to 1st Lieutenant and wears one silver bar once he earns it. A captain commands a *company* which is made up of multiple platoons. Majors command *battalions,* made up of multiple companies. A lieutenant colonel commands a *regiment* comprised of multiple battalions. *Divisions* of 12,000-13,000 Marines are made up of regiments and are usually headed by a (two star) General. Generals rank from brigadier (one star), major general (two stars), and lieutenant general (three stars). There are four-star generals and five-star generals appointed during periods of combat.

poncho Plastic cover and hood used for rain protection and for covering our cots during constant dust storms.

punji stick A piece of dried bamboo sharpened into a weapon and tipped with a poison such as excrement. A cluster of these sticks were stuck strategically in the ground to inflict dangerous puncture wounds to Marine jungle patrols.

ready room Operations lounge where pilots gather to brief, debrief for flight operations, and generally shoot the bull. Plenty of card games and checkers on rainy days.

rice Honda Reward from profits earned by increasing rice yields with new hybrids introduced by American agricultural advisors.

roger Radio talk for *"I understand. Got it, okay."* **Wilco** means *"will comply."*

R&R Rest and recreation. A five day holiday from the action spent in places like Tokyo, Hong Kong, Bangkok, and Hawaii.

Richard M. Nixon was the fourth president to preside over the Vietnam War. After the TET Offensive in 1968 that caused Johnson to retire, Nixon won by a narrow margin in the next election. He spent most of his term as president coping with the Vietnam War and scheming to get reelected. He and his Secretary of State, Henry Kissinger, devised a four point plan to manage these issues. Trying to convince a restless American public that they had a plan to end the unpopular war, Nixon courted Russia with the concept of "détente," a fancy word for rebuilding relations through foreign trade, and playing on the distrust between Russia and China. With North Vietnam, Kissinger's strategy portrayed Nixon as a madman who had an unpredictable personality and might push a nuclear button at any moment. While these political games ran their course, the troops languished in the jungles. For the most part, they were abandoned, betrayed and forgotten. One year into his second term, in 1974, Nixon became the only US President to resign his office, turning it over to Gerald Ford. Ford could not convince Congress to send additional troops or support to Vietnam. The communist offensive began in April 1975, and Ford ordered the small remaining contingent of U.S. embassy and security personnel to leave. The final evacuation produced painful pictures of Americans in retreat, with officials scrambling to board helicopters while Marines held back crowds of Vietnamese who had loyally supported the United States.

scuttlebutt Hearsay, rumor, water fountain gossip.

Skipper The commanding officer of a squadron or a ship; derived from shipboard slang.

slick Stripped-down Huey used as the pickup plane for medevac missions and VIP sorties. Weight considerations often dictated a light fuel load.

sortie A single flight mission. It could be from here to the mailbox or all the way to China.

snafu Yet another witty military acronym describing a snarl in the original plan; stands for "situation normal, all f***** up!"

squid(s) Marine slang for Navy personnel.

swagger stick   A short stick carried by affected high ranking infantry officers.

tango uniform   Dead; a clever, but irreverent, phonetics pun for the letters *t* and *u*, for *"tits-up."* Also applies to crashed airplanes.

III MAF   Third Marine Amphibious Force established when the Marines completed the amphibious landing in 1965 that formed the Chu Lai enclave. This became part of General Lew Walt's command and the III MAF headquarters was located in Danang.

tracer   Rounds of ammo that burn with a red tail providing a visual reference to allow the shooter to guide them onto the target. Gunners usually made every fifth round a tracer.

triage   Prioritizing medical attention, time, and resources.

VMO-1   Marine Observation Squadron One, headquartered at New River, in Jacksonville, North Carolina in 1966.

VMO-2   Marine Observation Squadron Two, headquartered at Marble Mountain Air Facility in 1966. Our call sign was DEADLOCK.

VMO-6 Marine Observation Squadron Six, headquartered in Chu Lai in 1966. Their call sign was KLONDIKE.

Vietnam Today   Modern-day **Vietnam** is a kaleidoscope of its war-torn past, its economically-stifled socialist present, and an unclear vision of its future. The cultural life is deeply influenced by a government-controlled media and unproven socialist programs. Western opportunities, shunned for decades in favor of communist nation's influences such as the Soviet Union, China, Cuba and others, are gradually, but slowly being accepted into the Vietnamese economy. With per capita income of less than 1000 US dollars annually, Vietnam is among the poorest nations in the world. Unlike the Japanese economy after WWII, Vietnam has been slow to adapt to the new world economy. The collapse of the Soviet Union, on which Vietnam heavily depended, was a critical blow to the idealistic dreams of most third-world Communist countries. Rice continues to be Vietnam's mainstay, and today it ranks as the world's second largest exporter, due largely to the introduction of IR8 during the Vietnam War.

This recent email from Donna Suddeth, a friend who visited Vietnam in September, 2010, paints a realistic picture from an American tourist's perspective.

"Ho Chi Minh city (Saigon) has a population of about eight million people and there are about four million motor scooters, with another 1,000 being registered each day. Most scooters have one or two people on them, a fair number have three, and occasionally, four. The record that we saw was five people on a normal, small-size bike. You would not believe all the things they manage to transport on these bikes. What is amazing is how the cars, trucks, buses, motor scooters, and bicycles all flow together with no road rage -- only polite honking in order to pass someone.

We left the opulence of the Park Hyatt Saigon hotel to go on an all-day Mekong Delta tour, working our way to Hanoi. We rode buses, several types of boats, motor and row, and even a cart pulled by donkeys. The roads are not good. There are a few stretches of decent highway, but for the most part, the roads are poorly maintained two-lane roads shared by every conceivable vehicle. The scarcity of roads makes traffic jams horrendous, as they were this morning. The driver tried to make up for the lost time, and we somehow managed to get there alive. We saw jungle, jungle and more jungle. The water is muddy brown because of the silt, but the farms are very fertile. We have more than 5,500,000 Vietnamese dollars, less than $300 in our possession; apparently inflation has ravaged their economy.

(The exchange rate was 118 dong to one US dollar when I was at Marble Mountain, making 5,500,000 dong worth over 46,000 dollars in 1966.)

A number of the major hotel chains are putting resorts along the beach, including Hyatt and Le Meriden. Hue was the last Vietnamese imperial city, and, the Perfume River divides the city. Again, our hotel, the La Residence, a portion of which was the residence of the French governor during France's occupation, is right on the river. It occupies a beautiful setting and is very well done in a Colonial style.

We learned that school is compulsory through the primary grades. After that, it becomes expensive to attend school. After children start school they are no longer indulged and are expected to excel.

In Hanoi we stayed at the Hilton Hanoi and enjoyed a cruise of spectacular Ha Long Bay, with limestone mountains rising out of the water. There are many things to like about Vietnam, but the standard of living and infrastructure are not among them. The living conditions are not pretty, and most houses and buildings are in a deplorable state. There are a few nicer areas and some new construction here and there, which is nice, but rare. The houses are built of crude brick and steel and then covered with stucco. They are narrow, two to four story structures, with a workshop or garage on the first floor. Sometimes, only one or two sides are painted.

There are piles of rubble, bricks, dirt, whatever, on the streets. Yet, interestingly, it doesn't feel dirty, and the Vietnamese people are clean and neat. We spent our last night in Hanoi in the Metropole Legends (a Sofitel hotel). There may be many things about the Colonial periods that were not good, but the architecture from that time is beautiful, especially when it has been artfully restored. We had a great Vietnamese meal in a lovely small restaurant right across the street. I mention that only because we were the only Americans, so we knew it was authentic." We had our last harrowing ride to the Hanoi airport this morning. My favorite sign in English was in the bathroom over a toilet-- **"Out of work."**

Resources for Further Study:

The Vietnam War Years - 1965-1973

By 1967 a half million soldiers were serving the U.S. in Vietnam. During the U. S. War in Vietnam, 8.7 million men and women served the armed forces, more than two-fifths of those in SE Asia. Vietnam was at war, i.e. the French-Indochinese War, in 1950 through 1975, at the fall of Saigon.

Nearly three and one half million troops fought in Vietnam. More than 58,148 were killed, 304,000 wounded. Average age of those killed in action: 23. Two-thirds of those who served were volunteers. More casualties occurred in Vietnam than in the Pacific theater during World War II.

TEN SELECTED BOOKS:

Ashwill, Mark A. & Thai Ngoc Diep,
Vietnam Today: A Guide To A Country At A Crossroads,
Yarmouth, ME: Intercultural Press, 2005

Balaban, John, *After Our War,*
University of Pittsburgh Press, c. 1974 (poetry)

Eastlake, William, *The Bamboo Bed,*
Simon & Schuster, New York, c. 1969

Greene, Graham, *The Quiet American,*
Penguin Classics, 2004, New York (reprint: c. 1955)

Mailer, Norman, *Armies of the Night,*
Plume, c. 1995 Re: Protest March on Pentagon, 1967.
Pulitzer Prize Novel

Maraniss, David, *They Marched Into Sunlight,*
War and Peace, Vietnam and America, October 1967,
(nonfiction) Simon & Schuster, c. 2004 Pulitzer Prize
for History, 2004, J. Anthony Lucas Book Prize.
(Film by Universal Pictures intended release: 2013)

Moore, (Ret.) Lt. Gen. Harold G., and Joseph L. Galloway,
We Were Soldiers Once ... and Young,
(historical non-fiction)
Random House, c. 1992

O'Brien, Tim, *The Things They Carried,*
(reprint) 1970, Penguin, New York, 1991
O'Brien, Tim,
If I Die in a Combat Zone, Box Me Up an Ship Me Home,
Dell, c. 1973, New York

Plaster, John L.
SOG, The Secret Wars of America's Commandos in
Vietnam, NAL Caliber ™, New American Library,
(Penguin Group) USA 1997, (maps by Jeffery L. Ward)
SOG: code-named Studies and Observations Group,
Secret U.S. military unit serving in the Vietnam War.
(Major John L. Plaster, author, is a three-tour SOG Veteran.)

Rubin, Cyma, Curator/Editor, *The American Soldier*
From the Civil War to the War in Iraq (pages 92-109)
A Photographic Tribute, The Exhibition Catalogue
with Historical Text by **Gary Helm Darden**, Ph.D.,
Fairleigh Dickinson University. c. 2008 Business of
Entertainment, Inc.Exhibition sponsored by John B.
Stetson Company,EADS North America and Business
of Entertainment, Inc.

SIX SELECTED MOVIES:

Apocalypse Now, 1979, Film conveys action in Vietnam War, however, content is based on novel, *Heart of Darkness*, by Joseph Conrad, c. 1902. Director: Francis Ford Coppola

Born on the Fourth of July, 1989, True story of a soldier's tour in Vietnam and what he faces after coming home. (Ron Kovic played byTom Cruise.) Director: Oliver Stone

The Green Berets, 1968, Guerilla Warfare, John Wayne, Director: Ray Kellogg; one of the earlier films on Vietnam War.

The Deer Hunter, 1978, A group of friends, steelworkers, who experience the war together. From book by E. M. Corder. Director: Michael Cimino

Good Morning Vietnam, 1987, Disk jockey (Robin Williams) on military radio In Vietnam during the 1960's. Director: Barry Levinson. Adrian Cronauer is the jockey portrayed by Williams in this film.

Full Metal Jacket, 1987, Marines, basic training and into The Tet Offensive, from a novel (1980) by Gustav Hasford, *The Short Timers.*

Web references:

http://www.gwu.edu/~nsarchiv/NSAEBB/NSAEBB101/index.htm

http://www.leatherneck.com/forums/archive/index.php/t-544.html

Chronology of Vietnam War, 1962-1975
Headquarters Company 9th Marine Regiment
3rd Marine Division, Republic of Vietnam 1964 ~ 1969

Shulimson, Jack
THE MARINE WAR: III MAF IN VIETNAM, 1965-1971
U.S. Marine Corps Historical Center

Notes from the editor: *Book & movie listings are selected from catalogues of novels, memoirs, and movies and do not include collections of television drama, artist's exhibits, biography, music of the Vietnam War era, or theatre. All listings are easily accessed on the Web, and in most Libraries. Selections included here, specifically, are for content, or, relevance to the stories in this publication, <u>Marble Mountain</u> by Bud Willis. All efforts herein honor United States Military Veterans, when or wherever they served, men and women, and their families. In appreciation of all that was learned while contributing to this book from 1966-1967 while editing stories of leaders, politicians, or officers, pilots and crews serving with Bud Willis in Vietnam ... this work has been an incredibly-worthwhile experience!*

Veita Jo Hampton, Bluestocking Editorial Services
Bluestocking Hollow Road, Shelbyville, TN

www.windowstovietnam.com   www.lighttravels2.com

CPSIA information can be obtained at www.ICGtesting.com
225641LV00002B/2/P